Passport
to Poverty

Passport to Poverty

THE '90S STOCK MARKET AND WHAT IT CAN STILL DO TO YOU

Peter Erickson

To order additional copies of this book, contact:
Xlibris Corporation
1-888-795-4274
www.Xlibris.com
Orders@Xlibris.com
18622

Contents

TO MY MOTHER

CHAPTER I

DÉJÀ VU?

Writing when the stock market was near its top in late 1999 or early the next year, Robert J. Shiller, Professor of Economics at Yale declared that "if the Dow were to drop to 6,000, the loss would represent something like the equivalent value of the entire housing stock of the United States."[1]

The stock market has been in general decline since April 2000. Already, ominous questions are being asked about the real estate market. Is that, too, a bubble? Are Freddie Mac and Fannie Mae sound?

President Bush said some cheery words last summer about a bright tomorrow, as he should have—for much depends upon an uplifting attitude. But so did President Hoover some twenty months after the famous crash in October 1929. On June 15, 1931, he said to the Indiana Republican Editorial Association in Indianapolis: "I am able to propose an American plan to you . . . . We plan more leisure for men and women and better opportunities for its enjoyment. We plan not only to provide for all the new generation, but we shall, by scientific research and invention, lift the standard of living and security of life of the whole people. We plan to secure a greater diffusion of wealth, a decrease in poverty and a great reduction in crime. And This Plan Will Be Carried Out If We Just Keep On Giving The American People A Chance."[2]

Of course, material abundance was restored and then some, but the crime rate grew. The sense of well-being never quite returned—only briefly during the fifties—after which, it flickered on and off.

Today, Americans are asking if they can escape another great depression. Are there important parallels between the '90s and the '20s of the last century? Some say that the parallels are more like that of the '70s. But are they? The stock market did crash in 1973-74, but the major participants were the wealthy and the gamblers. At that time, the average citizen was more interested in the price of gasoline than he or she was in such equities. Unlike that period and more like the '20s, a significant part of the gross wealth of private citizens was invested in stocks.

In the nineteen twenties, like the middle nineteen hundreds, there was tremendous technological progress. The automobile was replacing the horse everywhere. It was said that Henry Ford had enabled innumerable farm women who had never traveled more than twenty miles beyond where they grew up to go to distant places hundreds of miles away. Less than two years before the market crash, Lindbergh had made his solo flight across the Atlantic; yet, the piston-driven aeroplane had not even been perfected. Air transport for people was by dirigible. But engineers were already theorizing about the jet. The radio was not perfected; only a few years back, radio stations with regular programming had first been set up; FM would not be developed until the end of the '30s. In 1913, a Junior High School student, Philo T. Farnsworth, had figured out the principle behind television; experimental devices were under construction. Talking movies appeared in theaters in 1929. Color movies were in their experimental stage; by 1935, they would be practical. The chemical industry was predicting artificial silk. Near the end of the next decade, this would be an accomplished fact. Opportunities abounded; bright skies lay ahead.

Because of hindsight, we tend to think that the stockbuyers of that day were somehow more careless than the modern ones. Images of men in raccoon coats drinking bathtub gin out of

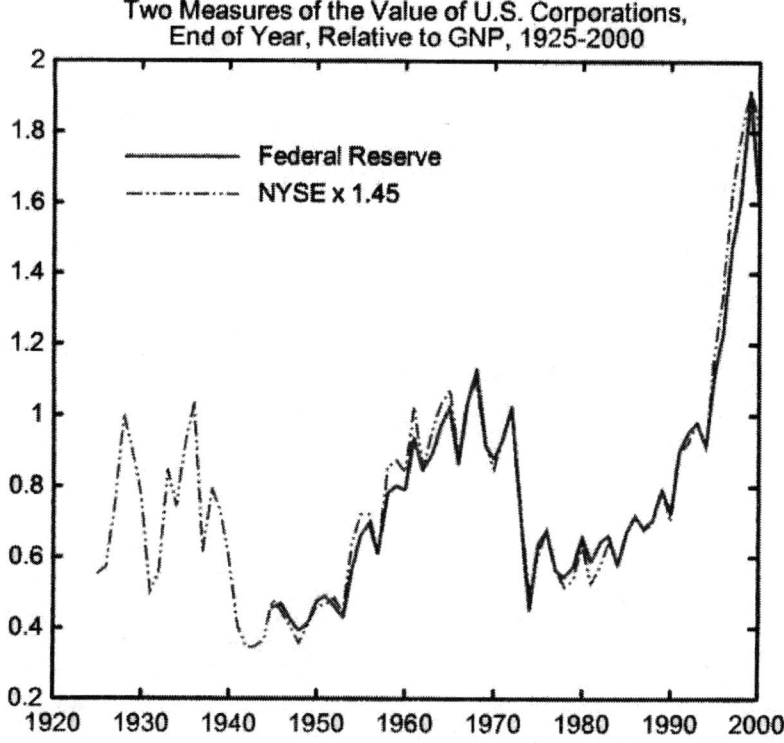

Two Measures of the Value of U.S. Corporations, End of Year, Relative to GNP, 1925-2000

——— Federal Reserve
—·—·—·— NYSE x 1.45

flasks come to mind; of flappers dancing all night to tinny records, etc. Yet, a comparison of the gross domestic products of the two eras shows that theirs was the more conservative. Look at this chart from a study prepared for the Federal Reserve Bank of Minneapolis.[3] Note that the total value of U. S. Corporations as a percentage of GNP was nearly twice as great at the end of the 1990s as it was in 1929. Note also that the percentage in the late 1930s when the depression was in full swing was about the same as it was during that tragic year. The difference, of course, is that GNP was so much smaller. Note also that the percentage was also about the same in the mid-'60s, which had a bull market—but there was no general decline until near the start of '70s when the percentage was markedly higher. To ascribe a special frivolity to the '20s, therefore, is presumptuous. By this measure the recent adventure was far worse.

One can even argue that they had more to look forward to. Just compare the sunlit expectations of that era with the dark, nearly narco, android touting stuff issuing from *Wired*, the leading Internet magazine. The cover story in their April 2000 issue—just before the market began to crash—featured a scrap from a dictionary, defining the word "human" and the title of the lead article, "'Why The Future Doesn't Need Us' by Bill Joy." Mr. Joy is not an obscure scribbler, but a Silicon Valley billionaire. Contrast that attitude with Henry Ford, who could still say on October 3, 1930, more than eleven months after the stock market debacle and while sales of his automobiles were plummeting: "The crash was a good thing . . . You watch!"[4]

America then had a Christian-style culture. It could contain the socialist agitation of the years which followed. Today, where is the unity? Would the almighty dollar be enough? The veneration of democracy?

Some attribute bubble markets to the madness of crowds; that people condense themselves into such a crowd, each one encouraging the other like so many reinforcing wavelets, many of them secretly hoping to get out of it in time, should it prove to be mainly a surge. Then there are the momentarily sincere touts, their pitches rising and falling in sync with the moods of the market. And of course, the mutual funds stressing their expertise to those who try for safety in numbers; in a famous TV ad, one of these organizations suggested that buying and selling stocks without them was like a dog chasing its tail. This madness certainly played a part, but it is not the whole story by any means. Before men can put themselves in such a state of mind that they march together, buying and selling on some other basis than a reasonable expectation, something else has to put them into that state.

Probably the reader has heard of the great tulip market in Holland in the 17th century, how people were paying ridiculous prices for rare bulbs until the whole thing collapsed. But the ownership of American production is something better than throwing money at a mere decorative thing. The 17th century tulip market did not seriously damage the Dutch economy. In both the '20s and the '90s, Americans believed that the economy was basically sound. With better reason than those investing in stocks 75 years later, the people of the '20s could claim that they had a balanced budget; taxes were really low; also, inflation was also imputed to be low. Then as now, America was the richest country in the world; by the end of the nineteenth century, it was both the world's biggest agricultural and industrial power; as a result of WWI, New York had become the world's financial center, replacing Paris and London.

Investors of the 1990s believed that its enemy, communism, had been defeated and that capitalism and democracy were safe. Those of the 1920s saw that their young country had surpassed Europe in many respects in a little more than a century. George Gershwin's "Rhapsody In Blue" was a materialistic celebration of that fact. If the visionaries at the close of the 20th century imagined a "new economy," they saw a "new era." In 1929, America's only open enemy was Soviet Russia, which was far away and not yet a major power. Hitler would not be in office until 1933.

In both times, as we shall see, the people in charge made some errors.

Jorge Augustin Nicolás de Santayana was an American philosopher. Today, he is best remembered for having said that those who do not learn from history are condemned to repeat it. Contemporary Americans hardly study that subject anymore. The public schools in New Jersey have taken George Washington out of their history courses.

To answer the question as to whether America will enter another great depression, history is a fruitful mode of study. Under all its vicissitudes, human nature is the same. Statistics will also be used when needed; but they are at base generalizations from the numerical aspects of some past. They are also history.

The method of study is a short history of the last bubble market and the beginning of the present decade up to January 2003, interspersed with quotations from major figures of the opening years of the last depression, such as President Hoover, Secretary of the Treasury Andrew Mellon, financier John J. Rascob, economist Irving Fisher and others. They are printed in SMALL CAPS. No lengthy analysis is used to conclude emotionally what cannot be proven through their words. They are plain enough. Let the reader draw his or her own conclusions.

Many of these quotations from the earlier depression were collected by Edward Angly and combined into a book published in 1931, titled, *Oh Yeah?* The present book is an adaptation of his premise with frequent short editorial remarks clearly distinguished from the text by being placed in *italics.*

The actual feelings and attitudes of the people as they were experiencing them are of great value. All too often, writers give a picture of some grand sweep of history which is almost never experienced as such by the people actually living then and there. The reader tends to forget that there may be circumstances in his own life that he may not fully understand. The method chosen here allows the reader to think not only the thoughts of those who were wise at the time, but also some of those who were caught up in a folly which they either could not discern or, if they could, they did not know how to extricate themselves out of it. The shameful words of those who knowingly led others to their destruction are also set down. Also are the words of the blind.[5] Many of these quotations are followed by short, clearly distinguishable editorial remarks.

Throughout this little study, the time line—the sequence of events—is stressed. When the reader is instead presented with a study by categories, the fact that causes are always before and effects afterwards is sometimes obscured, even though the distinction is understood by the author. Or, if, causality is stressed, the reader is apt to forget that it is men and not abstractions who are doing the acting.

What is a depression? Government economists define a

recession as a period when a significant number of important business indexes are down for more than two quarters. Obviously, if one of these lasts long enough, it will turn into a depression. It took from October 24, 1929, until June 30, 1932, for the stock market to reach its bottom; then it dragged on until the onset of WWII. Do we have one now? Will the economy ratchet past the stock market? In the final chapter, the author will offer his conclusions. Please don't skip ahead, as a person's conclusions are less important than the reasoning by which they are reached. Being right for the wrong reasons is not good. What is more important is that the readers increase their understanding of these times so recent as they read through the short history.

This book is to be read as a whole from start to finish. (It does not, however, need to be read in a single session). There is not the usual index. However, sources are completely identified, either within the text or in the endnotes.

But before we commence the countdown of the speculative market and its aftermath, it is necessary that there be a brief look at the two individuals who were most prominent during its build-up.

CHAPTER II

THE TWO PRINCIPALS

All of those who participated in the financial markets during the '90s—bankers, C.E.O.s, accountants, bureaucrats, pundits, stockbrokers, investors—had their effect. But the two most influential were U.S. President Bill Clinton and Federal Reserve Chairman Alan Greenspan. Before we begin our countdown of the salient events of the bubble market, a few words need to be said about both.

President Clinton

Many recall the famous slogan from the successful 1992 Clinton-Gore presidential campaign, "It's the economy, stupid!" Many people generally get the idea that Bill Clinton won the election solely on the supposedly dismal economy under George Bush. This is not the full truth. Recently, former Vice-President Al Gore spoke of having inherited "the worst economy in fifty years" and bequeathed "the strongest economy in history." Actually, during the last six months of the first Bush Administration, the economic rate of growth was 4.2%; not a stellar performance, but much greater than the .08% that the economy grew in the concluding half year of the Clinton-Gore administration—in fact, five times as great.[6] But of course, it is impossible to perceive the future.

Even so, the economy was a contributing factor to President Bush Senior's defeat. Very important is the fact that the Democrat did not beat the Republican in a two-party context.

There was also the third-party candidate, H. Ross Perot. In the final returns, Clinton got 43.01%, Bush, 37.45% and Perot, 18.9%. Since it is widely believed that about seventy percent of Perot's constituency preferred Bush over Clinton, it is very possible that if it had been a race between the two, the Republican might have been re-elected.

At first, Democrats had high hopes for him. The press flashed an old photograph of the teenaged Bill Clinton and JFK just moments after they had shaken hands. The picture was captioned with phrases like "The Torch Is Passed."

But some people noticed something else. In his acceptance speech at the Democratic National Convention on July 16, 1993, Governor Clinton said that "as a teenager I heard John Kennedy's summons to citizenship. And then, as a student at Georgetown, I heard that call clarified by a professor named Carroll Quigley, who said to us that America was the greatest country in the history of the world because our people have always believed in two things: that tomorrow can be better than today and that every one of us has a personal, moral responsibility to make it so." What was remarkable about these words was not the intoning of commonplace American ideals, but the name of the man who, supposedly, had conveyed them to him. Carroll Quigley, Professor of history at the Foreign Service School of Georgetown University, was once notorious for reporting in his opus, *Tragedy and Hope,* that a network of very wealthy people had been working behind the scenes for many decades to transform society, and that he had "no aversion to it or to most of its aims and [has] for much of [his] life, been close to it and to many of its instruments."[7] For a week or so after this tribute, there were quite a few mentions in the press, but then the whole matter was forgotten. The idea that Wall Street would play a huge role in the new administration did not seem likely. Most critics expected it to veer toward the traditional Left, as indeed it did at first.

The first two years of the Clinton Presidency were unsuccessful. By the end of that period, many were writing him off as a one-term president.

There were the scandals—Whitewater, travel-gate, Mrs. Clinton's improbable commodity winnings, Vince Foster's mysterious death; the Waco killings made many suspicious.

In his State of the Union address on January 26, 1994, the President pledged to push legislation on health reform. He also said that he would veto any health care bill that did not provide medical care for every American. He placed his wife in charge of drawing up the appropriate program. Her attempt to have the Federal Government take over the health care industry angered millions of conservatives and libertarians who had before been only mildly critical. A novelty timepiece, "The Clinton Watch," came out with a picture of him on the face and with the hands running backwards. Rush Limbaugh built a huge national following over the radio—also a well-received TV show—lambasting Clinton to the delight of his audience. Even the same man who would later become so useful to Clinton as Treasury Secretary was the subject of a February 3, 1993, derisive front-page story in of all places, the very liberal *New York Times:* "Robert F. Rubin, a former co-chairman of Goldman & Sachs & Company, who is President Clinton's top economic adviser, sent a letter in December to many of his clients urging them to continue doing business with the investment banking firm and to stay in touch with him at the White House."[8]

Democrats were beginning to think that Clinton was inept. A cover story in the liberal *Time* magazine depicted a shrinking President. He felt the need to tell the TV cameras that his presidency was not irrelevant. When he proposed new legislation, many Democrats went their own way. In 1994, The Financial Accounting Standard Board proposed that companies charge against current earnings the value of stock options given employees. Clinton supported it. But so many Democrats did not go along that the initiative was defeated. Arthur Levitt, Clinton's SEC chairman, was very disappointed with Senator Lieberman, but the latter considered the proposal to be of little value.[9]

The President seemed inept when he tried to resist the downward movement of the stock market. In April 1994, the stock market was full of jitters. After over three years of stable increases, the Dow Jones Industrial Average declined nearly nine percent in two months. Clinton ventured to say to the Press that "these corrective things will happen from time to time, but there's no reason to overreact. What I'm trying to do is to reassure people so that we don't go beyond skittishness. No one believes that there's a serious problem with the underlying economy. It is healthy, and it is sound."[10]

This was not the first time that a President went forth to help the stock market. Students of history were reminded of the time that President Coolidge tried to reassure skittish investors. In that day, it was considered very bad taste for a President to involve himself in the stock market

JANUARY 6, 1928, AN ASSOCIATED PRESS DISPATCH FROM WASHINGTON STATED THAT "PRESIDENT COOLIDGE IS OF THE OPINION THAT THE RECORD—BREAKING INCREASE IN BROKERS' LOANS IS NOT LARGE ENOUGH TO CAUSE UNFAVORABLE COMMENT."[11]

"NEVER BEFORE HAD A STATEMENT OF SUCH IMPORTANCE TO SPECULATION BEEN ISSUED BY AN OCCUPANT OF THE WHITE HOUSE. ECONOMISTS AND STUDENTS OF FINANCIAL AFFAIRS THROUGHOUT THE COUNTRY WERE DUMBFOUNDED." RALPH ROBEY, *ATLANTIC MONTHLY*, SEPTEMBER 1928.[12]

President Coolidge's remarks took place less than two years before the collapse. Since FDR, that kind of behavior on the part of a President has seemed less out of place. But there still remains some danger in doing it. More often than once, when somebody would propose to the President that he ring the bell at the opening of the New York Stock Exchange, Rubin would remind him that if the market went down, the film clip of him ringing that bell would be played over and over again.[13]

In 1994, the disbelief in Clinton was so high that the

Republicans captured the House of Representatives that November. It was the first time since the Eisenhower election of 1952 that this happened. Clinton knew it was then or not ever.

After that year, his fortunes improved. On April 19, 1995, a government building was blown up in Oklahoma City. Clinton blamed his opponents for creating discord in the country in a manner reminiscent of how the Press held the conservatives responsible for the assassination of President Kennedy, claiming that they had created a "climate of hate." Rush Limbaugh spent the next three or four weeks explaining to his listeners that he was not a terrorist. Pretty soon, the TV show was gone. (There are, however, some important contradictions in the government's account of the Oklahoma tragedy. But that is another story.)

The second development was more important for the long run. This was the change in his strategy. His strategist Dick Morris had convinced him that the way to win was to accept some of the Republican positions and run with them. He recommended that Clinton embrace welfare reform and a balanced budget by a certain date.[14] The idea, as Morris would explain later, was this: "The most potent word in politics is 'yes.' Political strategists for the opposing camp spend their waking hours preparing for 'no.' They amass arguments and ammunition, allies and advisers, to meet the enemy attack that 'no' represents. But when you answer 'yes, I agree with you,' they are disarmed."[15]

This is a difficult strategy which cannot work against all opponents. If the opponent is inwardly convinced of the truth of his position, he can say with conviction that the admission proves he has been right all along; from there, he can argue that the points still in dispute should be surrendered as well. But if the opponent is mostly using the position as a club, then Morris' ploy has a much better chance for success. Once deprived of the club, the opponent must look elsewhere for weapons. But even then, it has to be used adroitly. Clinton was successful with it.

Federal Reserve Chairman Alan Greenspan

That difficult strategy might never have been attempted, were it not for Greenspan. Although a Republican ofttimes associated with conservatives, he was friendly from the beginning. At Clinton's first State of the Union address before Congress, people were surprised to find Greenspan in the galleries, seated between Hillary Clinton and Vice-President Al Gore's wife, Tipper. In his speech Clinton proposed the largest tax increase in history. Two days later, Greenspan diplomatically told the Senate Banking Committee that "leaving aside the specific details, it is a serious proposal . . . ." Greenspan made no criticism of the tax hike, but instead praised the President for his efforts to cut back on spending.[16] Obviously, he wanted to get along with this man.

In June, when Clinton's approval rating in the polls had dropped to 36%, the lowest recorded of any president after his first four months in office, David Gergen, one of Clinton's Republican advisors, asked Greenspan to see the President to offer him some encouragement.

Here is the meeting as described Greenspan enthusiast Bob Woodward:

"On Wednesday, June 9, Greenspan went to the White House to see the President. The Chairman was upbeat. The new consumer price index due out the next day was expected to show an increase of only 1/10 percent, suggesting inflation was in check, he said. They could feel some relief. The long-term economic outlook was the best and most balanced in 40 years, he told the President.

"'If I have to do something [i.e., raise an interest rates, ed.] it will be very mild,' he assured Clinton. A small increase would signal to the markets that the Fed was on top of the situation, and it likely that the long-term rates would come down.

"Clinton spoke yet again with such depth and passion about his deficit-reduction plan that Greenspan concluded once more than unless Bill Clinton was the best actor ever, the statements were genuine."[17]

It was Greenspan who originally proposed to him the idea of making substantial reductions in the federal deficit, thereby encouraging the stock market.

In August, Congress passed Clinton's deficit-reduction program, which mandated a $500 billion reduction over four years by increasing taxes and cutting some government spending. The only important Republican that supported it was Greenspan.[18]

The older man's background would at first seem incongruous with an alliance with a Democrat President.

Greenspan has studied the actual economic performance of American industries since 1948—resulting in a view of economic reality which may unique due to the duration of the inquiry alone. In 1953, he became a part-owner of Townsend-Greenspan & Co, which analyzed industrial statistics for business clients

During the early fifties, Greenspan became a close disciple of the novelist-philosopher Ayn Rand, who was then writing her final and most ideological novel, *Atlas Shrugged*. Rand was a principled advocate of laissez-faire capitalism at a time when most American intellectuals were flirting with socialism. She proclaimed reason in all aspects of life. But she was no conservative, for she was also a dogmatic atheist.

Their relationship centered upon her ideas. At first, she was a little contemptuous of him, even calling him "the undertaker," but she soon concluded that he had a "first-rate mind." They got along most of the time.[19]

In 1966, Greenspan wrote the essay, "Gold and Economic Freedom" which was carried in an journal which Rand and her principal lieutenant owned. It was later included in her brisk selling book, *Capitalism: The Unknown Ideal.*

Basically, the essay extolled gold as a monetary medium and condemned central banking, as exemplified by the Federal Reserve. In a passage which has been repeated over and over again, he blamed the Fed for the collapse of the 1929 stock market. Here are his oft quoted words: "When business in the United States underwent a mild contraction in 1927, the

Federal Reserve created more paper reserves in the hope of forestalling any possible bank reserve shortage. More disastrous, however, was the Federal Reserve's attempt to assist Great Britain who had been losing gold to us because the Bank of England refused to allow interest rates to rise when market forces dictated (it was politically unpalatable). The reasoning of the authorities involved was as follows: if the Federal Reserve pumped excessive paper reserves into American banks, interest rates in the United States would fall to a level comparable with those in Great Britain; this would act to stop Britain's gold loss and avoid the political embarrassment of having to raise interest rates.

"The 'Fed' succeeded: it stopped the gold loss, but it nearly destroyed the economies of the world, in the process. The excess credit which the Fed pumped into the economy spilled over into the stock market—triggering a fantastic speculative boom."[20]

This essay made him famous. He became a leader in the movement for capitalism and monetary reform. In 1968, when Richard Nixon made his successful run for the White House, Greenspan was his chief counsel on the economy. In 1974, President Gerald Ford appointed him to be Chairman of the Council Of Economic Advisors. The news services carried a photograph featuring the President, Mr. Greenspan, his mother, and Ayn Rand and her husband, Frank O'Connor.

Ayn Rand died on March 6, 1982. That was Greenspan's birthday. Reportedly, the conjunction still haunts him.[21] A few years ago, when asked what he thought of her ideas, he answered: "What was a syllogism back then is still a syllogism."[22]

By December 1981, the Social Security system was in trouble. President Reagan appointed a bi-partisan commission, chaired by Greenspan. There was considerable consternation over his appointment, inasmuch as he was a known foe of the system. After much wrangling, the members came to an agreement. Greenspan said it was "fixed" for about seventy-five years.[23]

In 1987, President Reagan nominated him to be head of the Federal Reserve. At the time, there was much discussion over the anomaly that a prominent critic of the Fed would receive such an appointment. Many of those who had followed his career with admiration spoke of his "selling out."

The question as to whether he had really been converted to the idea of central banking or had simply taken the position because of the power and glory involved has been asked many times. In 1997, he gave a speech in Belgium in his usually careful language. He contended that there is virtually no possibility of a monetary collapse under a gold standard, but that there is one under the present banking system.[24] So, at the deepest intellectual level, he has not moved far from his former position. Its importance to him will be plain to the reader by the time this book ends.

On October 19, 1987, about two months after Reagan had appointed him, the soaring stock market went into a tailspin, falling 508 points from 2,246[25] in a single day. Needless to say, this was the cause of much consternation. Had he followed the pure capitalist line on the Federal Reserve, he would not have intervened, but simply let the market seek its own level. Instead, he directed the banks to inject money into the wounded market. For doing so, he was praised in the same liberal and moderate quarters which had previously met his appointment with skepticism.

Let us conjecture what might have happened had he not rescued the stock market. It might have gone down some more. But this fall was partly due to some technical peculiarities of the computer-driven investment programs. Once this was explained, first the bolder investors and then the others would have ventured into the market. Within a few months, it might have returned to a similar level. A Fed Chairman who was still following Ayn Rand and orthodox Misean economics would have been satisfied with this answer and would have simply waited through the ensuing storm of criticism until conditions returned to normal.

But a man who was not altogether convinced by this line of reasoning might have asked himself: Suppose that it did not react that soon? In that case, there might have been a recession. If that were the case, he might have decided to risk it and endure it if it happened. And had it taken place, it would not have been as severe as the one Americans are now experiencing, because in the nineteen eighties, the market was not as much out of kilter as it was later to have become; further, a much smaller proportion of the population was then investing in the stock market—and they for the most part in smaller amounts. But suppose the recession continued. In that case, it is possible that the result would have been the election of a Democrat—but it would have been someone other than Clinton.

Suppose now the more improbable, and it got much worse. The '87 crash was similar in percentage to the '29 crash. What if the S & L's unraveled soon after the stock market? Is anyone really sure that it would not? Yet, by intervening in favor of the stock market as Greenspan did, he stood an excellent chance of cauterizing the wound, as it did. But by doing so, he went against some of the things he had once proclaimed in print to the world, unhinging part of the philosophy which had once directed his thought. He now believed in central bank intervention in emergencies. What further changes would there be?

After that, he returned to normalcy. During the administration of Reagan's successor, George Bush, Greenspan followed the policy of keeping monetary expansion down. Critics were accusing him of confusing inflation with an increase in economic activity and fighting inflation by suppressing growth. But he continued with the restrictive banking approach anyway. In 1992, President Bush reappointed him. In a TV interview in 1998, the ex-President would lament that he was defeated because of the tight-money policy of the Federal Reserve: "I think I would have been re-elected president, because the recovery we were in would have been more visible. I reappointed him, and he disappointed me."[26]

Obviously, Greenspan did not put the Republican Party first in that election. One might think he was dedicated to monetary stability, regardless of the immediate political consequences—a grey, bureaucratic version of the Dutch boy with his finger in the dike.

But that was to change. By the end of the decade, some critics would start calling him "Al, the speculator's pal."

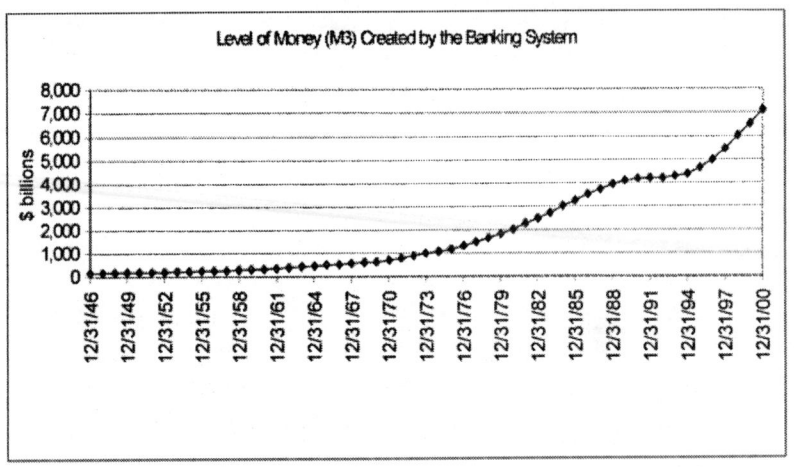

Figure 1: *Level of Money (M3) Created by the banking system* (Source: Federal Reserve *H.6 Series* for the period 1959 to present; and the *Historical Statistics of the United States: Colonial Times to 1970*; Series X-415, X-418, X-419; U.S. Department of Commerce for the period 1946-1958.)

Above is a graph showing the monetary expansion of the bank system from 1946 until year-end 2000.[27] This includes the entire bull market of the last decade of the century past.

Note some facts about it. During the first Bush administration, there was very little monetary expansion. The chart is almost flat. During this period, Greenspan was carrying on a very restrictive policy. Note also that this policy continued into 1993, the first year of the Clinton administration. The trend was not broken until 1994, when it was very slight. After that began the greatest period of money creation in American history.

If we take the second greatest period, the Carter-Reagan years, and draw a straight line to the end of 2000, we can see that rate would have been somewhat less than what happened during the Clinton years. If we go back to the Nixon years when inflation was an issue and the price of gold took its great rise, carrying Alan Greenspan to the forefront of national attention, the monetary expansion was tiny by comparison. Going back to Lyndon Johnson and the hugely expensive Vietnam War of the sixties, the rate was close to nil.

Clearly, Mr. Greenspan had abandoned his restrictive policies during this period. Yet, we were told by the Clinton Administration and by Greenspan that there was little inflation during those years. What gives? How could America have had a fantastic monetary expansion and little price inflation? If he was afraid of some hidden disaster breaking through the stops mentioned in the discussion about 1987, shouldn't he have evidenced more consternation at this development? These questions, the reader should address. The answers will be found in the succeeding chapters.

CHAPTER III

DID GREENSPAN REALLY EXPAND

THE MONEY SUPPLY THAT MUCH?

This chapter contains a slightly technical discussion of the money system. It shows in what way Greenspan can be blamed for the huge amount of M3 money created during his years as Chairman. Readers who don't like to read about these things may want to skip it and begin with Chapter IV, which is quite short.

Some will object that this $7 trillion number is too much—that the amount of genuine money creation is a lot smaller than seven trillion dollars. And furthermore, that the only part of the money supply for which Greenspan's Fed is really responsible is the creation of new currency outside of coin (which is the responsibility of the Treasury Department).

The Distinction Between M1, M2, & M3

There is some truth in this: but, as we shall see, Greenspan does bear a lot of responsibility for it.

M3 is the sum of M2 + large time-deposits + repos of maturity greater than one day at commercial banks + institutional money market accounts.[28] In other words, M3 includes M2 plus certain interest-bearing instruments and an investment account.

M2, in its turn, is the sum of M1 + savings and small-time deposits; + repos at commercial banks.[29] In other words, it includes M1 and some other elements.

Last and least in size, M1 is the sum of all the currency held by the public + all of the money held in checking accounts + travelers' checks + NOW accounts + automatic transfer service accounts + balances in credit unions.[30] Since M3 contains M2, which includes M1, this last is the one major component all three measures have in common.

M1, although it is the smallest of the three, is the classification in which almost all of the creation of new money takes place. Savings accounts generally use money that is already in existence. Before one can put money aside, one must first already possess it. The same with CDs, both large and small. Ditto for the traveler's check. Owning a money market account is impossible, unless one has money to put into this somewhat speculative financial pool The new money is that which did not exist at an earlier date. This category embraces demand deposits and currency. Currency is the responsibility of the Treasury. It is a small part of the monetary system and is only peripherally involved in the creation of new money. It can safely be ignored here.

It is from demand deposits that loan proceeds normally originate. The converse is not true, however; one can open a checking account with non-borrowed money—money one received in a salary, through a sale of some sort, or from a gift or inheritance. Therefore, while not every demand deposit has been created as a result of a loan, most loans are set up as demand deposits. NOW accounts and automatic transfer accounts can sometimes be originated as the result of loans. So they are included.

Loans created through our banking system involve money creation. At this point, however, if the reader does not already know that fact, he or she is asked to accept it, provisionally. Under the current banking system, loans bring money into existence which otherwise would have no being. As one of Mr. Greenspan's predecessors put it bluntly: the new money is "created out of the *right* to create credit money."[31] So it is true that the Federal Reserve and the banking system did not create all of the $7 trillion dollars of M3 that has been added from 1946 through 2000.

How Money Creation Affects
The Magnitude Of M3

But it is also true that they provide the yeast, as it were, for the ultimate M3 expansion. How is this so? Suppose that a bank lends a butcher $100,000 so that he can buy a house from a baker. To make this simple, let us ignore the source of the money which the bank used for the loan to the butcher and concentrate upon what happened to it after it had given it to the baker in exchange for the latter's house. Now suppose that the baker takes all the money and opens a savings account. Next, his bank takes $90,000 of it and lends it to the candlestick maker to make improvements on his shop. The extra $10,000, the bank retains as a reserve to cover withdrawals. The baker still has a balance of $100,000 in his savings account, drawing interest; if he were to close his account, the banking institution would have to give him his money. This is independent of the candlestick maker's situation; the latter has an installment loan; as long as he meets his payments in a timely manner, they cannot get any more than the small monthly payment from him. So, in fact, out of $100,000 the additional money lent to the candlestick maker, the greater sum of $190,000 has come about. The sum of money has almost doubled since the baker opened his savings account. If they had just taken the $90,000 out of the baker's account and left him with only $10,000 from which he could make withdrawals, there would be no money creation. If that were the case, the baker would have to wait until the loan to the candlestick maker was all paid back before he could get all of his original principal back.

Speaking mathematically: Since both the baker and the bank each have a perfectly legitimate claim to $90,000—to the equivalent amount, not to the exact same physical lump of money—the result is not a cancellation, but an addition.

Stated differently: A checking account is a claim on a bank for an amount of that currency equal to the account balance. Generally speaking, the bank may lend out to a third party almost all the money that is in the account. But the bank must keep enough reserves on hand to pay out any depositors who might wish to close their accounts.

M2 adds the money in savings accounts to M1. Such an account is also a claim, against which the bank pays interest as well. If, for instance, an S&L uses the money to lend to a third party for a house, the seller of the house gets the money; this party may in fact open up a checking account; in which case, both the S&L passbook holder and the bank depositor have a valid claim on the same amount of money, though neither has any legal claim on each other. The claims on the currency are greater than the amount of currency itself.

M3 adds large CDs to M2. A Credit Deposit (CD) is a sum of money which a bank may use for a given amount of time. (Terms like three months, six months, and one year are common.) Unlike a regular savings account, which can be liquidated at any time, the bank may not have to the close the account if asked to do so ahead of maturity; and, if they do, they will charge a high fee. This money, which the bank has the right to use for a specific time, it may lend out to a party which will then open up a demand account, of which the balance in the latter can be lent to a party which may use it to pay for something of value, the new owner of which may open up a savings account. And so it goes on. In fact, the current ratio of M1 to M3 is about 6 to 1.

This is the major reason for M3 being a multiple of M1. Part of the money that was originally created through a loan in times past has been converted from demand deposits to savings accounts of various kinds. Over the years, this adds up. In the United States, the quantity of this already created money is greater than the newly created money for any given year. And again, there are M1 checking accounts which did not originate from loans; as explained above, this is money which a depositor may have received through earnings or through a gift, etc.[32] It had to start somewhere.

Greenspan's Responsibility For M3

Alan Greenspan, therefore, must bear responsibility both for the size of M3 and its rapid increase during the period from 1996-2000. Greenspan is not only head of the Federal Reserve, but also a life-long student of money. He must know the consequences of the part over which he has some control. He can, therefore, be held accountable for the magnitude of M3.

Having understood that, one can appreciate this statement by the exasperated editor of *The Wall Street Digest* who was disappointed that the money supply had not increased more than it did in year 2002. "During his tenure as Fed Chairman Greenspan has created $4.646 trillion of M3, more than all other Fed Chairmen combined. Three trillion dollars, or 65% of $4.646 trillion, was created for Mr. Clinton. Over the past 15 years, Mr. Greenspan has served four U.S. presidents as Fed Chairman. Is Mr. Greenspan a Republican or a Democrat? Paul Volcker [his predecessor as Fed. Chairman] was neither."[33]

We shall find why this editor was disappointed and also confirm that Mr. Greenspan is in reality neither a Republican nor a Democrat.

Once we have ascertained the year when the bubble started forming, then the history of that folly may commence.

CHAPTER IV

WHY NO BUBBLE IN 1993 AND 1994?

The line of monetary expansion starts the very first year of the Clinton Administration. But the increases in 1993 and 1994 were quite slight—by the M3 measure, around $62 billion for the first year and around $82.5 billion for the second.[34] Contrast this with the $345 billion M3 increase in 1996, the first year of the bubble market. The difference is readily discernable.

During those two years, the Federal Reserve exercised restraint. In 1994, the Fed began raising the Federal Fund Rate for the first time in five years. This is the interest rate at which banks lend balances at the Fed to other banks overnight.[35] Increasing this rate restricts lending and therefore money creation. In this instance, the tightening began on February 7 with a quarter of a point boost and went on during the year. On March 22, it was again raised a quarter of a point, and also on April 18, and then a half point on May 17. That same day, the Fed also hiked the discount rate by half a percentage point.[36] This is another technical control the Fed has over money creation by banks.

Senator Paul Sarbanes (D-Maryland) complained to Greenspan that "every time the economy comes up out of the water to catch its breath, you move in and push it right back down again." Greenspan's answer: "We're not against growth. Quite the contrary. That's the reason we're endeavoring to do this."[37] It was during this period that he acquired the reputation of being *safe*.

Greenspan delayed making any more raises until after the

election. He then raised both the Fed Funds and the Discount rate an additional three-quarter point. According to a biographer, Jerome Tuccille, he did not want to hurt the Democrats, but the Republicans won big anyway.[38] That year, they got control of both the House and the Senate. In December, Greenspan said that the economy had been slowed down, and no more interest rate raises would be contemplated. At this time, the Fed was still keeping the M3 accumulation down. That year, several large banks raised their prime lending rates without any apparent prompting by higher authorities.

Monetary expansion and inflation are important, but they do not tell the whole story. It is possible to have a period of high money creation, but still have investors acting prudently. Instead of believing in automatic progress, they could pay strict attention to such considerations as the price-earnings ratio. Adults can act responsibly even in treacherous circumstances.

It is stock prices that tell the story. During 1994, the stock market behaved like a roller coaster, going up and down. On January 11, the Dow Industrial Average reached 3,865.61. From that point through April, it was in general decline. But in May it re-crossed the 3,000 mark; then rose until on June 15, it went above 3,800. Then it continued to go up and down, finally closing on December 30 for the year with a slight increase over January. No bloated bull there.

It should be said, however, that the dollar was declining in value overseas, at one point posting a post-WWII low against the Yen. As we shall come to find out, this problem will have much to do with what will happen in the stock market.

Real Government Obligations vs. Official Deficit

At an early meeting, Greenspan told Clinton of the "virtuous circle"; of how cutting the budget deficit would drop interest rates, which would increase the value of the stock market, which would in turn bring in more revenues, leading to greater tax revenues, more deficit reductions, and so on. Greenspan even left the new President a rule of thumb; For every $100 billion in deficit reduction, the interest rates would drop 1%.[39] Translated in the politics of the day that meant: a higher stock market, i.e., a President who could be re-elected.

But there was one problem associated with the budget that needs to be addressed before we can go forward. According to figures supplied by the Office of Management and Budget, total governmental obligations for 1994 were about *$36.2 trillion*—a total approximately seven times the obligations listed in the budget deficit. The greatest portion of it was entitlements ($14.952 trillion).[40] Like the total mortgage on a house as distinct from a monthly payment, this amount is not current, but it is an ultimate government responsibility.

Contemplating this astounding sum, H. F. Langenberg asked: " . . . will the federal debts be paid off in like kind? The answer from this corner is categorically no . . . . The next question is, how will the government approach the problem? The answer in short: via depreciated paper currency."[41] According to figures supplied by the Federal Reserve Bank of St. Louis, the national income for 1994 was only $5.140 trillion, of which the total government take was already 48.40%, leaving about $2.652 trillion for the people.[42] And this debt could be counted upon to grow every year. How could it ever be paid off, except by further monetary depreciation? Yet, it would not be long before Clinton Administration and Greenspan would be making the very claim that they were attacking this problem while maintaining low inflation.

Historically, high inflation has been bad for stocks.[43] During the 1970s, for instance, that market crashed in late '73 and remained in the doldrums for the rest of the decade; in that day, people went for such things as gold, silver, rare stamps, and real estate. An unscrupulous interest which wanted to promote stock investment in the '90s would skip mentioning this problem. "Low inflation" is what investors in that market liked hearing.

As the reader will discover, the bubble came into being in 1996. In order to provide the proper basis for understanding the causality, however, the countdown of the short history will begin with the year preceding—1995. The reader will receive the flow of events from the standpoints of the participants. In order to distinguish editorial remarks from the actual words of those who acted and reacted, thought or schemed during those years, they will be in *italics*. In the last chapter will my conclusions be given.

CHAPTER V

1995—THE YEAR BEFORE

There will be more editorial statements in this chapter than in many of the others. This is done so that the reader can more readily grasp the interconnection of events as the tragedy begins to unfold. Through this means, some of them will learn what it means to really read a newspaper. These statements are in italics and are marked either "editorial" or "edit."

Rubin Becomes Secretary Of Treasury

On January 11, 1995, Clinton's chief economic advisor is sworn into office. Before coming to Washington, he was co-chairman of Goldman & Sachs & Co. Mr. Rubin's predecessor as Secretary of the Treasury was Lloyd Benson, a former U.S. Senator and Democrat Vice-Presidential candidate in 1988.

Edit. By shifting from a career politician to a financier, the President is obviously moving closer to Wall Street. Goldman & Sacks is a leading New York investment banking house. The reader may recall the New York Times article which stated that Rubin had directed his former clients to stay in touch with him and continue to work with the investment firm. In the coming years, Goldman & Sacks will be an important source for IPOs.

Merrill Lynch Reduces Staff[44]

In January, the stock brokerage company which proclaimed most proudly that it was "bullish on America" is uncertain as to how the year would turn out. Apparently unaware of what will soon happen, they decide to reduce their staff by five hundred.

Edit. They are not the initiators of what will become the bubble market. Its origin must be sought elsewhere.

Republicans Now Control Both House And Senate

Edit. This is important, because it is the first time since the Eisenhower Presidential victory of 1952 that the Republicans have controlled the House of Representatives. Clinton is forced to work with the opponents of the party which elected him.

Fed Raises Rates

On February 2, the Federal Reserve increases short-term Interest rates ½ %.

Dow Sets Record

On February 24, the Dow Jones Industrial average closes above 4,000 for the first time. This is because of what *The Wall Street Journal* characterizes as a "growing optimism the Federal Reserve can engineer a 'soft landing.'"[45]

Editorial: There are three things to take notice of here: (1) Even though the Fed increased its short-term rate less than two and a half weeks before, the market is going up. (2) Many investors implicitly believe that the guiding hand of the Federal Reserve will protect them. This is not a "simplistic" belief in capitalism so much as it is a presumption in favor of a managed stock market. Naturally, most investors think that it is being managed in their favor. Those who stay too long will wish they had left sooner. (3)The metaphor "soft landing" was taken from the Apollo project for the moon. A strange analogy, since the moon landing required two safe landings, one to get the crew there, the other upon returning to Earth. Perhaps the idea is to take the earth with them as the stock prices go to the moon—that Greenspan and the Fed will supply the air and water, food and electricity which will enable them to thrive under those alien conditions. In this regard, these lines penned by Shakespeare have something for this time:

"It is the very error of the moon;
She comes more near the earth than
She was wont,
And makes men mad."

—*Othello, V, ii 109-111.*

"Currency's Slide May Mark End Of Reserve Role"

"LONDON—Undercut by years of U.S. deficits, the dollar's days as the world's reserve currency may be drawing to a close.

"On Friday, eighteen central banks spent a half-billion dollars in a futile attempt to resist that notion, following a similar $250 million effort by the Federal Reserve the day before. In Germany and Japan, finance ministries scolded dollar bears as wrongheaded. In the U.S. Treasury Secretary Rubin tried talking up a strong dollar as 'in our national interest.'

"Traders, unperturbed by the fuss, continued to dump dollars by the billions. As the greenbacks fell to another post-World War II low against the yen and continued sliding against major European currencies, foreign-exchange dealers and money managers predicted more to come."

Article by Michael R. Senit, *The Wall Street Journal*, March 6, 1995, p. C1.

Edit. Ironically, as the reader will discover, the dollar's slide will have much to do with the stock market's precipitous rise.

"Late Flurry of Program Trading Pulls Stock Prices Back From Loss"

"Late-breaking computer-guided program trading boosted

stock prices out of an otherwise depressing session marked by continuing concern about the ailing dollar.

"Prices ended mixed, with the Dow Jones Industrial Average—which at one point during the day was off nearly 35 points—rallying late to end with a gain of 7.95 to 3,997.56. Standard & Poor's 500-stock Index added 0.23 to 485.65 . . . .

. . . .

"Fears that an ailing dollar will force the Federal Reserve to raise interest rates, combined with worries that inflation may be brought on by rising import prices, haunted investors throughout the day, analysts said.

"'It's right to be worried. With the dollar at these levels, the question you have to ask is, 'Gee, why isn't the market down more?' said Robert Brusca, chief economist at Nikko Securities."

Article by Michael Gonzalez, WSJ, March 7, 1995, p. C1.

Edit. Indeed, how can it keep going with the dollar in trouble?

On March 9, The German Mark Reaches Its Highest Point Since WWII

"The dollar hit new lows against the German mark and Japanese yen yesterday, setting off needless calls for government intervention . . . .

"The Key facts are that the American economy is growing briskly and the current policies are sound . . . .

"The Fed could make a dent if it shifted its monetary policy to drive inflation lower and interest rates higher. Such a shift could persuade investors to buy dollars to invest in America. But monetary contraction poses a serious danger. The Fed raised interest rates last year to bring the growth rates down from unsustainable levels of over 4 percent. Further tightening could tip the economy into stagnation or recession—for little real gain."

Editorial—"Let the Dollar Drift," *New York Times*, March 8, 1995.

Edit. What can they do? If they raise interest rates much more, the stock market will sink. How will they reduce inflation? What they will decide to do will have much to do with the creation of the bubble.

"U.S. Jobless Rate Tumbles To 5.4% On Surge In Hiring"

"An unexpectedly large number of Americans found new jobs in February, and the unemployment rate matched a four-year low by dropping three-tenths of a point, to 5.4 percent, the labor department reported today.

"After a tumultuous week in the financial markets, as the dollar hit record lows against both the German mark and the Japanese yen before recovering somewhat, investors found something to cheer in the latest figures . . . .

"The jump last month in job creation might typically have led to a selloff in markets that are often unnerved by evidence of exuberant growth that could lead to higher inflation. But the traders were encouraged to buy United States assets because the economy appeared to be growing fast enough to keep any threat of recession at bay.

. . . .

"The dollar, which was helped by Mexico's announcement of a new austerity package, got an extra lift . . . .

"For stock traders, the jobless report meant that a recession was less likely and that Corporate earnings might continue to rise. It was party time for Wall Street because the jobs report was 'good news for profits,' said Todd Clark, managing director for equity trading at Mabon Securities."

Article by Robert D. Hershey, Jr., WSJ, March 11, 1995, pp. 1, 48.

Edit. It appears that the prognosticators made an error in the investor's favor. Many take this as a signal that they have more money to play with, just as in the Monopoly game.

PETER ERICKSON

Even Stranger

Under Greenspan, inflation is not held to be an increase in the money supply. According to his idea, as long as the plethora of new money does not result in people having to pay more for the same goods and services, there is no inflation. Up until now, whenever Greenspan said that he thought that the economy was "overheating," he would put the damper on it.

On Friday morning, March 10 at 8:30 A.M., comes the unexpected employment statistics—318,888 new jobs when only 220,000 were expected. One might think that the Fed would take this as evidence that the economic cauldron was in danger of boiling and raise the interest rates, but this is not what it does.

In anticipation of Fed intervention, the 30-year bond price would naturally go down, because it was issued at a lower interest rate. This key instrument is followed avidly by bankers all around the country and, indeed, by serious investors throughout the world. But to the surprise of the market, it moves up, not down—which means that those buying anticipate lower, not higher interest rates. It did not move up just a smidgen either.

Manipulation Suspected

Critics are asking, how would they know that interest rates will not go down, when it is a common practice for Greenspan to raise the rates in this circumstance? As of them puts it: "The [30-year bond]" moved up 19/32nds or $5.94 for a $1,000 face value. Its yield, which moves in the opposite direction, fell to 7.46% from the close on Friday of 7.51%. In other words, these economic statistics, showing a strongly growing economy, should have forced the rates higher; instead, they actually fell.

"Economists have absolutely no explanation for the activity. Here's where the suspicion of Federal intervention arises. The FED desperately needed these strong statistics to allow the dollar to stabilize."[46]

Edit. Some might say that this is only a coincidence—that one swallow does not make a summer. But if it was not the Fed or some governmental agency, what would induce these entrepreneurs to risk large sums of money when they could so easily lose, should the monetary authority raise the rates before they were able to unload them? Were they just being reckless, or did they have inside knowledge?

Lower Unemployment Becomes A Bullish Sign

On March 10, the Dow Jones Industrial Average leaps 52 points, to close at a record 4,035.

Edit. The whole key to this move is that there is no inflation as the Fed defines it, i.e., no significant price increases.

On March 13, Greenspan Says Cost Of Living Index Is Too High

Edit: Greenspan is telling the investor that it is not inflation which needs to be reduced, but the index which measures it, i.e., the dollar is stronger than official government figures would lead one to suppose. This is extremely bullish for stocks. At this time, Greenspan has a lot of credibility, much more than the President. He is reputed to have what they call "integrity." In the past, the general criticism was that he worried too much about currency depreciation, that he longed too much for the fabled discipline of the gold standard.

On March 27, the Dow Crosses the 4,100 Point Threshold For The First Time

Edit: With a boost like the one which Greenspan just gave, there is no surprise there.

On April 19, A Federal Building In Oklahoma City Is Bombed, Slaying Hundreds

After the 1996 elections, Clinton will tell a group of

reporters that he owes his political survival to that event. "It
broke a spell in the country as people began searching for our
common ground again," he added.[47]

*Edit: Instead of continuing to question Clinton, many are trying to
find common ground with him. More are giving him the benefit of the
doubt.*

Clinton Administration Intervenes In Support Of Dollar

In March and April are some fairly quiet dollar rescue
operations. Thereafter, the currency will generally rise until
the year 2002. (Previously, the Administration intervened in
behalf of its currency in May-August 1993 and June November
1994.)[48]

"The birth of a new dollar standard"

"Behind the turmoil afflicting global currency and financial
markets . . . . economist John H. Makin of the American
Enterprise Institute discerns an intriguing pattern: 'I think we
are witnessing a major shift in U.S. economic policy vis-vis
Europe and Asia,' he says, 'the emergence of a monetary
Monroe Doctrine—a hemispheric dollar standard.'

"This policy shift, claims Makin, is implicit in the stance of
the Federal Reserve. Resisting pressures to prop up the
plunging dollar against the yen and the mark, the Fed has
instead emphasized the trade-weighted dollar's stability over
the past year. And surprisingly, the stock markets have
responded by mounting rallies in spite of the dollar's weakness
against major currencies.

"The irony is that the dollar's overall stability comes from
its strength against the shaky Canadian dollar, the fallen
Mexican peso, and other weak Latin currencies. In part, the
recent U.S. equity-and-bond-market rallies have been fueled
by the huge volume of dollars rushing out of Latin America in

search of a safe haven. Declining U.S. interest rates relative to rates in Europe and Japan, in turn, have fostered the flow of short-term cash out of dollars into yen and marks.

"In short, the U.S. has confronted Germany and Japan with what amounts to a competitive dollar devaluation. And this strategy is already boosting the prospects of U.S. exporters to Europe and Japan while undermining the competitiveness of European and Japanese exports to America and other nations with currencies tied to the dollar.

"Pushed too far, warns Makin, this 'devaluation' could feed on itself, touching off a wholesale run on the dollar, with calamitous consequences for the world economy. But pushed just far enough, it could propel Germany and Japan to further loosen their highly restrictive monetary policies and convert their current hesitant recoveries into the full-fledged global expansion." observers have long anticipated."

"A Monetary Turning Point?' by Gene Koretz, *Business Week,* April 24, 1995, p. 26.

Edit: Dr. Makin makes an excellent case that the dollar can continue to be the regional currency for the Western Hemisphere. By itself, however, this local preeminence will not be enough to maintain its basis as the world's reserve money. Latin America is a third-world area and Canada is an economic satellite of the U. S. The author says that the Germans and the Japanese are somewhat stymied. Sooner or later, however, unless something is done about this—or there are currency collapses elsewhere-the dollar will be in danger of losing the position it has held since WWI, when it replaced the British Pound and the French Franc as the chief international currency.

"Companies' Profits Grew 48% Despite Slowing Economy"

"Profits at major U.S. corporations surged in the first quarter in spite of signs that the economy is slowing down. Companies with international operations were helped by the strong performance of European and Asian currencies.

"According to a Wall Street Journal survey, 674 major companies reporting net income rose a cumulative 48% from the 1994 period. In the 1994 fourth quarter, cumulative net income increased 61% from a year earlier."

Article by Fred R. Bleakely, *WSJ*, May 1, 1995, p. A7.

Edit: U. S.-based international corporations can gain from a diminishing dollar; so can exporters. But purely domestic corporations with a fundamentally American market usually cannot. The gain is temporary for many of the others as well.

On May 5, The Commerce Department Announces It Will Overhaul Its Statistics

Edit: This seemingly bland announcement presages great changes in the relationship between Wall Street and the Commerce Department with respect to the handling of government statistics. Greenspan has already called for a revision of the cost of living downward. With a go-ahead signal from such an august source, the Administration has gotten just what it has wanted all along. (The Secretary of Commerce is Ron Brown).

"Mutual Funds Plan to Make Buying Easier"

"WASHINGTON, May 19—Potential buyers of mutual funds will get their first peeks in 30 to 60 days at an easier-to-understand offering prospectus, the documents that details a mutual fund's risks and previous performance, Arthur Levitt, Jr., chairman of the Securities and Exchange Commission, told an investment industry . . . ."

Article by Edward Wyatt, *New York Times*, May 20, 1995.

Edit. No general reduction in staff for them. Mutual funds will soon be easier to buy.

Clinton Veto

Clinton vetoes Republican-passed bill with $16.4 billion in spending cuts. It is his first veto.

On June 19, the Dow Skips Across the 4,500 level

On June 28, the U.S. and Japan Reach Agreement

"Tokyo—Just a day after the United States and Japan reached an automotive trade agreement, the two sides started arguing Thursday over what the accord meant, underlying its ambiguity and weaknesses."
Article by Paul Blustein, *The Washington Post,* June 29, 1995.[49]

"Washington is doing what it accused other nations of plotting to do"

"GENEVA. June 30—Leaving the United States isolated after it rejected a global plan for liberalizing trade in financial services, a large group of industrial and developing nations said today that it favored pressing ahead with a plan of its own.

"The effort won support from all 15 nations in the European Union, which endorsed it at a hastily convened meeting of ministers here tonight. It was supported by a number of other nations, including Canada, Switzerland, Hong Kong, India, Pakistan, Morocco and Uruguay.

"The Governing council of the World Trade Organization, the body created earlier this year to oversee world trade, also gave its support to the European approach, as well as to the exclusion from the plan of the United States.

On Thursday, American officials said they would not enter into a global agreement because certain other countries were not offering American financial institutions enough access to their markets. Under the agreement, each of the more than 80 nations would offer banks, insurance companies and brokerage houses from other countries access to their financial markets.

. . . .

"The United States, meanwhile, formally notified the trade organization today that it was closing its financial services market to all new foreign entrants, although foreign financial companies already in the country would continue to be treated as if they were American companies.

. . . .

"Under the European plan, any trade concessions that the countries agreed upon at the end of the month would be automatically extended to the United States because the trade organization's rules forbid discrimination among its members.

"That means the United States would become a 'free rider' in the system, gaining improved access abroad without opening its own market any further—precisely the accusation it made during the negotiations against Asian and Latin American countries that were seeking greater access to the American market than they were willing to offer."

Paul Lewis, "Financial Services Plan Advances Without U.S.," *New York Times,* July 7, 1995, pp. 33-34.

Edit. The U. S. government is doing the very thing that it has been bashing Japan for doing. In this case, it is keeping the increasingly lucrative U.S. financial services market for American firms—especially Wall Street firms like Goldman & Sachs. Foreign stock brokerages will not be able to send advertisements to America; Canadian credit card companies will not be able to solicit business here. At the same time, as we will see, millions of blue-collar industrial jobs are being sent overseas— "the mighty sucking sound" warned about by Ross Perot.

On July 6, The Federal Reserve Cuts Short-Term Rates By 1/4%

"Under mounting political and economic pressure, to stave off a possible recession, the Federal Reserve reduced short-term interest rates for the first time since 1992.

. . . .

"'As a result of the monetary tightening initiated in early 1994, inflationary pressures have receded enough to accommodate a modest adjustment in monetary conditions,' Alan Greenspan, the Fed's chairman said in a statement today.'"

Keith Bradsher, 'Federal Reserve Trims A Key Rate . . . .", *The New York Times*, July 7, 1995, p. 1.

"Japan Joins U.S. to Block Fall by Dollar"

"Washington, July 7—Seeking to prevent the Federal Reserve's Thursday interest-rate reduction from weakening the dollar, the Japanese government pushed down interest rates slightly in Tokyo today and then intervened in American currency markets with the United States to prop up the dollar"

"The combined effort was a sharp rise in the dollar's value against the yen, as many traders concluded that Washington and Tokyo were more closely coordinating their economic policies and would prevent any further fall in the dollar. In late trading, the dollar has surged 1.80 yen, to 86.70 yen to the dollar.

Keith Bradsher, *The New York Times*, July 7, 1995, p. 33.

Edit. Backed up by Japan, the Fed takes an important step. Because the currency is shaky, there is fear of a stumble.

"Dow Gallops Past 4,700, Riding on Fed's Rate Cut"

"Just two days after the Dow Jones Industrial average first topped the 4,600 mark, it soared past 4700 yesterday, as the stock market enjoyed its best week since last August."

"The Dow closed at 4,702.73, up . . . 146.63 points for the week. Less than five months ago this key indicator exceeded 4000 for the first time.

"Much of yesterday's market advance was attributed to the lowering by the Federal Reserve of the target for the Federal funds rate by one-quarter of a percentage pint, to 5.75 percent . . . ."

Leonard Sloane, *NYT*, July 8, 1995, p. 37.

Edit. This maneuver is succeeding, so far. But can this keep up?

"Jobless Rate Dropped to 5.6% During June"

"The unemployment rate dropped .01 percentage point to 5.6% of the work force, the Labor Department reported, the second consecutive monthly decline since the rate hit 5.8% in April. Payroll employment rose 215,000 last month, the department said, the most since a 313,000 increase in February."

Christopher Georges, *The Wall Street Journal*, July 10, 1995.

Edit. This unexpected good news from the Department of Labor about the June unemployment rate does not increase the market very much, but it gives it the appearance of underlying solidity.

Mushy Data

"On the other hand, the June survey period was later in the month than is typical, and the additional time to capture workers in the statistical net swelled the gain by 50,000 to 100,000, according to a rough estimate by the Bureau of Labor Statistics."

Article by Robert D Hershey Jr., NYT, July 8, 1995, p. 1.[50]

Edit. The delay lowers the employment increase from 46.5% to 23.25%. This is quite a difference. What is remarkable about the initial report is that the increase was expected to be a lot lower—about 115,000. Now, it appears that it might even have been as low as anticipated. This contradiction is buried in the back of a New York Times article extolling the 215,00. Was this a covert attempt by the authorities to back up the Fed, or was it simply an accident? Would Clinton's Labor Department stoop to that? Obviously, the situation requires watching.

Dow Transportation Average Accelerates

The Dow Jones Company posts and reports on other Averages, besides the Industrials, which will be tracked throughout nearly the whole of this book. Another is the Transportation Average, covering 20 stocks, such as Alaska Air, Conrail, Delta Airlines, Santa Fe, and Union Pacific. On Friday, June 7, and Monday, June 10, the average was suddenly driven up 51 points[51] from 1,843 to a new record. The old record was 1,862. It now stands at 1,994.

This is of great significance because of the Dow theory, which holds that the market will rise as a whole when the Industrials and the Transport rise together. For the many people who follow this theory, it means that a new bull market may have begun.

Critic Charges Manipulation

" . . . on July 7th and 10th, the transportation average suddenly gapped higher on two consecutive days. Normally when this happens, it is a sign that the gap upward will be equaled by a downward movement. It is significant to note that there were no earnings reports for the 20 stocks in the transport average that could justify such a run up. It was clearly manipulation."

. . . .

"Heretofore . . . [it] had failed to breach the previous high, thus preventing the Dow theorists from declaring a FORMAL DECLARATION—of a new bull market—in accordance with the Dow theory. In other words, the government has purposely manipulated the averages—so as to deceitfully trick and defraud the American public into believing that we have a new bull market when in fact—we have a currency crisis, which is forcing the

Government to prop up stocks in an attempt to avoid a run on the dollar."

L. Patterson, July 31, 1995.[52]

Edit. Was it the autonomous market that nursed and rehearsed the birth of this bull? Or is this critic right? Is it just some champaign bubbles issuing from the Fred's action, Japan's support, and the dubious employment statistics, or an attempt to support the dollar by hiking up the stock market? What about the other strange events that have been going on, such as the 30-year bond, and the number of last-hour recoveries bringing the market up? Keep tuned.

On July 19, Accountants Decline To Vouch For House Of Representatives' Books

Edit: Good thing we've got Alan Greenspan. He'll keep things clean.

On September 18, The Dow Closes Above 4,800

"Skilled Workers Watch Their Jobs Migrate Overseas—A Blow To Middle Class"

"College-educated Foreigners Are Doing High-Technology tasks for far Less Pay"

Article by Keith Bradsher, *The New York Times*, October 28, 1995.

Edit. While foreign financial service companies which would compete with Wall Street and U.S. banks are kept out, educated foreigners are brought in to compete with ordinary citizens.

On October 10, The Nasdaq Falls

The Nasdaq composite index loses 2.7% of its value, falling to 984.74. This is a reaction against the high priced technology stocks.

Edit. Investors still price such stocks according to realistic standards. Woe to them if they change!

Clinton Claims Budget Deficit Reduction

On October 25, Clinton holds a press conference in which he claims credit for reducing the budget deficits for 1993 and 1994, because of his tax increases.

The Joint Economic Committee of U. S. Congress Demurs

According to their *Economic Update of October 1995*, "a review of the budget figures from 1993, 1994, and 1995 demonstrates that the deficit declines are not driven by the Clinton tax increases, a policy which even President Clinton now acknowledges was a mistake.

. . . .

"As the 1994 JEC report pointed out, the deficit did decline from 1992 to 1993: $290 billion (1992) - $ 255 Billion (1993) = $35 Billion deficit reduction.

"This decline had nothing to do with Clinton policies, but with large swings in deposit insurance outlays and other non-policy factors. Also, since the fiscal year ended several weeks after the Clinton tax increases were signed into law, there is no way that these policies could have had a direct effect on the fiscal 1993 deficit." (**Emphasis** removed).

On November 22, The Dow Struts Across the 5,000 Mark

Significant Clinton Veto

On December 7, Clinton turns back a Republican bill to balance the budget in seven years.

Edit: Will he stay with this stand, or will he co-opt the Republicans, as Dick Morris advised? To put it differently, will he continue the traditional

Democrat approach, or will he work more closely with a certain prominent Republican?

Hundred-Year Corporate Bond To Be Eliminated.

On December 7, Clinton looks to raise revenue through changes in corporate tax laws, such as eliminating 100-year bonds. The argument is that the hundred-year corporate bond is in fact an equity and not an expense. The administration hopes to gain $28 billion in taxes from this measure over seven years.

Edit. Although Clinton's favor is shifting toward the stock market, there are still elements of traditional Democrat thinking left in his actions.

Congress Overrides Clinton's Veto

On December 26, Congress overrides Clinton's veto of a bill cutting the types of lawsuits for fraud which can be made against firms selling securities. At this time, however, it is not considered as a party issue. Twenty Senate Democrats, including liberal stalwart, Senator Edward Kennedy of Massachusetts, and 89 House Democrats join the Republicans in overriding the veto.[53]

Edit. Clinton's veto is in line with the traditional Democrat approach. It might have made a tiny difference in the final outcome At present, Clinton is moving in both directions, sometimes toward Wall Street and sometimes the other way. But, more and more, he will be seen to be s shifting into the new economy orientation.

Dow Breaks Record 69 Times In 1995

On December 14, the Dow attains 5,200 and set a new record for the sixty-ninth time, finishing at 5,216.47.

Edit: The beat goes on.

On December 20, The Fed Cuts An Interest Rate

Short-term rates are cut 1/4%. The reason given is that

inflation is low. This is in keeping with Greenspan's contention that the cost of living is less than the government indexes might lead one to think.

Edit. Aw-a-a-y we go!

"What A Year For Greenspan"

Bob Woodward's Admiring Estimation Of 1995 For Greenspan

"In most respects, he had the economy right where he wanted it. Inflation was low, at less than 3 percent for the year. Unemployment was also low, steady in the 5 1/4 percent range, with the addition of 1.8 million jobs for the year. After 3 ½ percent growth the previous year, the annual growth was down in the range of 1 ½ percent. There had been no recession. Greenspan had delivered. The economic analyses he had given Clinton were evident. By keeping inflation low and cutting the federal deficit, the intermediate—and long-term interest rates—the key rates for businesses, home buyers, and consumers—were 2 to 2 ½ percent below their levels at the beginning of 1995. Bond prices, which move in the opposite direction as interest rates, were up substantially, and the stock market was up about 35 percent with the Dow at 5117—its best year in two decades."

"He was available [for reappointment]."[54]

A Problem With The Way The Administration Cuts the "Deficit"

As H.F. Langenberg, C.F.A., put it that year: "In 1990, 68% of the national debt was funded at maturities of five years or less. The current Administration in its attempt to cut expenditures turned to shortening maturities and, by 1994, 74% of the debt was funded at maturities of five years or less with nearly 33% at one year or less. This manipulation created an immediate savings of almost $50 billion. Multiplying that five years ahead and assuming no change in rate, the theoretical savings amounts to

$250 billion. Add the increase in revenues of $50 billion a year for five years, and it would appear to be a deficit reduction of $500 billion. However, this reduction of maturities was quite the opposite of every other previous Administration since World War II which tried to extend maturities as long as possible. The latter policy protected the budget from swings in interest rates and was regarded as the conservative and sane policy of financing. This change in policy has now endangered the economy. The dramatic decline in bond prices last year and the weakness in the dollar are just the first warning signs. With short-term rates almost double of a year ago, and 33% of the debt now funded in one year or less, the deficits will rise far faster than most observers are prepared to forecast. For every percentage point rise in short term rates, another $200 billion or more could be added to the debt by 1998. The widening deficit will once again become an issue of the capital markets."[55]

Edit: The dollar's weakness implies higher and higher interest rates on short maturities. Unless the dollar can somehow be propped up on a continuing basis, the Administration's short-term policy seems doomed.

But the Stock Market Is Still Within Reason

Below is a chart of price-earnings ratios as prepared in April 2002 by the Federal Reserve Bank of Chicago.[56]

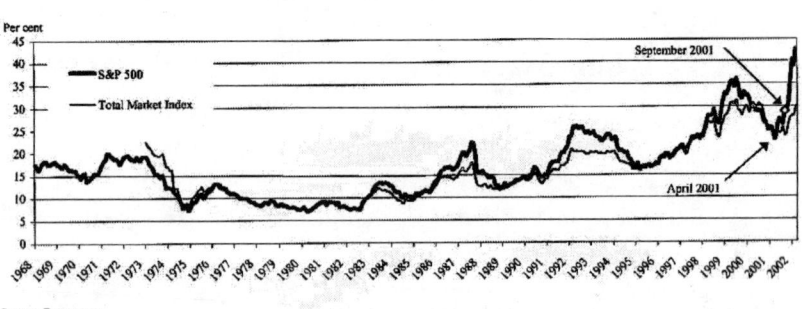

Figure 2. **Price earnings ratios for broad stock indices in the United States**

Source: Datastream.

This is the ratio between stock price and earnings.

Historically, the ratio is in the neighborhood of 14-18, which means that the stock price is from fourteen to eighteen times earnings. This means annual earnings of between 7.14% and 5.5%. Based on this graph, it is clear that even the higher S & P ratio is within historical averages.

The chart actually shows the ratios dropping from a local high in 1993. The trough takes place in 1995.

Looking at the years ahead, the S & P price-earnings ratio progressively increases, peaking early in the year 2000 above 35, dropping earnings to 2.8%. Then, as the stock prices plummet, the P/E ratio descends, reaching a nadir in the low twenties in April 2001. Thereafter, the ratio will rise once more, despite the drop in stock prices. This is because so many companies are in bankruptcy or are simply making less money. Looking ahead of 1995, the ratio will peak early in 2001.

1995 was not a year of ridiculous asset prices for stocks. It was instead the come-on, the invitation through the gateway to destruction.

Editorial: The onrush of dollars out of the ruined economies of Latin America and the declining Canadian dollar brings money into the stock market. In turn, the rising stock market, bolstered by behind-the-scenes manipulation, saves the day for the dollar. 1995 stock prices, although they scrape the sky, are not altogether atmospheric. It is possible for the market to come down a little without wiping out a lot of people; the 5,200 level on the Dow could be maintained, even surpassed a few times within the next year or so, without triggering a vigorous downpour through up-swellings of turbulent speculation. There would many corrections, but no general disaster.

This situation was brought about through adept manipulation— at this stage principally by Greenspan; there is also strong evidence of the increasing use of legerdemain by the Administration.

In the next chapter, the short history of the bubble market will begin. As with this chapter on 1995, the people writing and talking about it then will be allowed to speak in their own words. Opinions expressed by myself will be in italics, as before. As the reader follows the brief history, he or she might ask these questions: How was the fragile market kept up? Why it is that a libertarian Fed Chairman should abandon the policies which he followed under the Republicans who had appointed and reappointed him in favor a huge expansion of the money supply during the administration of a very partisan Democrat?

CHAPTER VI

1996—THE BUBBLE IS HATCHED

Edit: "The bubble began in 1996, when the ratio of stock prices to corporate earnings went out of kilter. By the late '90s, the ratio had reached about 30 to one—double the historic average."[57] *These are the words of Jonathon Chatt, a writer for the traditionally liberal, New Republic. And he was correct. Look back on the two charts.*

1996 was the centennial year for the Dow. That year it climbed above 6,000, doubling what it was when Clinton came into office.

Nasdaq Drops

On January 8, the Nasdaq drops to 986.81, the first time it hit below 1,000 since October of 1995.

Edit: But there will be another day.

Rubin Vs. House Republicans

"House Republicans yesterday turned up the pressure on the Clinton administration by suggesting they might initiate impeachment proceedings against Treasury Secretary Robert E. Rubin if he continued to ignore the will of Congress by borrowing money for the Treasury.

"Reps. Gerald Solomon (R-N.Y.) and Christopher Cos (R-Calif.) raised the impeachment specter after Rubin met for 90 minutes with key legislators at the Capitol to discuss the impasse over increasing the $4.9 trillion ceiling on federal debt.

Raising the debt ceiling is mired in the larger battle over balancing the federal budget.

"'Those of us who are concerned with the constitutionality of Secretary Rubin's behavior will be watching him closely and will support impeachment proceedings should he continue to bypass the Constitution,' said Solomon, chairman of the House Rules Committee.

. . . .

"Solomon and other Republicans were enraged last year when Rubin, in an effort to avert a first-ever default on U. S. government obligations, invoked his authority under the law to replace government securities held in two federal employee retirement accounts with IOUs. Rubin then issued new debt to pay off bondholders when their Treasury bonds came due.

. . . .

"Republicans, backed by legal opinion prepared by former Republican Attorneys General William Barr and Edwin Meese, argue that the Constitution vests Congress with the sole authority to decide how much debt the government can take on. When Rubin exchanged federal debt for non-interest-bearing IOUs in two federal employee retirement funds last November, he effectively usurped the power of Congress, they said."

Steven Pearlstein, *The Washington Post*, January 5, 1996.[58]

Edit: Some people might sympathize with Mr. Rubin, because he was only trying to hold off a major default; that it was during a squabble with the Congressional Republicans, who were deliberately holding back money from the federal government in order to get their way. But he still did something of questionable legality, and he did use the sleight-of-hand technique of exchanging one debt for another, thereby making the federal retirement fund less secure. The reader should be on the lookout for such devices in situations less easy to minimize.

"The Money Plane"

"Five nights a week, at least $100 million in crisp new $100 bills is flown from JFK nonstop to Moscow, where it is used to finance the Russian mob's vast and growing international crime syndicate. State and federal officials believe it is part of a multi-billion dollar money laundering operation. The Republic National Bank and the United States Federal Reserve prefer not to think so.

. . . .

"The Russian mob, according to numerous well-placed law-enforcement sources interviewed by *New York*, has been using an unimpeded supply of freshly minted Federal Reserve notes to finance a vast and growing international crime syndicate. American C-notes are the unofficial currency of Russia, of course, and can get things done there that rubles cannot; but the hundreds are also being used to fuel the Russian mob's flourishing dollar-based global drug trade, as well as to buy the requisite villas in Monaco and Cannes. The Russian *Mafiya* has also used laundered funds to set up operations abroad, including its American offshoot in Brooklyn's Brighton Beach . . . and has began investing in legitimate businesses in the United States.

. . . .

"A 1994 CIA report identified ten of the largest Russian banks as mobbed-up fronts. And in his speech to the United Nations last October, President Clinton declared money laundering a threat to national security . . . .

"So then why are Republic National Bank and the U.S. Federal Reserve continuing to supply millions of crisp, clear $100 bills to banks that so many money-laundering experts agree are tainted? 'Republic's guilty of willful blindness, though not in technical violation of any existing laws,' says a former

New York State Banking Department official. 'That money is used to support organized crime; it's used to support black-market operations,' agrees the federal Comptroller of the Currency office, which regulates Republic: 'In my personal opinion this is an absolute abomination. It should not exist. Yet it appears that at least part of the federal government sees nothing wrong with it.'

"A provision in the 1992 Annunzio Wylie Anti-Money Laundering Act requires banks to make sure that they're not knowingly doing business with criminals or their agents. For the record, the Republic National Bank, which makes millions off the currency sales, insists it is certainly not *knowingly* selling $100 bills to mobsters.

"'That's my responsibility, to make sure we don't sell to the banks that have organized-crime ties,' says Richard Anricharico, one of Republic's compliance officials. 'That's the hardest thing to find. In fact, if you know of any, let me know.'

"And the U.S. Treasury, which makes $99.96 off of any $100 bill that leaves the country and never comes back, is similarly blissfully ignorant. 'What do we know of Republic's customers?' says New York Fed Spokesman Peter Bakstansky. 'We don't. It's their responsibility to know who they are sending it to.'

. . . .

"Amricharico acknowledges that a federal money-laundering task force had contacted him about Republic's currency trade with Russia: 'The task force told me that they think Russian organized crime is involved in money laundering. But so what?' he says. 'Who? What's the crime? Tell me—I'll stop! I can't find them. I'm not being facetious.'"

Article, Robert I. Friedman, *New York Magazine,* January 22, 1996, pp. 26-28.

Edit: Here are the Federal Reserve and the Treasury Department cooperating with New York's Republic Federal Bank in sending money to international drug dealers. Not only is this less worthy of sympathy than Rubin's maneuver with the retirement funds, but it suggests that Greenspan's allegedly stodgy Fed is not as upright as the image concocted by the media would allow one to suppose. Treasury is also involved. Why doesn't someone tell Rubin?

Mrs. Clinton Says She's Innocent

On January 29, Hillary Rodham Clinton says she doesn't know why the long-missing billing records from the Rose law firm were located in the White House residential quarters, after having testified before a Whitewater grand jury that she didn't know where they were.

Greenspan Reduces Fed Fund Rate

On February 2, the Federal Reserve cuts interest rates by 1/4 point. The Fed also cuts the Federal funds target rate to 5.25%.

During Week Of February 12-16, Dollar Slides Against German Mark

Edit: The same problem as last year.

Bankers Indicted

On February 21, a Whitewater jury indicts two bank owners on charges of conspiracy, fraud, and misappropriation of bank funds for donations to Clinton's 1990 gubernatorial campaign.

Clinton Reappoints Greenspan

The date is February 22, 1996. The President also announces the nominations of Democrats Alice Rivlin and Laurence H. Meyer to the Federal Reserve. A reporter asks, "Mr. President, do you think these three people will be able to engage in the kind of debate you were talking about last week?" Answered Clinton, "I do." Then he explains: "I think that the truth is that *we're entering a new economy* and it's a subject that ought to be open to honest debate."[59] (*Emphasis* added).

> CALVIN COOLIDGE—U.S. PRESIDENT—WHITE HOUSE, 1927
> "[AMERICA IS] "ENTERING UPON A NEW ERA OF PROSPERITY."[60]

> MISS GERTRUDE M. COOGAN—ECONOMIST 1935
> "THE NEWSPAPERS AND WELL PUBLICIZED PAID 'ECONOMISTS' REPEATED DELIBERATE FALSEHOODS TELLING THE PEOPLE THAT AMERICA WAS IN A 'NEW ERA.' WE WERE ASSURED ETERNALLY RISING PRICES, AND ALL OF THE OLD MEASUREMENTS OF STOCK VALUES WERE OUT-OF-DATE. THE NEW YORK STOCK EXCHANGE WAS AN ALADDIN'S LAMP. THE NEWSPAPERS DID EVERYTHING POSSIBLE TO FAN THE FLAMES AND 16,000,000 PEOPLE IN THE UNITED STATES WERE ACTIVE PARTICIPANTS IN THE PURCHASE AND SALE OF SECURITIES." [61]

Dow Jones Industrial Average Soars

The very day that Greenspan is reappointed, the Dow gains 92.49 points to 5,698.46. There is also some economic news, claiming lower inflation. And on March 18, after a dip, the Industrials rise 98.65 points to a record 5,683.50.

Edit. The investors really respect this man.

Economic Writer Finds That CPI Has Been Rigged

"Energy prices have been zooming. They are up 25%-to-45% over the past five months. Crude oil has soared $6 a barrel from its October lows. During February alone, energy prices rocketed up close to 20%.

"Yet the February CPI showed a 0.7% DECREASE in energy

costs! Because of that, the CPI showed only a 0.2% increase for February. The PPI showed a 0.2% decline.

"This made no sense to me. So I confronted one of the economists at the Department of Labor. He helps calculate the CPI and the PPI. First, he tried to blow smoke. But finally he admitted the energy number was bogus. No market goes straight up: in the report they had used the brief dip in energy prices that took place earlier in January.

"'Our orders are to hide inflation as much as we can,' he told me.

"He also said they have a real problem, because everyone watches the report. The best they could do, he said, was postpone the bad news for as long as possible.

"I could not believe my ears. This guy was admitting they were under enormous pressure to lie. Of course, the powers that be benefit from keeping the public trolling along in blissful ignorance. Why? It's just like the balanced budget malarkey. As long as they can keep the masses sleeping, the more wealth they can confiscate.

"If people believe the no-inflation lie, they will do the exact opposite of what they should do to protect themselves from the ravages of inflation. They will dig their own graves, and have to pay the cruel inflationary tax. Government can try to inflate its way out of trouble."

The Underground Wall Street, March 1996, pp. 12-13.[62] *Http:/ /www.wallstreetunderground.com/NewsLetter/Filles/0396.asp*

"Russians greet new $100 bill with open arms: U.S. education program worked"

"Somewhere in Siberia, there may be people who haven't heard about the new U.S. $100 bill. But it wasn't for lack of trying by the U.S. Treasury, which spent millions preparing people around the world for the redesigned U.S. currency.

"The campaign appears to have worked. Officials in the United States and Russia say Russians—many of whom keep their life savings in dollars—have accepted the redesigned $100 bill with aplomb."

Sandra Block, *U.S.A. Today*, April 1, 1996.

Edit: This illustrates that the U.S. dollar is still the world's major currency; some of it, however, is being shipped by airplane to Russian drug gangs.

INS Chief Says Immigration Down

It is March. Congress is considering some legislation that would restrict immigration. There is bipartisan support and also opposition to it from both parties. President Clinton is on record as being against it. Doris Meissner, commissioner of the Immigration and Naturalization Service, testifies before Congress that immigration had gone down ten percent in 1994 and also in 1995.[63]

Edit: The new immigrants, both legal and illegal, compete with Americans for their jobs, keeping wages down by competition. This lowers business costs, which temporarily improves their bottom line; which can add to the upward thrust of stock prices. The bill threatens that. But, if it is true that immigration is decreasing, there is less reason for changing the law.

Meissner Testimony Not Truthful

In April, there is a leak to the effect that legal immigration has climbed up by 41% above the 1995 level and the same is expected for 1997. Senator Alan Simpson (R-WY), a sponsor of the beleaguered bill to lower immigration, says, "If the INS had projections about the dramatic hike in legal immigration and did not release it to Congress before debate on the effort to lower immigration numbers, its actions were unconscionable."[64]

Edit. Keeping down the cost of labor is crucial to the pretense of low inflation. The public thinks that inflation is just an increase in the price level. Actually, inflationism is the policy of increasing the money supply. It is possible for inflationism to exist without raising prices. This could happen in a time of rapidly improving technology. In the '90s, the cost of computer hardware is going down. There, inflationism is disguised because prices which would have gone down much further in its absence are higher, or the same, when they might have been lower.

"Up to 20 are subpoenaed in criminal probe of Brown"

"Federal investigators have subpoenaed as many as 20 witnesses in the criminal investigation of Commerce Secretary Ronald H. Brown for appearances before a grand jury in Washington.

FBI and IRS agents are focusing on claims that an Oklahoma gas company—Dynamic Energy Resources.—was used to enrich Mr. Brown's son, Michael, and gain influence in the Commerce Department. Investigations also are trying to find out if any of the hundreds of thousands of dollars paid to Michael Brown was funneled to his father."

Article, Andy Thibault, *The Washington Times*, March 29, 1996

Edit. The evidence against him is strong. If Brown is guilty and should decide to plea bargain in exchange for involving some more Clinton people, the whole Administration would be at risk. The election is slightly more than seven months away.

On April 3, Ronald Brown Dies In Balkan Airplane Crash

Clinton Denies Involvement In Fraud

On May 10, Clinton states in a video testimony in court that he did not participate in a $300,000 allegedly fraudulent government-backed loan in behalf of one of the Whitewater defendants.

Edit. The election is about six months away.

Stock Market Rises In May

On May Day, the Nasdaq composite reaches a record high of 1,199.86. On May 13, the Nasdaq hits 1,221.87. That same day, the Dow Jones Industrial Average gains 84.46 points, attaining the level of 5,582.60.

On May 29, A Jury Convicts All Three Defendants In Whitewater Case

More Whitewater Trouble For Clinton

On June 17, a second Whitewater trial in Arkansas begins; two bankers are accused of having stolen money in order to cover political donations to two campaigns, including Clinton's 1990 Gubernatorial race. On July 18, Governor Jim Tucker, Clinton's hand-picked successor as Arkansas governor resigns. He has been convicted of fraud.

Edit. The election is about four and one-half months away.

Republicans Pick Candidates at July Convention

Former Senate Majority Leader Bob Dole of Kansas is chosen as their Presidential candidate, and former Congressman and later HUD chief, Jack Kemp, is selected to run for the Vice-Presidency.

Stocks Go Down In July

Comes July 8 and the Dow falls 114.88 points; on the 16th, the Dow loses more than 161 points in a sell-off of technological stocks. It is not until July 17 that the Dow makes a slight recovery, ending with a gain of 9.25 points.

Clinton Denies

On July 18, Clinton testifies by videotape at the 2nd

Whitewater trial that he did not give two bankers state jobs in exchange for donation to his political campaign.

Greenspan Rides To Clinton's Rescue

"The one event that could have stopped Clinton was a sudden downturn in the markets and the economy. In the first two weeks of July 1996, amid concerns about inflation and corporate profits, the Dow did fall 7 percent. But once again, Alan Greenspan rode to the rescue. On July 18, he told Congress, 'There are a number of reasons to expect demands to moderate and economic activity to settle back toward a more sustainable pace in the months ahead.' That meant he probably wouldn't have to raise interest rates. His remarks sparked a huge bond rally, sending the rate on the long bond from above 7 percent to 6.92 percent; the Dow rose 87.3 points, or 1.6 percent."

Daniel Gross. *Bull Run: Wall Street, The Democrats, and the New Politics of Personal Finance.* [65]

Edit. Mr. Gross is a Democrat intellectual. Greenspan was once a major intellectual for the other party. Here, Gross is showing how Greenspan helped a Democrat beat the Republicans.

Clinton Gets Another Break

On August 18, the Reform Party meets at Valley Forge, Pennsylvania, to nominate Ross Perot for the Presidency.

Edit. In 1992, Perot gave Clinton the edge he needed to defeat President Bush from being reelected. Can he do it again?

Another Whitewater Figure Is Jailed

On August 20, Susan McDougal goes to jail, after refusing to tell a grand jury whether Clinton had lied to the jury that convicted her of fraud.

Edit. Two and a half months before E-day and the media is full of pictures of Mrs. McDougal in chains. Many wonder if there will be more like that.

Clinton's Former Agriculture Secretary Implicated In Bribe Trial

On September 25, Sun-Diamond Growers is convicted of having made illegal gifts to Secretary Esby and his brother.

Edit. Despite some convenient developments, Clinton is still immured in scandal. If the economy were to slump, even a weak opponent might be able to defeat him.

Republican Candidate Claims Economy Not In Good Shape

Bob Dole proposes a 15% tax cut, which boosts his standing in the polls. Along with that, he expresses doubts about the economy's sustainable pace.

On October 6, during the first Presidential debate, he tells the voters: "He [Clinton] inherited a growth of 4.74 percent, now its down to about 2.4 percent. We've got stagnant wages . . . .

"We have the highest foreign debt in history. And it seems to me that if you take a look, are you better off? Well I guess Saddam Hussein is probably better of than he was four years ago . . . . Are the American people? They're working harder and harder . . . and paying more taxes. For the first time in history you pay about 40 percent of what you earn. More than you spend for food, clothing, and shelter combined . . . ."

Stock Market Rises In October

On October 1, the Dow passes the 5,900 mark for the first time, closing at 5,904.90. Thirteen days later, the Dow closes above 6,000, increasing that day by 40.62 points to 6,010.

More Happy News For Clinton

In September, the Labor Department states that energy costs have fallen, that the core PPI rate is down 0.1 %.

The Labor Department also claims that August unemployment dropped to a seven-year low of 5.1%. At the first debate with Dole, Clinton asks the same question Reagan did when he was unseating Carter, namely, Are Americans better off than they were four years earlier? Clinton rebukes Dole's pessimism: "It is not midnight in America, Senator." On October 28, at University City, Missouri, he brags that the deficit had been reduced by 63%.while he was President.[66]

John M. Berry, *The Washington Post's* Federal Reserve observer, writes an article, headlined: "U.S. Sails on Tranquil Economic Seas, Recessions No Longer Seem Inevitable."[67]

A Behind the Scenes Explanation

"Normally, the FOMC [Federal Open Market Committee] meeting is a no-event, even if the Fed moves rates. We have been predicting higher rates all year. And rates have steadily gone up from 5.75% to 7% . . . .

"Right before the FOMC meeting, 8 of 12 Fed regional bank presidents were demanding the Fed raise rates significantly. They didn't just want a .25% raise. They wanted a .5% raise, at the September meeting. They were so desperate that they took an unprecedented action. They risked criminal prosecution, by leaking their demand for higher rates to Reuters News Service.

"Why? . . . Clinton appointees to the Fed, plus administration arm-twisting, have fatally politicized the Federal Reserve Board. They are flirting with disaster: destroying the entire U.S. economy, to appease Bill Clinton. And now, for the first time in memory, the Fed refused to raise rates, despite the pleadings of the overwhelming majority of its regional members. This clearly shows how successful Clinton has been at destroying the Federal Reserve's independence.

"You have to understand the orientation of regional Federal Reserve Banks. They nearly always want LOWER interest rates. It is extraordinary for these guys to demand a big rate increase.

To go public with the demand is unprecedented. Inside information I have says the Fed presidents are really concerned . . . . By the time inflation hits the nightly news, it's embedded. It takes a hell of a lot more pain (in the form of higher interest rates) to stamp out. Remember the early 1980's? Inflation became embedded. The Fed had to raise rates to 18% to stamp it out. This wiped out the life savings of millions of people."

. . . .

"The bubble market is a disaster waiting to happen. In the shock of the century, the biggest ever wipeout of the average Joe is about to take place. Blame will be placed squarely on the shoulders of the Fed. they have *not* reeled in derivatives. They *have* given mutual funds a blank check, to do as they please. They have aided and abetted the biggest stock market orgy ever. The history books will record this as the worst Ponzi scheme of all time. Wall Street created mutual fund mania: the Fed ignored it; the politicians give it their full support.

"Trillions of dollars have been unthinkingly thrown at the market. The market can't begin to efficiently utilize that kind of money . . . ."

The Wall Street Underground, Vol. 3, No. 1, August/September 1996.p. 17.

MISS GERTRUDE M. COOGAN—ECONOMIST—1935
"IN AUGUST OF 1927, DESPITE OPPOSITION FROM ELEVEN OF THE TWELVE FEDERAL RESERVE BANKS, WHO SAW THE DANGER, THE CENTRAL FEDERAL RESERVE BANKS WERE ORDERED TO LOWER THEIR REDISCOUNT RATES AND BUY ADDITIONAL GOVERNMENT BONDS. IN OTHER WORDS, THE STEPS WERE TAKEN TO INCREASE THE RESERVES OF THE CITY BANKS. CITY BANKS RESPONDED BY INCREASING THEIR PROMISES-TO-PAY (LOANS). THESE LOANS WENT ALMOST ENTIRELY TO FINANCE STOCK PURCHASES. LOANS WERE MADE ON ANY AND EVERY KIND OF

COLLATERAL. IT BECAME A VERY COMMON PRACTICE FOR CORPORATIONS TO ISSUE RIGHTS TO BUY ADDITIONAL STOCKS, AND FOR INDIVIDUALS EXERCISING THOSE RIGHTS TO BORROW THE ENTIRE AMOUNT AT THEIR BANKS, USING THE STOCK AS COLLATERAL. IN OTHER WORDS, BANKS WERE CREATING PROMISES TO PAY AND THE FUNDS THUS CREATED WERE FLOWING INTO THE TREASURIES OF CORPORATIONS, THERE EITHER TO LIE IDLE AS DEPOSIT CASH OR TO BE USED IN BUILDING PLANTS. OF COURSE, THEY WERE UNSOUND."[68]

Edit. The reader may recall that in his famous 1966 article, Greenspan played down the significance of the 1927 episode, focusing instead upon the Fed's attempt to help England. We shall see that even The Wall Street Journal would years later chide him for his overruling the regional Fed presidents and governors. Greenspan is living the kind of reality that he had mis-reported earlier.

A Little bit Of Bad News For Clinton, But . . .

On October 29, bond prices reach six-month highs because of news that the economy has not been growing as much as expected.

First Democrat Since FDR To Be Elected President Twice

Clinton is re-elected with 49% of the vote, Dole, 41%, and Ross Perot, 8%. By December, the Dow will have advanced 26% over the previous year. Dole still carries the majority of those making at least $100,000 per year—54% to 38%—but Clinton's share rises above what he had in 1992.[69]

A top aide of Clinton's is reported to have explained: "People dismissed Bob Dole's argument that the economy was in terrible shape, because they know that everyone was making money in the market" [70]

Reminiscent of Election Of FDR's Unfortunate Predecessor

In November of 1928, Herbert Hoover, Secretary of Commerce under President Calvin Coolidge, defeated New York Governor Al Smith for the Presidency of the United States. But, as the world knows, Mr. Hoover was not long to enjoy his victory, for the stock market would take the most famous plunge in recorded history eleven months later. In the next election, he would come down in crushing defeat to N.Y. Governor Franklin Delano Roosevelt. For many years afterwards, Hoover's name would become a byword for economic collapse. By contrast, the Bubble of the 90's would not receive the first strike from the lance until nearly 3-1/2 years after Clinton's momentous victory. Mr. Hoover's short-lived triumph was based upon the six years of Republican Prosperity under Coolidge which preceded it. Below are some statements made by supporters during his successful campaign.

OTTO H. KAHN—INTERNATIONAL BANKER EXTRAORDINARY—OCTOBER 25, 1928

"THE KIND OF PROSPERITY WHICH MR. HOOVER IS SO EARNESTLY SEEKING TO PROMOTE AND PERPETUATE, AND WHICH, THROUGH HIS DIRECTION OF THE DEPARTMENT OF COMMERCE, HE HAS DONE SO MUCH TO AID, IS WIDELY DIFFUSED PROSPERITY, PERCOLATING THROUGH ALL SECTIONS OF THE COUNTRY, BENEFITTING THE PEOPLE, ADDING TO THE CONTENTS NOT MERELY OF THEIR POCKETBOOKS, BUT OF THEIR LIVES"

CHARLES EVANS HUGHS—CHIEF JUSTICE OF THE U.S. SUPREME COURT—OCTOBER 24, 1928

"THE POLITICAL AIMS OF THE GREAT MAJORITY OF THE AMERICAN PEOPLE MAY BE SUMMED UP BROADLY IN THE WORDS, PROSPERITY AND PROGRESS . . . . PROSPERITY FEEDS UPON ITSELF . . . . DELEGATIONS FROM FOREIGN LANDS ARE VISITING US TO ASCERTAIN OUR SECRET . . . . I BELIEVE THAT IT IS VERY IMPORTANT IN MAINTAINING THE CONFIDENCE THAT UNDERLIES OUR PROSPERITY

THAT WE SHOULD RETAIN A REPUBLICAN ADMINISTRATION. EVERY ONE MUST REALIZE, AS IT SEEMS TO ME, THAT IF THE ELECTION RESULTS IN A REPUBLICAN VICTORY, BUSINESS ALL THROUGH THE COUNTRY WILL BE HEARTENED AND STIMULATED."

ROGER W. BABSON—ECONOMIC LETTER PIONEER— SEPTEMBER 17, 1928
"IF SMITH SHOULD BE ELECTED WITH A DEMOCRATIC CONGRESS, WE ARE ALMOST CERTAIN TO HAVE A RESULTING BUSINESS DEPRESSION IN 1929 . . . . THE ELECTION OF HOOVER AND A REPUBLICAN CONGRESS SHOULD RESULT IN CONTINUED PROSPERITY FOR 1929."[71]

Stock Market Soars

On November 8, the stock market reaches its third largest post-election rally since 1928. Passing the 6,100 level for the first time, it closes at 6,177.71. On November 28, the Dow streaks past the 6,500 level.

Greenspan Gets Cold Feet

It is Thursday, December 5, 1996. Greenspan is the main speaker at a $400 per place black-tie dinner at the Washington Hilton. Earlier that day, the Dow closed at 6,400. It increased nearly 25% in 1996; the year before, the gain had been 33%, although the base was, of course, correspondingly lower. During the course of his speech, Mr. Greenspan asks: "How do we know when irrational exuberance has unduly escalated asset values, which then become subject to unexpected and prolonged contractions as they have in Japan over the past decade? And how do we factor that assessment into monetary policy?"[72]

The stock exchanges in Tokyo, Hong Kong, Sidney fall three percent. London's descends 4.2%, Paris's drops 4.9 % and Amsterdam's slumps 6.5 %. In New York, the Dow decreases 145 points—more than 2 percent.

Stock Market Rebounds

Technology stocks lead the ascent. On December 6, the Nasdaq increases 2.22%, reaching the record of 1,316.27. On December 18, the Dow climbs 126.87 points, its second greatest point gain to date. It closes at 6,473.84.

Ed. "Up, up and away in my beautiful balloon . . . ."

U. S. Stock Market Exceeds GDP

On November 25, *Barron's* magazine carries this chart, which shows that for the first time in history, the U.S. Stock market exceeds the Gross Domestic product (GDP).

Greenspan might have seen this chart. *Barron's* is a sister publication of *The Wall Street Journal* and is read by the more conservative type of investor.

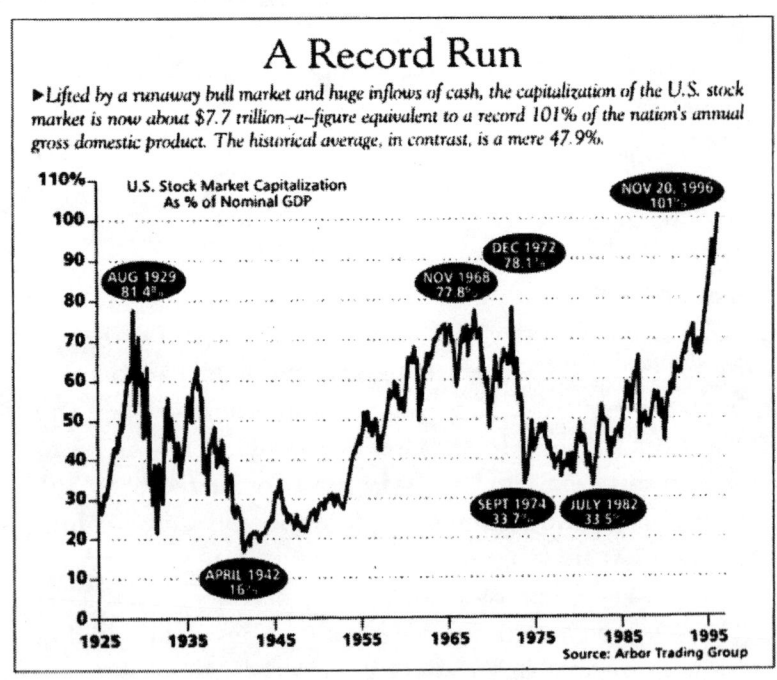

A Record Run

▶ *Lifted by a runaway bull market and huge inflows of cash, the capitalization of the U.S. stock market is now about $7.7 trillion—a figure equivalent to a record 101% of the nation's annual gross domestic product. The historical average, in contrast, is a mere 47.9%.*

U.S. Stock Market Capitalization As % of Nominal GDP

NOV 20, 1996 — 101%
DEC 1972 — 78.1%
AUG 1929 — 81.4%
NOV 1968 — 77.8%
SEPT 1974 — 33.7%
JULY 1982 — 33.5%
APRIL 1942 — 16%

Source: Arbor Trading Group

Administration Says CPI Too High

"Clinton administration officials Dec. 8 praised a congressional-appointed panel for recommending that the Consumer Price Index be adjusted downward, while congressional leaders said it is up to the White House to initiate action to remedy the problem.

"A panel, headed by former Council of Economic Advisors Chairman Michael Boskin, suggested that the current method of calculating the CPI exaggerates inflation by 1.1 percentage points annually, causing the government to overspend on cost-of-living adjustments pegged to spending programs such as Social Security.

"'1 think Boskin had it exactly right,' said Treasury Secretary Robert Rubin, appearing on NBC's *Meet The Press*.

"The administration plans to work with Congress to study the panel's report, Office of Management and Budget Director Franklin Raines said on CNN's *Late Edition*. The panel's recommendations will be studied in an 'expeditious way,' he added."[73]

Evidence Of Deliberate Understatement

"We've been robbed and cheated, by none other than the U.S. Department of Labor. On September 12 and 13, Labor released the August PPI and CPI reports. August PPI was up .3%, a significant upward move. The markets chose to ignore that move. Instead they paid attention to the core rate, which was down .1%. But the really big news was the CPI report. That showed a .1% increase, well off this year's 3.2% annual rate.

"I was shocked. In the PPI report, gasoline was up .9%. In the CPI report, energy somehow fell .8%!

"As shocking as it may sound, they are reporting that energy prices have gone down 3.2% for the past three months. That's at the very time crude went from $18.50 to over $25 a barrel!

Gasoline prices over the same period went up from 54 cents to 66 cents. Every single component of the energy index went up. So excuse me if I'm a little stupid. I don't understand how they can show a 3.2% decrease in prices—when at the same time prices went up over 20%.

"Oh, there was one other surprising decrease. Despite huge increases in sales, apparel prices were reported down 1.4%. That was on a seasonally-adjusted basis. The real drop was .2%.

"As a direct result of the market's mistaken belief that there is no inflation, bonds rose 1 ½ points. The Dow went up over 100 points . . . .

. . . .

" . . . Government is not coming close to reporting the true energy scenario . . . .

"Let's recalculate the CPI, to accurately reflect the present increase in energy prices. The August CPI then goes up a whopping 1.26%. That's an annualized inflation rate of over 15%, energy led. That's versus the .1% increase reported by the Labor department. Friday's extraordinary rally is based on mythological assessment of the real inflation rate."

The Wall Street Underground, Vol. 3, no. 1, August/September 1996. p. 14.

Edit. So much for the good news in August which helped the Clinton balloon clear the rocks of scandal and waft past Dole's cloudy words about the economy. But he couldn't have done it without Greenspan's help. That man certainly delivered.

TIME Magazine Announces Clinton's "Economic Dream Team"

[Cover Story] "A bunch of investment bankers and lawyers, friendly to the stock market, heavily focused on balancing the federal budget. Sounds like the kind of [men] whose ideas of government traditional Democrats would instinctively distrust . . . . In fact, it is the team chosen by Bill Clinton to shape economic policy in his second term.

"The firm—er, team—is still adding partners—er, members. Robert Rubin, of course, is thoroughly entrenched as Treasury Secretary and a kind of managing partner; Erskin Bowles left his North Carolina investment firm to become White House Chief of Staff immediately after the election. Last week Clinton formally added Franklin Raines, a former partner at Lazard, Freres & Co., by announcing that he would keep Raines as head of the Office of Management and Budget, ... Daley, son of the famous Chicago mayor, who as a lawyer might be thought of as counsel for the firm, was named Secretary of Commerce.

"Gene Sperling, another lawyer, became in effect the junior partner of the firm when he was named head of the National Economic Council. Sperling, nicknamed 'Gene the Machine,' is more noted for his ability to grind out thorough policy-option papers than for being a brilliant academic economist. So while on paper the NEC is supposed to be an economic counterpart to the National Security Council, under Sperling it is unlikely to have as much clout as it did when Rubin ran it before moving to Treasury.

"If the appointments proved anything, it was that Clinton does not need Dick Morris to stick to a centrist course. The Administration's most noted liberals . . . are leaving.

"In contrast, the new men 'are don't rock-the-boat appointments, and they are exactly what Wall Street wants,' says David Jones, senior economist at Aubrey G. Lanston, which is really an investment-banking firm . . . . Clinton praised the 'vibrant' stock market as increasing not only the wealth of the rich but also the retirement savings of the middle class."

"The Economic Dream Team" by George J. Church, *Time This Week*, December 25, 1996. www.cnn.com/ALLPOLITICS/ 1996/analysis/time/9612/23/church.html

Edit. The Time reader might think that being Wall Street financiers, they are sure to increase the retirement savings of the middle class.

PETER ERICKSON

On December 27, The Dow Ends At 6,546.68, One Point Below Record

Edit. Quite a year for both Clinton and Greenspan.

CHAPTER VII

1997—THE BUBBLE STALKS

Administration Source Advocates Combining Stocks With Social Security

January 7, A presidential panel suggests that the government use common stocks to beef up social security, so as to protect baby-boomer's retirement.

Edit. This is a trial balloon. The idea is to prop up social security with stocks, and also, probably, stocks with social security—a hoped-for double whammy against poverty. Of course, it is possible that they would then fall into each other.

The Dollar Soars

On January 23, the dollar reaches a 31-month peak against the German Mark.

Edit. The ploy is succeeding.

Inflation-Indexed Bonds

On January 30, the government auctions off $7 billion of these special 10-year Treasury Inflation Protection Securities. The issue is so popular that it is oversubscribed. This is despite the claims by Greenspan and the Clinton administration that the official inflation measurements are too high. These buyers believe that the government is going to give them a fairly accurate and sincere estimate of inflation.

Clinton Proposes "Balanced Budget" In State Of Union Address

"In two days, I will propose a detailed plan to balance the budget by 2002. This plan will balance the budget and invest in our people while protecting Medicare, Medicaid, education, and the environment. It will balance the budget and build on the Vice-President's efforts to make our government work better, even as it costs less. It will balance the budget and provide middle-class tax relief to pay for education and health care, to help to raise a child, to buy and sell a home.

"Balancing the budget requires only your vote and my signature. It does not require us to rewrite our Constitution. I believe it is both unnecessary and unwise to adopt a balanced budget amendment that could cripple our country in time of crisis and force unwanted results, such as judges halting Social Security checks or increasing taxes. Let us at least agree, we should not pass any measure—no measure should be passed that threatens Social Security."

February 4, 1997.

Edit. This is one of the key claims of his second term. The stock market loves this kind of talk. The election is over, and he is still helping it get bigger.

"Greenspan: End CPI bias"

"The government should quickly change its inflation measure in ways that will trim increases in Social Security and other benefits and raise taxes for millions of Americans, Federal Reserve chairman Alan Greenspan told Congress Thursday.

"In his strongest comments to date on the matter, Mr. Greenspan took issue with critics who have called such changes a 'political fix' to give lawmakers a backdoor way to solve the government's budget problems."

Article by Martin Crutsinger, *The Cincinnati Inquirer,* January, 31, 1997, p. C1.

Ed. Once more, Greenspan returns to his theme that America is experiencing low inflation. Putting this claim into law would reduce social security costs for government and raise taxes. This will help make the dollar seem more solid. But it will decrease the money available to retirees. It will also have the effect of encouraging stock market speculation.

Dow Rises Above 7,000 For 1st Time

On February 13, the Dow Jones Industrial Average reached 7,022.44, rising 80.81 points.

"Job Insecurity gets Promotion: Fed Chief Treats It as Important Indicator of Inflation"

"For months now, the Federal Reserve board has been poised to raise interest rates, but has held off. Why?

"The answer lies mainly in what the Fed's chairman, Alan Greenspan, describes as a powerful recent force in the American economy: job insecurity. Now, in testimony to Congress, he has clearly elevated this insecurity to major status in central bank policy.

"'Workers have been too worried about keeping their jobs to push for higher wages,' he testified, and this has been sufficient to hold down inflation without the added restraint of higher interest rates."

Louis Uchitelle, *International Herald Tribune,* February 28, 1997.

Edit. Greenspan sees high economic value in the discomfort of the employee—especially those of the lower echelon. What happened to the positive value— "my best for your best"—capitalism of his old mentor, Ayn Rand?[74] *However that may be, this fits in with the Administration's policy of encouraging immigration; after the party's over, the more competition for jobs, the more fear.*

Greenspan Expresses More Doubts About Stock Market

On February 27, 1977, more than two months after the "irrational exuberance" speech, Greenspan tells the Senate Banking Committee that "caution seems especially warranted with regard to the sharp rise in equity prices during the last two years."

"These gains have obviously raised questions of sustainability," he adds. Since the beginning of 1995, the Dow has jumped a staggering 80 percent. On this news, the Dow Industrials falls more than a hundred points, but comes back to close at 6,983.18, down 55.03.

Edit. From such statements as that, one might think that Greenspan is pursuing a restrictive policy.

"Contrary to Popular belief, the Fed Isn't

Taking Away the Punchbowl, It's Spiking the Punch"

"Last December, [Greenspan complained about] a burst of irrational exuberance . . . For a time, ... stock prices retreated . . . ."

"The Fed chief reiterated his concern last Wednesday, with a similar impact on financial markets. Long term U.S. Treasury bond prices tumbled by 1-1/2% points or $15.00 per $1,000 bond. Stocks, the object of Greenspan's main concern, actually fared better. The Dow's losses were cut in half from their widest level, to 55 points, or about 0.8%.

"The capital markets strongly inferred that Greenspan's warnings augured a tightening in U.S. monetary policy, just as they had last December. Fed policy actually has turned more accommodative since then. In other words, while Greenspan was suggesting population control for financial bulls, his minions actually were supplying the genetic material to clone more of them.

"That is not apparent from the overnight federal funds rate, which has remained anchored at the 5-1/4% target prevailing for just over a year. Outwardly, this appears to be a stable monetary policy.

"But William V. Sullivan Jr., the sharp-eyed chief money-market economist at Dean Witter Reynolds, observes that the Fed actually has had to provide a markedly expanded supply of reserves to the banking system just to keep the fed funds rate from rising above the central bank's 5-1/4% target.

"Sullivan points to an acceleration in the monetary base, as measured by the St. Louis Fed, which can be viewed as the raw material for the nation's money stock. The three-month growth rate in the base has risen to 8.3%, sharply higher than the 4.8% growth rate in the three months ended Dec. 18, around the time Greenspan first warned of irrational exuberance in the capital markets.

"The Fed's need to pump increasing amounts of liquidity into the banking system just to hold the funds rate steady shows 'credit-market fundamentals argue for some increase in the rate on its own accord,' Sullivan says. The monetary authorities 'have been exhibiting increasing accommodation of rising credit requirements from a strong economy, effectively offsetting the upward pressures' on the key overnight rate, he concludes.

"Or to use a different metaphor, while the markets worried that Greenspan & Co. were about to take away the punchbowl because the party was getting too hearty, they actually were spiking it.

"Given the Fed's own easy-money policies, it's little wonder, then, that investors paid scant heed to Greenspan's original warnings . . . ."

Article by Randall W. Forsyth, *Barron's*, March 3, 1997, p. MW10.

Edit. Contrary to common opinion, Greenspan has been accelerating money creation. Back in 1994, he refused to do so, openly telling a U. S. Senator that by so declining he was promoting economic growth. This is further signification of a behind-the-scenes shift in monetary policy.

"Final Minutes Matter Most in Today's Market"

"Once upon a time investors could watch the stock market's direction take shape over the course of the six-and-a-half hour trading day.

"No longer.

"Traders today can't hazard a guess how stock prices will end up until the final hour of trading. The problem: A flurry of last minute trades are triggering sharp gyrations that leave the stock market bearing little resemblance to its earlier self.

. . . .

"' It's like having a scud missile land on you,' sighs Ned Collins, head of U.S. stock trading at Daiwa Securities America Inc. after one such late-afternoon swing sent the Dow Industrials plunging nearly 100 points. 'You go get a coffee, come back and you're facing a total reversal, with no apparent cause.' he says.

"This kind of volatility, concentrated late in the day and characterized by heavy trading, is emerging as a hallmark of the stock market this year. (Until now, analysts say late afternoon price swings were far less frequent and usually took place in thinly-traded markets) . . . .

"It's kind of making the stock market like an NBA basketball game. It's only the last bit that counts. And the rest of the day is either entertainment or agony,' says Greg Smith, chief stock market strategist at Prudential Securities. He says he has never seen so many moves of this magnitude so late in the day in nearly 30 years of tracking markets."

Article by Suzanne McGee, *WSJ*, March 3, 1997, p. C1.

Edit. In the former days, when smart operators anticipated an up-day, they would invest early in order to gain from the anticipated shower of gold. But this movement is late in the day. Why? Could it be that the objective is not to make a profit on some projected windfall, but instead to influence the next trading day? If they want the market to go up soon, by coming in late they can increase the day's closing price, so as to fool the speculator not in the know. If they want it to go down, they can do the opposite. But who would have enough money to do it time after time? This is worth thinking about.

Who, besides a government, is big enough to do that?

"U.S. cash en route to Russia is stolen: Insiders suspected in Heathrow heist"

Headline, *Washington Times*, March 3, 1997.
Ed. Well, boys, you can't win all the time.

Dow Jones Changes Composition Of Its Base Stocks.

On March 13, the Dow Jones Industrial Average changes four stocks. Travelers, Hewlett Packard, Johnson & Johnson, and Walmart replace Westinghouse, Texaco, Bethlehem Steel, and Woolworth.

Editorial: This is a significant action which breaks continuity with the past. In strict mathematical terms, a comparison of the February 12 Dow of 7,022.44, for instance, with any trading day following this change could not be made, because the base has been altered. Over the short range, it will appear to work; most investors are influenced by the name of the index with its hundred-year associations. But in the long run, by choosing more fast-moving stocks, the Dow will produce a different result from what would have happened if the index had remained the same. Otherwise, why make the change? Just as with lowering the C. P. I., this will tend to accelerate confidence in rising stock averages.

Later in the course of the bubble market, the Dow Jones company will do this again. There, a fresh analysis by someone else will be featured.

Fed Raises Discount Rate

On March 25, the Federal Reserve increases the short-term interest rate by 1/4 point.

Stocks Fall

Stocks fall about a hundred points after Greenspan's announcement; they drop even more the yield on-20 year bonds.

Critic Refutes Greenspan Move

"The 'signals' used by Greenspan to raise the federal-funds interest rate on March 25th were not 'inflation' but the consequences of expanding the money supply (the true definition of inflation) set in motion by the banking cartel that Greenspan himself heads. The phony definition of inflation as rising prices is necessary for two reasons: It conceals the role of the Fed in the enormous scam of creating money out of thin air which decreases the purchasing power of every dollar we own, and it places the blame for this theft on business instead of the Fed.

"What Greenspan actually did on March 25th was a start on slowing down the creation of phony money. Statistics from the Federal Reserve Bank of St. Louis show that M3, the broadest measure of the money supply, increased approximately 20 percent during the past six years. The monetary base, which provides the foundation on which the money supply increases, rose dramatically during the same six years to an annual average of 9.1 percent, more than twice that considered 'normal.' These deplorable increases are a measure of the true inflation that the Federal Reserve System has funneled into the economy since 1990 under the auspices of Alan Greenspan."

Jane H. Ingraham, "Fed's Inflation Charade," *The New American,* May 26, 1997.[75]

Economist Proclaims New Economy

"Changes in technology, ideology, employment and finance, along with the globalization of production and consumption, have reduced the volatility of economic activity in the industrialized world. For both empirical and theoretical reasons in advanced industrial economies the waves of the business cycle may be becoming more like ripples."[76]

Steven Weber, "The End Of The Business Cycle", *Foreign Affairs*, April 1997, p.65.

"PRIOR TO 1927, MEN HAD CALCULATED WHEN THEY BOUGHT SECURITIES. IN 1928 AND 1929 THEY CEASED TO CALCULATE, AND WHEN OLD-FASHIONED VOICES WERE RAISED IN PROTEST, CALLING ATTENTION TO OLD LANDMARKS AND OLD STANDARDS, RAISING PROSAIC QUESTIONS REGARDING EARNINGS AND DIVIDENDS AND BOOK VALUE, THEY WERE DROWNED OUT BY AN INDIGNANT CHORUS, WHICH CHANTED THAT WE ARE IN A 'NEW ERA,' IN WHICH BOOK VALUES NO LONGER MEANT ANYTHING, AND DIVIDENDS LITTLE, AND IN WHICH WE MIGHT CAPITALIZE EARNINGS IN ANY RATIO THAT THE IMAGINATION SAW FIT TO SET. OLD ECONOMIC LAWS WERE SUSPENDED. WEALTH WAS NOT MADE BY RISING CAPITAL VALUES, AND BUSINESS WAS TO BE KEPT ACTIVE BY THE SPENDING OF PROFITS MADE THROUGH RISING CAPITAL VALUES."

BENJAMIN M. ANDERSON, JR, CHASE ECONOMIC BULLETIN, VOL. IX NO. 6, NOVEMBER 22, 1929, P. 5.

Stocks Soar

On April 22, the Dow Jones Industrial Average reaches its greatest mark in over a year. The industrials rise 173.30 points to 6,833.59—the second largest point gain to date.

April 30 arrives, and stocks go even higher. The Dow scoots 179.01 points higher, another record-setting event. This is because of a recent report which holds that inflationary pressures are easing.

Edit. By pressures, it is not meant that Greenspan and the banking industry have slowed down their fantastic expansion of the money supply. Rather it has to do with the behavior of people as they go about their lives. Americans are being conditioned to think of inflation as the resultant of a whole number of forces—the interaction of money with human action and other eventualities. Of course, it would take an expert to even be supposed to know all this. The technocrat of choice is Alan Greenspan.

Government Claims Record Surplus

On May21, the Administration posts an $83.94 million surplus for April, citing high returns from individuals.

Dow Re-crosses 7,000 Point In May And June And Passes 8,000 point in July

On July 18, the Dow reaches the 8,000 level for first time, closing at 8,038.88.

Greenspan Says Price Stability Attained

On July 22, 1997, Greenspan tells the House banking Committee: "We have come as close to stable prices as I have seen, certainly since the 1960s . . . . We do not now know, nor do I suspect can anyone know, whether current developments are part of a once or twice-in-a-century phenomenon that will carry productivity trends nationally and globally to a new higher track.'"[77]

Edit: Greenspan's attribution of stability to the financial house of cards is doing much to make people think that the stock market is not a mirage—his warnings to the contrary notwithstanding. He is widely regarded as lovable, but crotchety. Few suspect him of being an inflationist.

Awe

"Greenspan is willing to try this experiment of low unemployment and low inflation right before our eyes." Eliott Plat, Director Of Economic Research At Donaldson Lufkin, etc., July 24, 1997.[78]

Clinton Signs Capital Gains Tax Cut Bill

On August 6, 1997, Clinton signs a bill to reduce the capital gains tax. He says it will balance the budget in five years. This was a departure from the long-established Democrat position against such legislation. The new law cuts the tax on assets held for five years by ten percent—from 28% to 18%—but raises cigarette taxes. It also cuts spending by $270 billion. Some Democrats, notably House Minority Leader Richard Gephardt, did not vote for it.[79]

On Wall Street, many fear that if the law were passed, investors would use this as an opportunity to sell, as had happened before in both 1978 and 1980 after a capital gains cut. But not this time. The market is too bullish.[80]

Democrat Intellectual Interprets Significance Of The New Law

"The enactment of capital-gains tax cuts was a function of politics but also a result of the expansion of the markets and the changing character of the investing public. In 1992, the stock market was something that Democrats tolerated, at best, and vilified at worst. But, by 1996, being a responsible Democrat, and one interested in prosperity and opportunity for people at all levels in society, meant being concerned about the fate of the stock and bond markets. After all, between 1992 and 1996 alone, the number of households with mutual funds rose 42.6 percent, from 25.8 million to 36.8 million. In 1996, the Investment Company Institute estimated that 63 million Americans owned mutual fund shares. With the democratization of money, such a posture becomes not only mandatory but also a means for Clinton to distinguish himself from the irresponsible Republicans."

Daniel Gross, *Bull Run* . . . [81]

Edit. Gross wants to trade places with the Republicans on that issue.

Dow Reaches Top For Year

On August 8, the Dow Jones Industrial Average hits 8,259.31.

"Asia's Economic Tigers Growl At World Monetary Conference"

"After a decade of persuading nations to open their financial markets, American officials at a tense conclave here have run into a wall of resistance as angry Asian leaders charge that foreign investors and Wall Street-style trading exacerbated Southeast Asia's financial crisis.

"The most extreme of the accusations came from Prime Minister Mahathir Mohamad of Malaysia. In a fiery space on Saturday evening, he accused the 'great power'—a clear reference to the United States—of pressing Asian countries to open their markets and then manipulating their currencies to knock them off as competitors"

Article, David E. Sanger, *The New York Times*, September 22, 1997, p. 1.

Edit. As was mentioned earlier, the regional supremacy of the dollar would not be enough to maintain its position as the world's currency. This rupture of Asian currencies might do the trick, at least for the present. The U. S.'s roaring economy will seem inviting to investors from Asia's now limping tigers. The Malaysian Prime Minister accuses American interests of doing this, deliberately, of getting them into deeply in debt so as to knock them down.

Bank Card Loss Reaches Height On September 11

Edit. Part of the price stability Greenspan so recently praised was purchased by millions of ordinary Americans going into debt at high interest rates. Without this convenience, some prices would most likely be less.

Greenspan Questions Market Level

On October 8, in testimony to the House Budget Committee, Greenspan declares, "It clearly would be unrealistic to look for a continuation of stock market gains of anything like the magnitude of those recorded in the past couple years."

Edit. Greenspan is checking out again. Watch for Clinton!

The Stock Market Is Shut Down

On October 27, the Dow drops 554 points—the largest point plunge in history. The automatic circuit breaker which had been set up after the 1987 crash goes into action for the first time. Ironically, this takes place almost 10 years after the famous October 19, 1987 crash in which Greenspan became an interventionist. This time, he is silent. A Fed spokesman answers the reporters with this: "Obviously, the chairman has been busy today. We don't have any comment."

Clinton receives the stunning news of the shut-down, shortly after having delivered a speech to the Democratic Leadership Council in which he claimed that since he had taken over, the deficit has dropped by "more than 90 percent, even before the balanced-budget law saves one red cent." He chooses to say nothing in public about this. He does, however, send out his Myrmidons to sally forth, besieging investor doubts. White House Spokesman Mike McCurry says, "This is a market that has performed well. So let's just be calm and reasonable."[82] More authoritatively, Secretary Rubin takes his stand on the steps of the Treasury building and proclaims, "It is important to remember that the fundamentals of the United States economy are strong and have been for the past several years. *The prospects for continued growth—with low inflation and low unemployment— are strong.*" (Emphasis added.)[83]

—Then Roars Back

October 28, 1997—The Dow charges forward, posting its biggest single day point gain to date. The volume record is also smashed with more than 1.1 billion shares traded. The headline in *The Wall Street Journal* reads: "Stocks burst Back by 337.17 points On Record Volume as Bonds Drop."[84]

Shortly after the market opens, President Clinton says that the U.S. economy "is as strong and vibrant today as it has been in a generation."

"It may be disappointing, but I think it is neither prudent nor appropriate for any President to comment on the hour-by-hour or the day-by-day movements of the market." Instead, Clinton focuses on what he called the economy's basic strengths: lower-than-expected federal deficits, unemployment and inflation at their lowest level in two decades, and healthy banks and businesses.[85]

Greenspan delivers a speech at a charity dinner in which he assures the important people assembled that the economy is fine—in fact, "impressive."

Analyst Bill King Comments

"The market went from being grossly oversold to grossly overbought in six hours . . . Clinton was in Chicago to address a grammar school about 45 minutes after stocks opened. He crowed about his economic accomplishments. This guy doesn't do anything unless it is plotted, planned, and reviewed. He was not going to go before the cameras and crow about his economic prowess with stocks in the toilet. So, we must assume he had more than an inkling that stocks would recover. The low on the SPZs was in the first minute of trading. Some entities aggressively bought SPZs as soon as possible."[86]

Edit; There will be two more dramatic upsurges after a low in the second half of October during the Clinton administration, 1998 and

1999. Is this connection among these three events merely chance events? The coincidental is the rare phenomenon, not the common one. In science, it is usual to conclude that a coincidence exists only when no reasonable explanation can be found. Let the reader be the judge!

"China rejects moving forex reserves to euro"

Headline, *London Financial Times*, October 13, 1997, p. 1

Edit. On this occasion, by selecting the dollar over its soon-to-be operational European competitor, Red China is supporting the Administration and Chairman Greenspan. For their own reasons, they want to keep the beat going.

"Hong Kong Stocks fall Steeply, New Victim of Region's Ills"

Headline of Article by Keith Faison, *The New York Times*, October 23, 1997, p. C1.

Edit. More impetus for investing in the supposedly safer U. S. stock market.

Greenspan Testifies On Social Security

In his testimony before the Senate Task Force on Social Security, he advocates that the checks continue to be paid out to the older workers as previously agreed. But the younger workers should be allowed to "invest a portion of their accounts in equities and other private securities, thereby receiving higher rates of return and enhancing their social security." Because of certain complications, he advocates that this be done gradually.[87]

Edit. This is a sincere proposal and as a former chairman of the 1982 commission, he is not out of order in making it to the U. S. Senate. But if it were implemented right now, what kind of an economy would these young people be salting their retirement money into?

"U. S. Trade Gap Grew 24% in December"

Headline, WSJ, February 20, 1998.
Edit. The public is being told that there is nothing to worry about here; that in exchange for their money, Americans are receiving goods which they esteem more than the dollars they gave up. Leaving aside the question of the validity of that argument (which will be discussed in the final chapter), Americans are running up their credit cards, paying huge interest in order to get what they esteem. Many are in default.

U. S. Trade Gap Compared With Other Nations

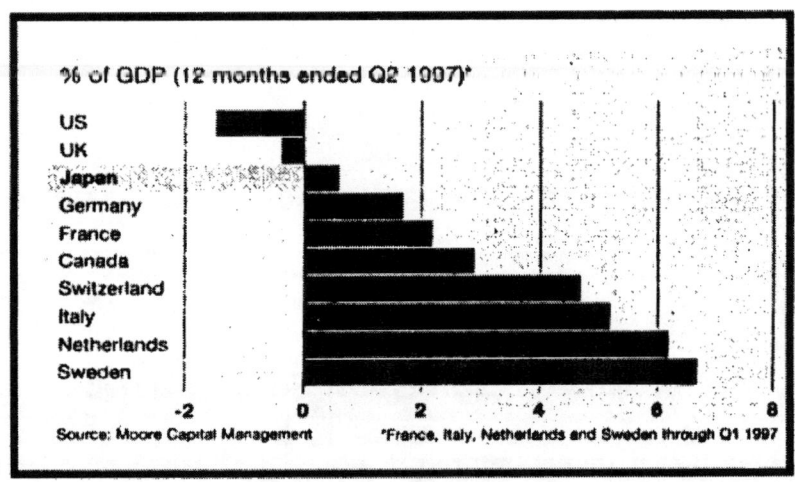

This chart appears in the *London Financial Times* on October 20, 1997. As a percentage of GDP, the U. S. trade gap is the largest in the world—about four times as great as the U. K.[88]

Record Number Of Personal Bankruptcies

In 1997, the number of personal bankruptcies reaches 1.35 million. The total cost was an estimated $44 billion; this included cancelled debt, collection costs, and legal fees.

As a result of this, credit card companies seek laws tightening bankruptcy laws. The rate of business bankruptcies have not changed much for nearly two decades.[89]

Poll Says Majority Of College Students Think They Will Be Rich

In 1997, a survey of American college students conducted by the five largest accounting firms finds that 77% expect to be millionaires, someday.[90]

Edit. Some of their teachers are not smart.

"In a Surprise, South Korea ends Effort to Defend Won"

Headline, WSJ, November 18, 1997. An important trading partner is weakening.

Gross Federal Debt Increases

The National Debt, or "Public Debt," as the government sometimes calls it, stands at greater than $5.4 trillion on 09/30/1997—more exactly $5,413,146,011,397.34. This is an increase of $188 billion over what it was on 09/30/96.[91]

The National Debt includes not only the federal budget, but also such off-budget items as Social Security, which have to be paid out on a continuing basis. It is quite common for administrations to say that they are "cutting the deficit by such and-such" when they are referring to the on-budget items only. This makes it appear that they are making greater progress than they really are. But in the next chapter, we shall see how the Clinton Administration is going far, far beyond this.

CHAPTER VIII

1998—TROUBLE, BUT STILL THE BUBBLE

"Factory Orders Slump in Sign of Asian Fallout"

"Factory orders fell 2.5% in December, the sharpest monthly drop since 1991 and another sign that Asia's financial crisis may be having a damping effect on the U.S. economy."
Article by Elizabeth Daerr, WSJ, February 8, 1998, p. A2.
Edit. One might think that this would put a damper on the stock market. But see . . .

"White House Bailouts for Asia Draw Fire"

"Congress has been out of session for the last two and a half months as the Administration has worked, through the I.M.F. and on its own, to stabilize financial markets in Asia and limit damage to the economy.

"But the Administration's decision just before Christmas to lend $1.7 billion of taxpayer money to South Korea galvanized longtime critics of direct American involvement in such bailouts. The failure of the I.M.F. plans throughout the region has brought further criticism from Congress that the White House's approach is flawed.

"The first flashpoint in the debate will be the Administration's request for a $3.5 billion contribution to an emergency fund established by the I.M.F. to deal with sudden financial crises of the type afflicting Asia."
Article by Richard W. Stevenson, *NYT*, January 12, 1998, p. D3.

"Greenspan Heckled"

"Community advocates heckled the Federal Reserve Chairman, Alan Greenspan, today for defending financial aid to Asia while poor neighborhoods in the United States needed help."
Article from Reuters, *NYT*, January 12, 1998, p. D3.

"Steep Stock Losses Curbed Late in Day"

"The Dow Jones Industrial Average, which had traded well over 100 points lower during the day, ended down 3.98 points at 7902.27. The Nasdaq Composite Index failed to retrieve as large a part of its losses, falling 18.44 points to end the day at 1561.70."
Sub-headline of article, *WSJ*, January 8, 1998, p. C1.[92]

An Explanation

"Another late 'Market on Close' buy program forced the Dow Jones Industrial Average 82 points higher in the last 15 minutes of trading .... Every day of '98 plus the last day of '97, has had a late Market on close buy program to rescue the market. We feel this is a manipulation to make the market appear much healthier than it is ...."
Bill King January 8, 1998. [93]

Last Year, Greenspan Congratulated Central Banks For Low Inflation

"This brings me, finally, to the area of monetary policy— the fundamental responsibility of a modern central bank. In this area, I am pleased to say, there have been positive developments, especially with regard to inflation. The recent record on inflation reduction in industrial countries has been impressive. Measured consumer price inflation in G-10 countries averaged only about 2 to 2-1/4 percent last year, down more than 3 percentage points from what it was in 1990. Consumer price increases on average in the G-10 have been kept under 3 percent for the past five years—the longest such period of sustained low inflation in more than three decades."

Alan Greenspan, Speech at Catholic University, Leuven, Leuven, Belgium, January 14, 1997.

Edit. I don't know about inflation adjustment in these other industrialized countries, but as for the United States, there the . . . .

"Federal Government Fixed Numbers"

"Since the early 1990s, the federal government has been gradually altering the way CPI is computed by making various adjustments.

"According to economist John Williams, who directs the Shadow Bureau of Government Statistics, a private firm that monitors government number crunching, the federal government has been using several clever and questionable techniques to keep the stated inflation rate low.

"Mr. Williams estimates that the current annualized CPI is above 5 percent—more than double the 2.4 percent annual rate reported by the federal government.

"To create a false and artificially low rate, Mr. Williams reveals, government economists use the technique of 'geometric weighting.'

"Mr. Williams states geometric weighting 'gives a lower weighting over time to goods that are increasing in price.' . . .

"The thinking behind geometric weighting goes like this: if prices rise on a brand name product, consumers just move to generic brands, or use other types of products.

"It's a nice theory, but consider why such thinking might not apply to real people. Gas prices have increased dramatically. Have motorists stopped driving cars? Have they begun using buses? Bicycles? Walking instead? The answers are likely no.

"Quality adjustments are another way the government keeps the stated inflation low.

"For example, when the government required that an additive be put into gasoline to make it cleaner, the CPI was adjusted to not reflect the price increase that was directly related to the additive.

"In other words, the end consumer saw higher prices, but because the government thought they were getting a better product, they shouldn't think of this as inflation!

"Other quality adjustments include government-mandated changes to auto production such as the addition of catalytic converters. Mr. Williams says these adjustments are 'not legitimate if the buyer doesn't have any alternative.' The buyers are stuck paying the higher price."

Article by Christopher Ruddy and Ryan Troup[94]

January 22, Clinton Denies Sexual Fling With Intern

The President says he never told Monica Lewinsky to lie to lawyers in the Paula Jones sexual harassment suit; Ms Lewinsky denies the affair in an affidavit. There are reports that her admission had been secretly taped.

"New Stock Investments Are Slowing, Report Says"

"New Investments in stock mutual funds appear to be slowing sharply this month, a research group reported yesterday, after a year in which a record amount was poured into such vehicles.

This month [January], net stock fund purchases total about one-seventh of the $29.7 billion that was invested in equities last January, according to an estimate from the research group Trim Tabs Financial Services Inc. That is also down sharply from December's levels.

"'Clearly, investors are concerned about the world's stock markets and they're limiting investments as a result,' said Carl Wittnebert, director of research for Trim Tabs, who estimates that just $3.8 billion has been invested in equity tabs this month.

. . . .

"'This month, investors are redeeming cash from international stock funds and aggressive growth stock to low-risk money funds,' Mr. Wittnebert of Trim Tabs said."
Article by Bloomberg News, *NYT*, January 30, 1998, p. D2.
Edit: If that trend continues, it will bring down stock prices later in the year. With stocks being so high, what could induce the ordinary person to plunge further?

President Unveils Proposed Budget Surplus for Fiscal 1999

On February 2, Clinton states that his budget will be about $1.7 trillion and will show a surplus of $9.5 billion, the first officially balanced since Lyndon Johnson's in 1969. "This budget," he ululates, "marks the end of an era and the decades of deficits that have shackled our economy, paralyzed our politics, and held our people back."

Democrat Senator Refutes "Surplus"

The reader is by now familiar with distinction between the official budget and the complete budget, which includes off-budget—especially trust funds like Social Security. It has also been pointed out that when politicians speak of lowering the budget deficit, they mean reducing the first, not the second. But, in the instance of Clinton's alleged surplus, the situation is much worse. The on-budget itself is misreported. Senator Ernest F. Hollings (D-SC) proves this:
"It is easy to determine the truth. All one needs to do is

determine how much more one spends than is earned in a year, as every family does. Accordingly, one should ask: Does the president's budget receive more than it will spend, or does it spend more than it receives. Once again, as it has for the past 30 years, the government will spend more. In fact, the president's budget projects more spending than income each year for the next five years. Instead of surpluses 'as far as the eye can see,' deficits will be the order of the day . . . .

"While the president talks about reserving 100 percent of every surplus, his budget borrows the pension fund surpluses in order to report a budget surplus. These pension funds are then spent on food stamps or foreign aid or some program other than Social Security. The same is true of the gasoline tax, which is intended for highways. In reality, the deficit is not eliminated; the deficit is merely moved from the general fund into the Social Security trust fund or the highway trust fund.

"This gimmick is called 'unified budgeting' with a 'unified' deficit or surplus. It's a fraud. With the present surplus fever, the people think the government is finally on a pay-as-you-go basis. But in reality, the politicians continue to spend, running huge deficits in the trust funds. The following trust funds are in deficit for the following amounts of FY 1999: Social Security, $845 billion; Medicare $148 billion; Military Retirement, $140 billion; Civilian Retirement, $490 billion; Unemployment Compensation, $81 billion; Highways, $35 billion; Airports, $15 billion; Railroad Retirement, $21 billion, and all others, $58 billion.

"One can see that instead of making the airports safe with modern radar, we have spent $7 billion of airport travelers' money on everything but airports. No wonder the highways are crumbling, the bridges falling. We have spent $22 billion of the gas tax on everything but highways and bridges."

Senator Ernest Hollings, "What Surplus?" *The Washington Post*, February 5, 1998.[95]

Edit. What took off in early 1996 as a scrawny attempt by Rubin to defeat a partisan Republican maneuver has grown into a full-fledged fraud.

CBO Replies

In June, the Congressional Budget Office projects that the federal government will finish the fiscal year on September 30 with a surplus of between $43 and $63 billion, a little more than Clinton claimed.

Then Senators Byron Dorgan (D-ND) and Ernest Hollings write to the CBO Director, June O'Neill, explaining that "the rosy declarations of a surplus, touted by congressional leaders and President Clinton, are all wet. We believe you have a responsibility to report accurately to the American people that, until revenues exceed expenditures without using the Social Security trust fund, there is no budget surplus."

Ms. O'Neill answers, saying she agrees and promises to change: "I regret that the report you cited failed to report the on-budget deficit, excluding the surplus of the Social Security trust funds." But she will resign before the end of the fiscal year.[96]

"Surpluses" Endanger Social Security

In the same article cited above, Senator Hollings explains: "At the beginning of the fiscal year we owed the Social Security trust fund $631 billion, and are scheduled to owe $732 billion by the end of September this year, and under President Clinton's 'unified budget,' we will owe Social Security $845 billion. As he loots another $113 billion from the Social Security trust funds, the president cries, 'Save Social Security first.' Obviously, the first way to save Social Security is to stop looting it.

"By 1980 it was apparent that Social Security would soon be in the red. So the Greenspan Commission was appointed to solve the problem. In 1983 the Greenspan Commission Report not only called for a tax increase to balance Social Security's budget but instituted a graduated tax to build up a surplus to take care of the retirement of the baby boomers in the next generation. It's exactly this surplus that everyone wants to use to cut taxes or spend more.

"The Greenspan Commission planned for Social Security to be fiscally sound through 2056. Now we hear that it will be broke in 10 years. In fact, it's already broke. Owing Social Security $732 by the end of September this year and continuing with 'unified budgets' to obtain 'unified surpluses,' the U.S. government will owe Social Security $1.236 trillion by 2002. Who is going to suggest increasing taxes by $1.236 trillion to make Social Security sound?

"In 1983 the Greenspan commission provided against this disaster . . . . Finally, in 1990, the Senate Budget committee, by a vote of 20-1, reported legislation requiring that Social Security be removed from the unified budget. Congress overwhelmingly approved and President Bush signed into law (on Nov. 5, 1990) Section 13301 of the Budget Act forbidding the president or congress from reporting a budget using Social Security trust funds.

"This stricture is violated every day. Even today, submitting a budget with a projected $9.5 billion surplus, the president is in violation of Section 13301. Worse, he is in violation of his own admonition in the State of the Union message: 'Tonight I propose that we reserve 100 percent of the surplus—that's every penny of any surplus—until we have taken all the measures necessary to strengthen the Social Security system for the 21st century.'"

Senator Hollings, "What Surplus?"[97]

Edit. In 1983, Greenspan said that it would take "a very adverse economic scenario to create major financial problems for the retirement-disability side of the Social Security system."[98] Where's Alan? His deficit-cutting protégé is killing it.

Global Markets Ascend

On February 8, in response to rising world markets, the S & P 500 crosses the 1,000 point level, increasing 2.14% to 1,000.27. The Dow slithers up 201.23 points to 8,187.73.

N. Y. S. E. Alters Circuit Breakers

On February 8, it was decided that the big board will automatically close trading after once a 30% market drop has taken place. Before that, it was based upon points, not percentages. Under the new law, a 20% drop would halt the market temporarily, but not the whole day, unless it occurred after 2:00 PM. A 10% drop would halt trading, but not close the market.

Edit. What does this mean? It means that the market would have to fall much further than in the past before it could be shut down. At the January 1998 level, it will take a Dow plummet of about 2,400 points to reach the thirty percent level. From now on, investors are more at risk than ever. The clamps are tightening.[99]

"China Will Have To Devalue"

"Hong Kong—Despite repeated assertions to the contrary, China will be forced to devalue its currency by 30 to 40 percent within 18 months. When it does, the peg that ties the Hong Kong dollar to the U.S. dollar at a fixed rate of exchange is doomed.

"Hong Kong interest rates then go up permanently, factoring in a risk premium for future devaluations."

Article by David Roche, *The International Herald Tribune,* February 3, 1998.

Edit. Red China has been devaluing its currency, the Yuan, repeatedly since 1994. This has made the purchases of Chinese goods, including labor, cheaper than they would otherwise be. Since their exports cost less, the powers over there are able to sell at a lower price than any other country in the world. Experts say that this is forcing other Asian currencies to also devalue; otherwise, they would not be able to compete. When this is combined with the benefits from slave labor, the result has proved very much to their advantage. This is an important factor in the ongoing Asian crisis.[100]

"Wall Street Is Scavenging In Asia-Pacific"

"The turmoil in Asia is turning some Wall Street securities firms into scavengers.

"In the past month, Salomon Smith Barney Holdings, Inc., Morgan Stanley, Dean Witter, Discover & Co, and Credit Suisse First Boston have dispatched armies of bankers to the Asia-Pacific region to scout for brokerage firms, asset management firms and even banks that they can snap up at bargain prices.

"The hunt for Asian acquisitions is urgent because many U.S. Securities firms, led by Merrill Lynch & Co. and Morgan Stanley, have made overseas expansion their priority."

Article by Anita Raghaven, *WSJ*, February 10, 1998, C1.

Asian Economic Crisis Rages All Year

Some highlights. By the end of the year, Japan's per capita gross economic product will be down 10.7%. U.S. Monetary authorities will intervene in behalf of the Yen. Malaysia's gross economic product will be down by 30%; Thailand's by 40.1%; South Korea's will descend by 43.1 %; and Indonesia's would plummet by 72.8%.[101] Long-time ruler of Indonesia, President Suharto, will quit in the wake of student protests and rioting over financial controls insisted upon by international authorities.

Loan losses in China alone will be on the order of 20 times that of the United States during the savings and loan crisis of 1990-91.

Analyst Compares Asian Situation With Possible U.S. Parallel

"We need to understand what went wrong. Stanley Fischer of the International Monetary Fund believes Asian countries made three key policy mistakes. First, they allowed their economies to become overheated, as shown by their large external deficits and asset price bubbles. Second, they borrowed too much from abroad, and third, their banks lent badly. No other countries should, therefore, allow themselves to get into a similar mess. Unfortunately they already have. The U.S. has a large external deficit, the biggest stock market bubble in its history, huge overseas borrowing and a record level of bankruptcies."

Andrew Smithers, "Halt subsidized debt to damp down the flames of Asian contagion," *Business Day*, March 30, 1998.[102]

Edit. If Stanley Fischer, IMF Deputy Managing Director, were more candid, he would have added a fourth point to his list, to wit: the role of the Chinese devaluations in bringing about the horrendous situation over there. Then, his analysis would be more complete. Without it, the crisis facing these debt-ridden countries would not have been so great, and they might have gotten by with just a few massive bankruptcies.

It should be added that their predicament has been a temporary advantage to the dollar. Just as the earlier string of financial crises in Latin America served to bolster the dollar in 1995, so it is with this one.

With all that chaos going on abroad, one might think that the Dow would go down, or at least pause. And it has for a while, then
. . . .

The Dow Sets New Record

"After struggling and gyrating for six months, the Dow Jones Industrial Average hit a record, surging 115.09 points, or 1.41%, to 8295.61 [on February 10].

"That decisively smashed the previous high of 8259.31 set Aug. 6, 1997, and left the blue-chip benchmark with a gain of 387.36 points, or nearly 5%, so far this year. Standard & Poor's 500 stock index also marched 8.27 points, or 0.82%, higher to a record 1019.01.

"'This could be the beginning of a solid, sustainable move,' said Michael Driscoll, listed stock trader at Hambrecht & Quist in New York. 'A lot of the worries that have been around the market for the past few months are being put firmly on the back burner, and we're back to the kind of market in which people chase the winning stocks higher'"

Suzanne McGee, "Dow Industrials Jump . . . To A Record," WSJ, February 11, 1998, p. C1.

Analyst Discerns An Underlying Pattern

"It happened again. Amid excitement that Lewinsky's mother would testify before the grand jury, and Monica would appear on Thursday, [Clinton] held a news lecture (no questions) at which he proclaimed the greatest economy and economic team of all time. Stocks, as has been the case when this occurs, rallied sharply, keeping the correlation perfect."

Bill King, February 11, 1998.[103]

Nasdaq Rises

On February 25, in a tech rally, the composite index reaches 1,751.6, its highest attainment since October.

A Critic's Estimate

"As has been the case, when a new [Clinton] scandal, or clarification of an old scandal emerges, stocks and bonds rally sharply. The low for stocks was the week the Lewinsky scandal was unfolding, 1/12 to 1/16. By the end of the ensuing week, stocks were breaking out and running for the moon. The DJIA is up about 20% since the January low. In that time, earnings warnings by leading U.S. companies have proliferated."

Bill King, March 17, 1998.[104]

Springtime On The Dow

On April 4, the Dow Jones Industrials cross the 9,000 barrier; on May 14, it closes above 9,200 for the first time, reaching 9,211.84. But on June 16, there is a significant slump, as the index makes its second largest dip of the year and descends 207.01 points, or 2.34%, dropping to 8,627.93. Then on June 18, it makes its second greatest percentage increase of the year, moving up 184.17 points or 1.89% to 8,829.48.

Edit. Where is the Fed?

Fed Takes No Action

When The FOMC met with Greenspan on May 20, most of them expressed alarm at the high stock prices. Here is the report of Jerome Tuccille, a friendly biographer: "To the amazement of just about everyone in the room, Alan—the preeminent hawk on inflation in the world—raised his hand to silence the group and called for caution.

"Robert T. Parry, the San Francisco Fed chief who had long mirrored Alan's views on inflation . . . begged to disagree. Richmond Fed President J. Alfred Broaddus seconded Parry's view . . . Fed governor Lawrence H. Meyer concurred with the dissenters . . . . Alan suggested that they all adjourn for a coffee break, and when they returned to the conference table, Alan exercised his prerogative as Fed Chairman to speak first. Addressing the group in his usual slow, low-key, confident manner, Alan argued that things were different this time, that the economy was undergoing a significant change, and that emerging new technologies were yielding productivity gains that would keep inflation in check. As long as worker productivity exceeded wage demands, it was possible for the economy to grow at a greater clip without triggering higher inflation.

"It was a measure of Alan's persuasive skills that, when the assembled bankers voted on whether to raise rates or leave

them where they were, they opted for the status quo. Broaddus
cast the only dissenting vote."
Jerome Tuccille, *Alan Shrugged*.[105]

Clinton Administration Intervenes In Mid-June To Support The Yen[106]

On July 20, The Nasdaq Passes Beyond The 2,000 Milestone

Prominent Academics Extol New Economy

Robert Liton, director of economics, and Anthony
Santomero, director of the Financial Institutions Center at the
Wharton School states that "a correction may come—and may
even be in process-but a repeat of the hair-raising events of
1987 is highly unlikely."[107]

MAGNUS W. ALEXANDER—PRESIDENT OF THE NATIONAL
INDUSTRIAL CONFERENCE BOARD. 1927
"THERE IS NO REASON WHY THERE SHOULD BE ANY MORE PANICS."[108]

"Growth Forever"

"The notion that all expansions come to an end and
give way to recession is superficially attractive. It has
biological overtones and, of course, is a sheer fact of history.
This is already the 10th expansion to the postwar period and,
by the law of averages, it should already be over. Only one
expansion, from February 1961 to December 1969, has
lasted longer. Yet none of the postwar expansions died of
natural causes—they were all murdered by the Fed over
the issue of inflation. Once an expansion got under way
and unemployment came down, wage and price inflation
would pick up. Then the Fed, like a matron at a sock hop,
would, as the recently deceased Fed chairman William

McChesney Martin observed, 'take away the punch bowl just when the party gets going.'"

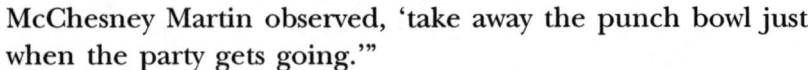

" . . . Inflation is at a record low while we have full employment. Granted, we do not know why this is so, and we suspect that it is too good to be true. But whether the explanation lies with the 'new economy' or the Asian crisis or some other factor, the point is that inflation figures give the Fed absolutely no excuse not to prop up the expansion should it need encouragement . . . .

"Just-in-time policy levers give the present expansion years of life. The payoff from a competitive and fully employed economy is low inflation and budget surpluses—double barreled anti-recession weaponry. They in turn carry the potential of a virtuous circle, in that monetary and fiscal policy are free to keep the economy from being accidentally derailed. That feeds back to longer horizons, deeper confidence, higher valuation and better performance."

Rudi Dornbusch, MIT Professor Of Economics, *WSJ*, July30, 1998, p. B1.

Edit. Note the acceptance of the legitimacy of the low inflation by a trained economist, even though he admits that he does not understand why. That the highest authorities in the land might be spiking the punch is a possibility he does not discuss.

Asian Turmoil Finally Dents Dow

On July 24, the Dow starts to fall. On August 2, the index plunges 289.42 points to 8,467.81, its third greatest loss to date—just shy of the mark that would make it a "correction."

Clinton Bites The Bullet

On August 18, Clinton Admits untruthfulness about Lewinsky but denies perjury. This follows his Grand Jury testimony.

The Dow Takes A Dive

On August 28, amid added questions over the Russian ruble, the Dow drops another 357.38 points, or 4.18%, to 8,165.99. Then comes September 1, and the Dow gets hit in the stomach and swoons 512.61 points to 7,539.07, thereby losing most of the year's gains.

Then comes the rally

On the September 2, there is a huge rebound of 288.36 points and again on the 4th, a gain of 380.53 points, the most stupendous increase to date.

The Fed Helps Out

On September 30, the central bank makes a 1/4 point cut in the short-term interest rate.

Fed Rescues Hedge Fund

On October 2, Greenspan defends intervention in behalf of Long-Term Capital Management before the House Banking Committee, claiming that its failure could have extremely deleterious consequences "on many market participants . . . and could have potentially impaired the economies of many nations, including our own."[109]

Despite its importance, this hearing is given very little coverage from TV and other media. The explanation that will be offered later on for this is that the public was preoccupied with Lewinski and the impeachment crisis.[110]

Here's a summary: Hedge funds make their money scouting opportunities, buying long when expectations look good and selling short when they do not. LTCM tried to be scientific by hiring dozens of Ph.D's and two Nobel Prize winners. The company was put together by a former Salomon Brothers Vice-Chairman and a Former Fed Vice-Chairman. When the Russian ruble went under, these scientific gamblers were in trouble; their computerized strategy had not projected that eventuality. Early in September, they admitted to their investors that they had already lost half of the capital, about $1.8 billion. Far beyond that, they were so highly leveraged that Bill McDonough, the New York Fed Chairman, estimated that there was a then a 10% chance that it could wipe out the U.S. bond market for a week or a month. There were even scarier scenarios than that.

The Fed came up with a plan. It was agreed that 16 investment banking firms will contribute $250 million each and take over Long-Term Management. Greenspan and McDonough were able to get them to kick in $3.2 billion.[111]

At the hearing, James Leach, the chairman of the House Banking Committee and normally a Greenspan enthusiast, objects that "the Fed's intervention comes at a time when our government has been preaching to foreign governments, especially Asian ones, that the way to modernize is to let weak institutions fail and rely on market mechanisms rather than insider bailout."[112]

Editorial: This intervention prevents the market implosion that will begin less than two years later when stocks will be at a much higher level. Had they dropped then, the result would have been much less of a catastrophe. Substantial damage would have been inflicted on fewer market participants and our own economy, as well as that of others, would have been less impaired.

Why does Greenspan not take his own advice and rely on market mechanisms? Is it the fact that the bubble would break and so, probably, would the Clinton Presidency? The atypical absence of TV coverage points to that possibility. By keeping the little investor in the dark, the show can still go on. If they become conscious of how fragile the value of their holdings is, many more will leave.

Govt. Announces Plan To Staunch Global Financial Crisis—Opens New Credit Lines

"Plunge Protection Team"

"Known officially as the Working Group on Financial Markets . . . . The team is led by the U.S. Treasury Secretary, Robert Rubin . . . . The permanent members include the Chairman of the Federal Reserve, Alan Greenspan, and the heads of the Securities and Exchange Commission. Decisions are made in conjunction with the National Economic Council at the White House, and the powerful governor of the New York Federal Reserve Bank. They have each other's telephone numbers at all times and are plugged into a sophisticated 'market surveillance' system that helps them to anticipate trouble. It works in close alliance with the British financial authorities . . . . It can extend open lines of credit, inject money into the system and cut interest rates."

Ambrose Evans-Pritchard, *London Telegraph*, September 2, 1998.[113]

Edit. These people intervene in markets. That includes Greenspan, despite his asseverations to the contrary.

Outstanding Margin Debt Declines

In the August—October 1998 period, margin on the New York Stock Exchange declined from $154.4 billion to $130.2 billion.[114]

Margin is the amount that a client of a brokerage house must deposit in order to obtain a loan for the purchase of some eligible security. The current minimum is 50% of the current price of the security or 50% of the proceeds of a short sale.

Edit. Most historians think that margin was one of the factors that triggered the famous 1929 market crash, Its recent decline, therefore, must be counted as one piece of good news on the horizon.

Greenspan Credited With Prosperity

"And without Greenspan, the stock market boom of the 1990s, the great bull run, which saw Wall Street putting equity prices around the World ever higher, would not have happened . . . . Sometimes, as in the autumn of 1998, this adulation went too far. One of the unintended consequences of Greenspan's rescue of global financial markets in the autumn of 1998 was that Wall Street embarked on a new and even more aggressive climb."

David Smith, "All good things do come to an end" July / August 2000.[115]

He-e-e-r-r-z Al-l-a-an!

On October 13, the Fed does something that is unexpected. It chops interest rates by a quarter point. According the WSJ, the decision reflects "worries about cautious lending and financial markets."[116] In response, the Dow shoots up 330.58 points, the third greatest to date.

He-e-e-r-r-r-z The Prez-i-de-e-nt!

"Developments Friday fueled a new sense of optimism about the U.S. economy. The Commerce Department reported that gross domestic product jumped at an inflation-adjusted annual pace of 3.3% in the third quarter, up from the second quarter's

1.8% pace. The reading was well above analyst estimates, and a far cry from recession. Meanwhile, leaders of the Group of Seven industrialized nations, long accused of foot-dragging amid the recent economic turmoil, unveiled a plan to shore up fragile world markets.

"At the same time, investors continued the stock-market rally—launched two weeks ago by surprise Federal Reserve interest-rate cuts—amid fresh signs that Japan is finally fixing its banking mess. The Dow Jones industrial Average rose 97.97 points to close at 8592.10, the highest level since Aug. 25.

"'Think what's happened in the past month,' President Clinton crowed from the White House South Lawn on Friday. 'I feel quite good about what my fellow G-7 leaders and others have done,' he added. And even 'in the face of world-wide economic turmoil,' Mr. Clinton said, 'our economy remains the strongest in a generation.'"

John Simons and Jacob M. Schlesinger, "GDP Rise Lifts Hopes for U.S. Economy," *WSJ*, November 2, 1998, p. A2.

Analyst Bill King Shows Dept. Of Commerce Report To Be A Sham

"Here's how those bogus GDP numbers were derived so as to produce the maximum political effect . . . ahead of the impeachment referendum: (1) This Commerce Department assumed inventories rose $57.2 billion, up from $38.2 billion the previous quarter. This assumption added .96 to GDP. (2) Commerce assumed U.S. exports surged in Q3 *[Ed., the third quarter]*. So instead of subtracting 2.0% from GDP for the trade deficit as they had in previous quarters, Commerce only subtracted .76, thus adding 1.24 to GDP. Last month's trade figures were a record trade deficit—how could anyone with a modicum of intelligence or integrity assume U. S. exports surged? To whom? This would be laughable if it were not so unconscionable. (3)

COLA adjustments are based on Q3's deflator. Ergo the government squeezes it to save $$, and increase the GDP (nominal GDP minus the deflator = GDP). (4) To validate huge consumption assumptions, Commerce put savings at 0.1% (lowest since '46), down from Q2's 0.4%. Thus Commerce's ludicrous assumptions, .96 (inventory) + 1.24 (export surge), added 2.2 to GDP. Without them GDP was only 1.1. Massaging the deflator and savings rate increased GDP a few tenths. In the old days of Wall Street, someone would quickly reveal the gimmicks behind the numbers. Where are the voices now? All Wall Street really has to peddle is information, and if the info is bogus, then what? The bogus GDP allowed [Clinton] to go on TV and crow, the raison d'etre for the chicanery."[117]

Democrats Gain On Republicans

After the November 2nd election, the Republicans still hold the Senate, but lose two key races. They barely increase their control of the House. The Democrats gain three state governorships, but George Bush wins re-election in Texas and his brother Jeb takes the governorship in Florida. According to the WSJ: "Results suggest Clinton's sex scandal wasn't the drag on his party many thought, and may make Republicans rethink their approach to impeachment."[118]

What Else The Votes Meant

According to Everett Caril Ladd, president of Roper Center for Public Opinion Research: "Forty-one percent of those interviewed in the voter News service exit poll said they are better off today than two years ago, only 13% that they are worse off. Those reporting improved finances voted for House Democrats 58% to 40%, while those calling their financial position worse went Republican by 57% to 30%."[119]

Edit. No Doubt about it! Clinton and the Democrats were helped by the seeming prosperity. The idea that the quality of political performance has little to do with private life has taken hold.

Fed Reduces An Interest Rate Again

On November 17, 1998, the FOMC convenes for its regular meeting. Although conditions on Wall Street have settled down, Greenspan asks for and gets another .25 % cut, just to make sure.[120]

"Low interest rates don't mean economic health"

"Very low, and especially, negative interest rates are a sure sign of depression. You know things are bad when people are willing to pay the Japanese government to hold their money because other options for investment are so likely to collapse to nothing that 'the return of capital' has become more important than 'the return on capital.'

"Equally troubling for North Americans contemplating what crony capitalism has done to Asia is the fact than an artificial bull market in stocks encourages individuals as well as businesses to overestimate future economic prospects. The damage that the rigging of the Japanese stock market did to the financial situation of Japanese households was limited by the fact that it coincided with a period of extraordinary high savings by aging Japanese facing retirement. In the United States, by contrast, the savings rate has dwindled to nothing. In fact, it actually turned negative in September for the first time since the great Depression. Americans will be in far worse shape to endure the down-side of the cycle than were the cashed-up Japanese."

Article by James Dale Davidson, November 18, 1998.[121]

"Clinton favors using stock market to pump up Social Security"

"President Clinton favors some use of stock market investments to boost returns for the Social Security trust fund, according to his top economic adviser, Gene Sterling."[122]

CNN.com, December 9, 1998.

"Liftoff Ahead"[123]

On November 24, the Dow reaches record levels, rising 2.34% or 214.72 points to 9,374.27, up from the August low. The Dow will finish up 18.5% for the year. This chart, which was prepared for Barron's, the first week in the following year, shows it continuing to grow. The expert consulted sees a target of 11,137.

The S&P 500 also makes a record, rising to 1,188.21.

The Nasdaq Composite Index also rises spectacularly, increasing 515 points above its August 31 low of 1,499.25.[124]

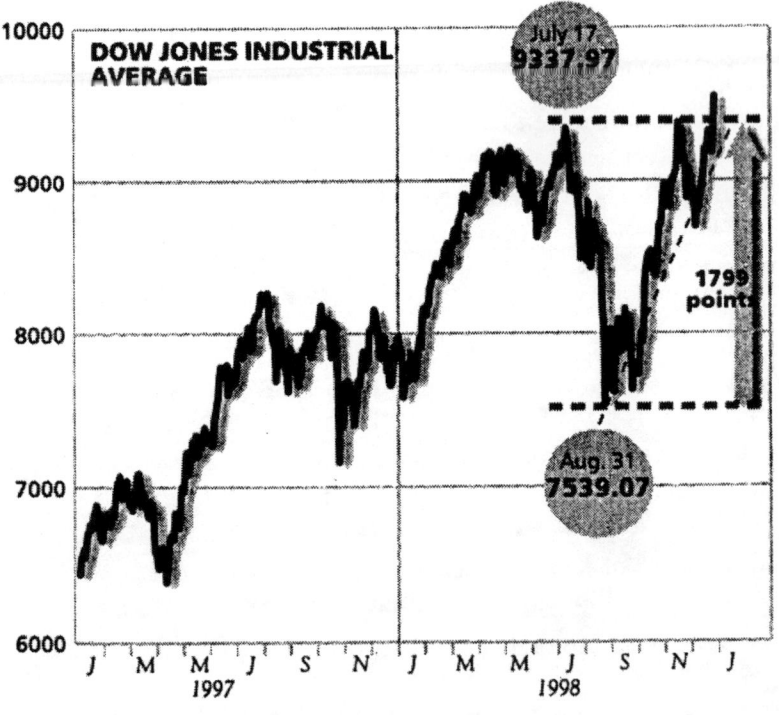

1998 Warning

"Just like the roaring '20s, the warning signs are everywhere. Back then, it was a non-stop party on Wall Street. People were sure the good times would never end.

"After the stock market crashed in October 1929, it rallied . . . .

"Today will be similar. Now, just like the dishonest politicians, the financial media and brokers are lying to the public. They refuse to tell you the truth. They don't want you to know about the huge job cuts; the downturns in earnings; the loss of sales, the soaring U.S. trade deficit. They don't want you to understand how severe the Asian, Latin American and eastern European wipeouts are."

Wall Street Underground, Vol. 4, No. 3. November/December, 1998, p. 10.

Importance Of Stock Options

"The trend in corporate management is moving away from set salaries toward ownership in the firm. According to a sample of 144 of the major S&P 500 companies, by 1998 employee stock options had attained 6.2% of the total shares outstanding."[125]

Robert J. Shiller

Margin Up Sharply After October

Gross Federal Debt Goes Up For Year

The Gross Federal Debt for the year does not go down, but increases by $113 billion to $5.526 trillion. ($5,526,193,008,897.62).[126]

Impeachment Crisis

After Clinton admitted lying to the public on August 18, he was on the road to impeachment and untimely removal from office. He made this admission in a brief television address, after having first testified before a grand jury. This caused an enormous amount of consternation. On December 14, the House Judiciary panel found it could agree on four articles of impeachment. On the 19th, the house approved two of those articles. Two days latter, President Clinton said he would not voluntarily resign.

During this tense period in the year's last month, the stock market is generally on the rise. It is generally expected that Clinton will prevail, since the Republicans have done much more poorly than expected in the recent elections. Indeed, the Dow posts its greatest day of the year less than three weeks after that election.

Editorial: Clinton is very popular with the investors. For some, he is considered to be good luck. His supporters are fond of calling him the "come-back kid," because of his ability to survive many crises. The sneering query, "Who needs character?" can be heard about the land. If he resigns late in '98, the market will probably begin its inevitable descent. Seeing the man who embodied so much of its realization fall, many will begin to listen to the voices which have been expressing alarm at the bloating bull; this is because when an important man falls, people look critically at that which came up with him. And the height of the market is far below that attained by the fifteen-month expansion which will take place between December 31, 1998, and April 4, 2000. At year's end, 1998, the Dow stands at only 80% of its eventual peak; the Nasdaq is at about 40% of what it will reach—no tech wreak. Enron and Worldcom might have a soft landing. The earlier the resignation, the smaller the damage to investors—and to America. It is probable that President Gore would behave in the very correct and legal manner that Gerald Ford adopted after President Nixon's resignation.

CHAPTER IX

1999—THE BULL PIROUETTES

Europe Challenges Dollar

On January 4, the Euro, a new currency is formed from the German Mark, the French Franc, and the Spanish Peseta makes it debut.

Edit. Recall that Red China declined moving important reserves into this currency.

Fed Research Official Issues Warning

On January 14, Mike Press, director of research and statistics at the Fed, told the Charlotte Economics Club in North Carolina: "Might people—business managers, consumers, investors—be taking risks that they would not have taken were it not for an exaggerated confidence in the ability of the Fed to cushion the economy and financial markets against any and all shocks? If so, there conceivably could be greater potential instability in the system than is readily apparent at this time."

Edit. Another timely warning from that source; it would be valuable to know whether it was initiated by Greenspan or by some other official.

Bigwigs Cheer Clinton During Impeachment Crisis

It is Friday, January 15, 1999. On the 107th floor of the World Trade Center is a conference hosted by Jesse Jackson's "Wall

Street Project." Richard Grasso, Chairman of the New York Stock Exchange, notes that the Dow has tripled during the Clinton years. But "my little corner of Manhattan is not what the U.S. financial markets are about." Referring to shareholders and pension beneficiaries, he announces that "two hundred million Americans have benefitted over these last six years from your unwavering commitment."

Michael Armstrong, the chairman of AT&T thanks Clinton for his choices to reduce the deficit and lower interest rates. "You made those tough decisions, and because of that a lot of us in our businesses look awfully smart." He concludes by saying: "So, Mr. President, my message is, you had the courage to get it started, and we all were along for the most wonderful economic ride in the history of this country."

Finally, the Reverend Jackson introduces Clinton: "How do you judge Bill Clinton? How do you judge Babe Ruth? How do you judge Hank Aaron? How do you judge Michael Jordan? . . . You judge them by their cumulative box score . . . . The only people at the end of the game whose uniforms are clean are those who do not have enough confidence in them by the coach to make it to the field . . . . Those who play have stains on their uniforms . . . Those who play, those who play . . . have stains."

Clinton is touched. "How can any American, of any station in life, not be proud of the financial markets we have built, and, as Mr.Grasso said, of our 260 million people who actually benefit from it. We are beginning to share the wealth." Turning his attention to Jack Kemp, the 1996 Republican Vice Presidential candidate who is also present, the man who defeated him says of the renowned supply-sider, "That's why Jack Kemp's here, and why I always like him." Kemp chirps back: "I like you too, Mr. President." Clinton closes his remarks by speaking about government's role in spreading the wealth even further. He pledges to "stay with the strategy that's got us this far." He adds that he would like to come up with more investment programs, but the main thing is "to keep the budget balanced and to keep the interest rates low and the confidence high."[127]

Edit. What sort of "Reverend" would imply that no one can accomplish anything great without getting morally dirty?

End Of The Millennium?

"Tonight, as I deliver the last State of the Union address of the 20ᵗʰ century . . . ."

Bill Clinton, *State Of The Union Address*, January 19, 1999

Edit. Of course, the real beginning will be 2001; but, many people insist on using the wrong calculation. Perhaps they dimly foresee the future and want to have time to celebrate.

Clinton Advocates Stocks For Social Security Fund

"From its beginning, Americans have supplemented Social Security with private pensions and savings. Yet, today, millions of people retire with little to live on other than Social Security. Americans are living longer than ever and simply must save more than ever.

"Therefore, in addition to saving Social Security and Medicare, I propose a new pension initiative for retirement security in the 21ˢᵗ century.

"I propose that we use a little over 11 percent of the surplus to establish universal savings accounts—USA accounts—to give all Americans the means to save. With these new accounts, Americans can invest as they choose, and receive funds to match a portion of their savings, with extra help for those least able to save.

USA accounts will help all Americans to share in our nation's wealth, and to enjoy a more secure retirement. I ask you to support them.".

Bill Clinton, *State Of The Union Address*, January 19, 1999.

Reactions To The Proposal

Generally speaking, there is little enthusiasm for Clinton's proposal to invest part of the Social Security trust fund in the stock market. The Dow closes at 9,235.91, down 19.31 points. The S&P rises 4.62 points, or .37%. The NASDAQ makes a record move up to 2,475.49, but the actual point increase is only 7.32. From that, one cannot tell anything.

Allen Greenspan is negative, saying that it would be "virtually impossible" to keep politics out.

The editorial in *The Wall Street Journal* is much harsher, naming the speech the "State of Shame:" It was, the newspaper said, "a fire bell, calling on every imaginable constituency in the Democratic village to rally toward the burning barn of his Presidency. Appealing to the old-style Democrats whose votes he needs to stay in office, he proposed that the government buy up the stock market (Jesse Jackson's dream come true) . . . ." [128]

A Dick Morris-like response comes from Lester Thurow, the well known Democrat economist: "As President Clinton sends up his budget proposal to Congress today, economically he has pulled a fast one on Republicans yet again.

. . . .

"President Clinton killed the privatization of Social Security by proposing that the government put $700 billion into the stock market to see what would happen. He had to know that the very next day the chairman of the Federal Reserve Board, Alan Greenspan, would come out against the proposal. Greenspan, and any other person who thinks about the issue for more than a microsecond, does not want some government agency buying and selling stocks. The government would be determining which stocks go up and down. The opportunities for corruption would be enormous." [129]

Clinton Says He Will Avert New Century Crisis

"We also must be ready for the 21st century, from its very first moment, by solving the so-called 'Y2K' computer problem. Now, we had one member of Congress stand up and applaud and we may have about the ratio out there applauding at home in front of their television sets. But remember, this is a big, big problem. And we've been working hard on it. Already we've made sure that the Social Security checks will come on time. And I—but I want all the folks at home listening to this to know that we need every state and local government, every business, large and small, to work with us to make sure that this Y2K computer bug will be remembered as the last headache of the 20th century, not the first crisis of the 21st."

Bill Clinton, *State Of The Union Address*, January 19, 1999

Edit. It will turn out to the last phony crisis of the twentieth century. The last genuine crisis will be the stock market bubble, which will start imploding in April of next year.

Greenspan And YK2

At a Senate Banking Committee hearing, Senator Charles Schumer of New York asks him: "You have mentioned that our financial institutions are doing quite well in dealing with the problem [of YK2]? A second and ancillary problem, but a serious one, is that citizens may be worried about what will happen and will take their money out of the financial institutions toward the second half of the year because they're worried about this. From what I understand, the Federal Reserve has set aside a certain amount of reserves for the end of 1999 to deal with that. As I understand, it's $50 billion."

Greenspan: "The concern that I have is that people are going to draw too much out, and walking around with a lot of hundred dollar bills is not the safest way to keep your money.

Senator John Edwards of North Carolina: "What advice

would you give a citizen in December of this year about what
to do with their savings account?"

Greenspan" "I would say the most sensible thing is to leave it
where it is. That's probably the safest thing. There's almost no
conceivable way in which I can envision that computers will break
down and records of people's savings accounts will disappear."[130]

Welfare Hits Lowest Point

On January 25, Clinton announces that welfare rolls have
fallen to the lowest level in 30 years.

A Critic's Answer

"When President Clinton signed Republican legislation to
'abolish' social welfare in 1996, it was greeted as the most
important conservative social victory in a generation. It was little
more than a bad joke.

"Welfare rolls have declined since then. But the punch
line is that the politicians did this by legerdemain. State and
local governments have been working with the federal
government in moving many welfare recipients onto the Social
Security disability rolls.

"The politicians like the fact that welfare recipients have
been moving onto Social Security rolls. During election season,
the politicians can say they reduced the welfare rolls.

"The former welfare recipients love it because the cash
benefits are much higher. For instance, a family of four can
receive twice as much cash on Social Security than the same
family on welfare.

"Claiming a minor psychological malady can get you on
disability. Once on the Social Security rolls it's a welfare cheat's
paradise because there are practically no reviews from the
government. Welfare recipients are more carefully scrutinized,
as many states have aggressive welfare fraud units.

"Thus, when President Clinton tells Congress the

anticipated budget needs to help fund the depleting Social Security trust funds, he knows what he is speaking about. Some of those funds have been used to cover the huge run-up in disability spending."

Article, Christopher Ruddy, NewMax. *com Vortex*, "November 1999[131]

President Acquitted.

On February 12, Clinton is acquitted by the U.S. Senate. Of the four articles of impeachment brought forth by the House, they decide to vote on only two of them. They vote 55-45 against perjury and 50-50 against obstruction of justice.

Hooray For The Nasdaq!

On that same day, the Composite increases 96.05 points to 2,405.55, a 4.16% gain, the largest so far. This can be attributed in part to Clinton's success and in part to some words by Greenspan with regard to banking reform and the economy.[132]

"The Committee To Save The World"

Time Magazine cover story featuring Greenspan, Rubin and Larry Summers, then Asst. Treasury Secretary under Rubin. "The three men trying to cope with these mid-ether collisions of dollars and expectations are an unlikely team. Greenspan, the data-loving analyst with government roots sunk back into the financial and moral chaos of the Nixon Administration, and shaman-like power over global markets. Rubin, the Goldman Sachs wonder boy who ran the firm's complex and dangerous arbitrage operation and then led it to rocket-ship international growth. And Summers, the Harvard-trained academic who is invariably called the Kissinger of economics, a total pragmatist whose ambitions sometimes grate, but whose intellect never fails to dazzle.

"What holds them together is a passion for thinking and an inextinguishable curiosity about a new economic order that is unfolding before them like an Alice in Wonderland world. The sheer fascination of inventing a 21st century financial system motivates them more than the usual Washington drugs of power and money. In the past six years the three men have merged into a kind of brotherhood with an easy rapport."

. . . .

"Greenspan has a theory about what holds them together: 'In analytical people self-esteem relies on the analysis and not on the conclusions.' That must be it. The three men have a mania for analysis that has bred a rigorous, unique intellectual honesty . . . . Rubin, Greenspan and Summers have out-grown ideology. Their faith is in the markets and their own ability to analyze them. 'It's unusual,' Greenspan says. 'In Washington, you come to the table, and everyone meets, and no one changes their mind. But with us, you have something else.'

"This pragmatism is a faith that recalls nothing so much as the objectivist philosophy of the novelist and social critic Ayn Rand (The Fountainhead, Atlas Shrugged) which Greenspan has studied intently. During long nights at Rand's apartment and through her articles and letters, Greenspan found in objectivism a sense that markets are an expression of the deepest truths about human nature and that, as a result, they will ultimately be correct."

. . . .

An example: "Hit by Asian turmoil, SOUTH KOREA teeters but does not fall { RUBIN talked Western banks into rescheduling their Korean loans, preventing a devastating default} + SUMMERS led his team through a fast analysis of

Korea's plight—and then passed key tips to Seoul} + GREENSPAN said Korea's recovery might be tough, but reassured markets by saying the crisis should pass in time} = RESULT Rubin's fast action—and Summers's advice—helped stall the Asian contagion and gave the U. S. economy a chance to adjust."

Article, *TIME Magazine*, February 15, 1999, pp. 39-40.

Edit. Their solution: Reschedule the old loans, creating more interest for the central bankers. Who but these three with "a passion for thinking" could come up with such a novel idea?

It is also interesting to see that the new pragmatism identifies itself with Rand's idea of capitalism; forty years ago, her capitalism was not mainstream.

"The Bailout of Banks"

"By all rights, one of the consequences of the crisis should be that the banks which made bad loans in South Korea and elsewhere in Asia should have to swallow hard and eat their losses. The amounts at stake are not insignificant: U. S. banks' exposure in South Korea is estimated to total more than $20 billion. BankAmerica alone reportedly has more than $3 billion in outstanding loans to South Korean firms, and Citicorp more than $2 billion.

"Now, due to the taxpayer-backed bailout engineered by Rubin and the IMF, it does not appear that BankAmerica, Citicorp or the other major banks with outstanding loans to South Korea—J.P. Morgan, Bankers Trust, the Bank of New York and Chase Manhattan—will lose a penny.

"Not only is the Rubin/IMF scheme an unconscionable bailout of the big banks which were complicit in the South Korean financial debacle, it is certain to create what is known as a 'moral hazard.' Simply put, that means we can expect to see more reckless lending by the big banks . . . ."

Russel Mokiber and Robert Weissman[133]

Crisis Continues In Third World

"Clinton's Secretary of the Treasury, Robert Rubin, pushed hard to increase the flow of American capital abroad. Poor countries welcomed the investment as the road to modernization, but it was too much, too fast. While one effect of uncontrolled American investment in the Third World was to create nations of sweatshops where union busting was enforced by the armies and American jobs went overseas in search of the cheapest labor, the end result was what the New York Times called 'a financial hurricane' that overwhelmed those nations. While U. S. banks encouraged foreign investment, the banking systems of the 'emerging markets' were unable to handle the speculation storm that overwhelmed them. Billions and billions of dollars were sent abroad—$93 billion in 1996 alone went to just Indonesia, Malaysia, the Philippines, Thailand and South Korea. Excess capital led to excess borrowing, cheap credit, and over-production. That led to financial collapse, unemployment, rioting, and suffering by the workers of those countries."

"The World financial Crisis: Made in the USA", *Institute For Global Communication*, by Albert Lannon, February 1999.

Chinese Trade Strategy

"In the past decade, with billions of dollars in grants and subsidized loans and enormous Western technical assistance, China has made astonishing strides in modernizing its electrical power generation, transportation, and manufacturing facilities. Its new state-of-the-art manufacturing facilities, together with its massive use of prison labor (including political and religious prisoners) and the payment of slave-labor wages to its 'non-prison' workforce, have enabled the PRC to capture huge segments of the U. S. market. Textiles, steel, clothing, shoes, auto parts, glassware, household goods, furniture, appliances, consumer electronics, hardware, tools, and toys—all once made in the U.

S—are now made in China. It is becoming increasingly difficult for the U.S. shopper to find goods that are *not* made in China.

"Besides taking several million U. S. jobs, this huge manufacturing shift has provided China with facilities which either produce items that are important to modern warfare and warfare support, or that could be converted to war production on short notice. The flood of products China daily deluges our ports with also provides Beijing's strategists with a steady, gigantic transfusion of cash, which it uses to purchase key military goods—and politicians."

Article by William F. Jasper, *The New American*, February 15, 1999, p. 26[134].

Now, Some Really Good News

In the month of February, outstanding margin credit at the NYSE declines by $1.7 billion to $151.5 billion.[135]

A decline in margin is a strong indication of a decline of speculation in the stock market. As David Jones, one of the best known Fed watchers on Wall Street put it: "Even though the margin requirement applies directly to only a small percentage of the market, it carries considerable symbolic weight, and it hasn't changed since early 1974.".[136]

Edit. But that is not to last.

The Dow Jets Upward

On March 17, the Dow Jones Industrial Average hits what at one time seemed to be an impossible barrier. It gets to above 10,000, but because of kick-ins by computerized selling programs, it closes at 9,930.47. But this is no fluke.

On March 30, the Dow closes at 10,006.78. The market average stands at more than 300% above its October 1990 level. On that same day, the S&P 500 increases 2.13% and the Nasdaq, by 3.08%

In response, Merrill Lynch comes out with a full-page

newspaper ad with a headline proudly proclaiming that "even those with a disciplined long-term approach like ours have to sit back and say 'wow.'" In the bottom left corner of the page, adjacent to a stock plot culminating at 10,000, appears the words "HUMAN ACHIEVEMENT."[137]

Edit. That sort of a self-promotion is very reminiscent of Greenspan's original mentor, Ayn Rand—although in fairness to her, she probably would have not invested in this kind of a market.

Margin Increases In March

Outstanding margin debt jumps $4.9 billion to $156.4 billion.

On April 20, the Nasdaq Loses Altitude

Internet stocks plunge, causing the Nasdaq Composite Index to drop down 138.43 points or 5.57% to 2,345.61.

Margin Jumps

Outstanding NYSE margin debt increases by 10.6 percent during the month of April. This is significant, because the rise from March 1998 to March 1999 was only 11.5 percent. The sum now stands at $179.9 billion.[138]

The Dow Gets even Higher

And May 4, the Dow rises 225.65 points or 2.09% to 11, 014.69. Since this is just 24 trading days after the first time the market closed above 10,000, it is the shortest time in history that it increased by a thousand points.[139]

Critic Notes Reasons For Despondency

"As I write this, the Dow is over 11,000. Quite a record. But underneath the surface, things are not so well. The average mutual fund was up a measly 1% for the 1ˢᵗ quarter. And the average share of stock is down 22% from last year.

"More stocks are at 52 week lows than 52 week highs. More stocks are declining in value than advancing. The question has to be, what in the world is going on?

"The answer is simple. The rally is over. The Dow has been putting in record highs. But vast bulks of stocks are not included in this narrow index. They are going *down* in value. One of the most complete measures of the stock market—the Russell 2000—is down 22% from its highs. This is the pattern we see when the market peaks.

Even more scary, corporate earnings are plunging . . . ."

"The oil industry is in a depression. So is copper mining. Gold mining. Steel. Aluminum. Computers. Chemicals. Agriculture. Manufacturing.

"Capacity utilization for companies in the U.S. is at a multi-year low. That is one of the best government stats we get. It shows how much of the total production capacity—factories, utilities, and mines—is being used. Above 90 is considered full use. 85 is a sign of an expanding economy. 80 and under is a sign of an economy slowing. Right now, the U.S. figure is 80.1, and falling."

Wall Street Underground, Vol. 4, No. 5 April/May 1999, p.7.

On July 1, The Fed Increases Important Rate By 1/4 Percentage Point

Edit: Greenspan is pulling back a little.

Clinton On The Business Cycle

"I believe in the New Economy. Technology is rippling through every sector of economic activity in ways that have given us dramatic increases in productivity and potential for growth without inflation. And I think most [economic] models have not accurately measured it . . . ."

"No one believes that we have completely repealed any tendency toward inflation, or that we've completely repealed business cycles. But we've dramatically improved [our chances] through this technological revolution."
President Bill Clinton, *Business Week online,* July 12, 1999.[140]

MELVIN A. TAYLOR, PRESIDENT, FIRST NATIONAL BANK OF CHICAGO, OCTOBER 1927.
"THERE ARE GROUNDS FOR THE BELIEF THAT THERE HAS BEEN A CHANGE FOR THE BETTER IN CERTAIN ASPECTS OF THE BUSINESS CYCLE AS IT BE EXPECTED TO OPERATE IN THE FUTURE IN THE UNITED STATES. CYCLES HAVE BEEN DESCRIBED AS CONSISTING OF PROSPERITY, CRISIS, DEPRESSION AND REVIVAL. CONDITIONS HAVE COME INTO BEING WHICH TEND TO SOFTEN THE SECOND OR CRITICAL STAGE SO THAT IN THE DESCRIPTION OF FUTURE CYCLES, WE MIGHT SUBSTITUTE THE WORD 'RECESSION' FOR 'CRISIS.' FURTHERMORE, WE MAY HOPE THAT THE TWO PHASES 'RECESSION' AND 'DEPRESSION' MAY BE RENDERED LESS DISASTROUS IN THE FUTURE THAN THEY HAVE BEEN AT MANY TIMES IN THE PAST."[141]

Big Business Starts to Shift Support To Democrats

The vaunted alliance between big business and the Republican party begins to show strains. In the first six months of 1999, business groups donate about the same to both parties. This is also the case with wealthy individuals. In 1998, support for Congressional Republicans among those making more than $100,000 slips from 64% in 1994 to 55%. In the bracket containing those making more than $75,000 per year, the Republican share declines from 62% to 53%. At the same time, Republicans see their support among those making less than $15,000 rise from 38% in 1994 to 41% in 1998. By 1998, 36.7% of Congressional Republican seats have come from the South— up from 1990's 26%.[142]

In the past, most of the support for Democrats among the wealthy came from financiers and show-business types. By 1999, that party has made serious inroads among business groups.

The Trade Deficit Also Soars

In June, it reaches the highest point in history, soaring to $24.62 billion. This figure will be released to the public on August 20.

On July 2, Rubin Resigns

"Defending the actions he and other policy-makers took to handle the worst global financial crisis in 50 years, Treasury Secretary Robert Rubin said in a farewell interview that there were nail-biting times when he feared that the situation could spin out of control.

"Praised by Clinton as the greatest treasury secretary since Alexander Hamilton, Rubin had to deal in his early days in office with the Mexican peso crisis of 1995 and for the past two years has struggled to fashion a rescue effort for the far worse Asian currency crisis, which began in Thailand in July 1997."

"Rubin in Final Interview, Defends Treasury, IMF, *BradyNet FORUM*, June 28, 1999.

Edit. How sad! Now there are only two left in the Committee To Save The World.

The Columbia Encyclopedia Lauds Rubin

" . . . 1938—, U.S. business executive and government official, b. New York City. A graduate of Harvard, he attended the London School of Economics before receiving his law degree from Yale in 1964. Rubin joined the investment firm of Goldman, Sachs & Co. in 1966, becoming a partner in 1971 and eventually (1990-93) co-chairman of the firm. He served as director (1993-94) of the National Council under President

Bill Clinton and in 1995 succeeded Lloyd Bensen as treasury secretary. During his tenure, Rubin worked to stabilize the value of the dollar. He held the post during a long boom, and some analysts credit his polices for the massive U. S. economic growth in the late 1990s. He resigned in 1999 and was succeeded by his deputy, Lawrence Summers; Rubin later became a co-chairman of the Citigroup financial services company."

The Columbia Encyclopedia, Sixth Edition 2001 www.bartleby.com/ 65/ru/RubinRob.html

Rubin Did Not Defuse The Asian Crisis

"Treasury Secretary Robert Rubin picked a good time to resign. As a senior White House official said, Rubin 'made his fortune selling at the top of the market.'

"But the disasters that Robert Rubin helped create in his four years at Treasury are still festering. There are tens of millions of newly impoverished people in Indonesia, South Korea, and the other Asian countries that were dragged into the swamp last year. The Russian economy, cut in half after seven years of Western management, is again contracting— spurring a seemingly endless political crisis. Brazil's economy is shrinking even faster, thanks to a treasury-organized bail-out of foreign investors that began last November. It is only a matter time before more of Treasury's chickens, dispersed throughout the globe, come home to roost.

"It is no exaggeration to say that the U.S. Treasury Department is the primary culprit in this continuing economic turmoil. It was at their urging that the Asian countries opened their economies to the massive foreign borrowing that pushed their financial systems to the precipice. For example, an internal Treasury department memorandum of June 29, 1996, listed 'priority areas where Treasury is seeking further liberalization' in South Korea. These included the short-term foreign borrowing by Korean companies that made their economy—as well as others—especially vulnerable to a sudden reversal of capital flows.

"Then they turned the financial crisis into a regional depression, by forcing 'austerity' policies on the injured economies of the region: high interest rates, tax increases, and budget cuts."

Mark Weisbrot, Research Director at Preamble Center, Wash., D.C. (May 13, 1999).[143]

Greenspan Favors Increased Immigration

On July 22, Greenspan testifies before the House Banking Committee. In response to a Congressman's question, he answers: "I don't know where the level [of unemployment] will trigger pressures [toward inflation], but I do know, because the law of supply and demand has got to work eventually, that there is a point at which if that pool of people seeking jobs continues to decline, at some point it must have an impact. If we can open up our immigration rolls significantly, that clearly will make that less and less of a potential problem."

" . . . I've tried to stop short of recommending any specific detailed program, because I do think that that's going well beyond, I think, anything that's appropriate for central banks or anything related to issues which are major value judgments of a society, which, in my judgment, are wholly within the realm, and should stay there, of the elected representatives."[144]

Critics Say No Labor Shortage

In June 1998, Representative Lamar Smith (R-TX), chairman of the House Immigration Subcommittee of the Judiciary, presented a survey which showed that 21 U. S. high-tech firms had let 121,800 workers go since December 1997. Norman Mattloff, a professor of computer science, stated in an interview with *Investors' Business Daily* that "the problem is that most employers prefer less-expensive talent. Most software firms surveyed hire less than 5% of the software professionals that apply for jobs. Microsoft Corporation hires 2%. Brodebur Software Inc. hires just 1%."[145]

Professor-Emeritus Virginia Deane Abernathy of Vanderbilt University writes: "Hardly mentioned in this debate is the *long-term* effect of responding to labor-management shortages by importing immigration labor: namely, to dampen wage increases that would otherwise occur, which is, of course, the subtext in industry's lobbying for additional immigrant workers. However, higher wages for skilled labor are not necessarily bad for the economy."[146]

"How to (Really) Get Rich in America"

This article that appears in the August USA *Weekend* attempts to show how a 22-year old college graduate with a salary of $30,000 and yearly income raises of 1% can get enough to comfortably retire. "If she saved only 10% of her income and invested the savings in an S&P index fund she'd have a net worth of $1.4 million on retirement at age 67, in today's dollars." The assumption behind the article is that the S&P index will consistently return 8% on average each year after inflation is taken into account.[147]

JOHN J. RASCOB—CHAIRMAN OF THE DEMOCRATIC PARTY—1929

"SUPPOSE A MAN MARRIES AT THE AGE OF TWENTY-THREE AND BEGINS A REGULAR SAVING OF FIFTEEN DOLLARS A MONTH—AND ALMOST ANYONE WHO'S EMPLOYED CAN DO THAT IF HE TRIES. IF HE INVESTS IN GOOD COMMON STOCKS AND ALLOWS THE DIVIDENDS AND RIGHTS TO ACCUMULATE, HE WILL AT THE END OF TWENTY YEARS HAVE AT LEAST EIGHTY THOUSAND DOLLARS AND AN INCOME OF AROUND FOUR HUNDRED DOLLARS A MONTH. HE WILL BE RICH. AND BECAUSE ANYONE CAN DO THAT I AM FIRM IN MY BELIEF THAT ANYONE NOT ONLY CAN BE RICH BUT OUGHT TO BE RICH."[148]

A Pension Program Rivals Largest Mutual Funds

Teachers Insurance Annuity Assurance (TIAA) began as an insurance company. It was established for college professors. By the early 1950s, it began to invest in stocks. In July 1952, a separate unit was established, the College Retirement Equities Fund (CREF).

By 1988, every dollar invested in CREF in 1952 was worth $36.74. As of May 1999, the value of CREF has increased 173 times, i.e., that for very $1 invested in 1952, there is now $173. As of October 30, 1999, TIAA-CREF has two million participants spread across 9,000 institutions with assets of $273 billion. Ranked by assets, it is the thirtieth largest company and the third largest insurance company in the United States. It is the largest pension fund in America. Its portfolio of stocks is larger than that of Fidelity's Magellan Fund and the Janus family of funds.[149]

Edit. What will happen the following year will be an injustice to those teachers who liked neither Clinton nor Greenspan.

The Democratization Of Money

"The age of the Masters of the Universe has given way to an era in which the masters—the CEOs—are increasingly being forced to answer to the servants, and in which the fiercest critics of capitalism clip bond coupons and collect dividends. The place of money and stockholding in politics has undergone a similar shift in the 1990s: The precinct of money, traditionally rock-ribbed Republican, has become one in which Democrats are more comfortable. In many ways, the democratization of money has led to the Democratization of money. As the 1990s wore on, Democrats, and in particular, the Clinton administration, grew not only to tolerate and appreciate the markets but even to love and embrace them."
Daniel Gross, *Bull Run* . . . , p. 80.

Murder-Suicide

On July 29, all-tech day trader Mark Barton has sizable losses. Too many margin calls. He goes insane and enters into the Atlanta trading house he has been buying from and kills nine people—and then himself.[150]

The Fed Increases Rates

On August 25, the Federal Reserve makes two small rate increases. The most important of the two is the lifting of the federal funds target rate from 5% to 5.25%. This move does not bother the stock market very much, as it was widely anticipated.

Edit.: People swallow the notion that it has already been "discounted."

IMF Official Expresses Alarm To Greenspan

It is late August. The scene is the Fed's annual Jackson Hole meeting. In his remarks, International Monetary Fund Deputy Director Stanley Fischer politely asks Greenspan to raise the margin requirement. Greenspan does not directly answer him in his speech, but claims that central banks like the Fed must "increasingly focus on changes in asset values" to discern whether high stock prices could hurt the economy.[151]

Edit. Open up any standard study of the origins of the 1929 stock market crash; they will say that broker's loans had much to do with fueling the speculative orgy.[152] It is not a necessary part of Greenspan's job that he comment on the stock market, but it is the responsibility of the Federal Reserve to determine margin requirements. Stanley Fischer is not a tyro on these matters. What is Greenspan doing?

"Greenspan plugs hi-tech"

"'Advancements in technology have allowed the U.S. economy to enter its ninth year of uninterrupted economic expansion, and the strides in productivity created can probably keep that expansion going,' Federal Reserve Chairman Alan Greenspan said Wednesday.

"In prepared remarks of a more historic than market orientation, Greenspan told an audience at Grand Valley State University in Grand Rapids, Mich., that information technology—particularly the advent of integrated circuits and other rapid forms of technology—have begun to alter the manner in which companies and people do business and create economic value,'often in ways that were not readily foreseeable a year ago.'

. . . .

"'It has also created new jobs as companies have allowed for changes in inventory management, distribution systems, customer service and other tasks,' Greenspan said. That has 'sharply reduced the degree of uncertainty confronting business management,' he added.

"'Today, economic value is best symbolized by exceedingly complex, miniaturized integrated circuits and the ideas—the software—that utilize them,' Greenspan said, claiming that 'most of what we currently perceive as value and wealth is intellectual and impalpable.'"

Article *cnnmoney*, September 8, 1999, pl 1 *http://money.com/1999/09/08/economy*

Edit. This softens the effect of the rate increase, as does his refusal to amend margin requirements.

Japan Intervenes In Behalf Of The Dollar

On September 10, Japan tries to stop the yen's advance against the dollar. The dollar recovers slightly, but then resumes its slow slide.

Edit. Last June, it was the U.S. that intervened in behalf of the Yen. This year, it is Japan's turn. Old economy thinking would definitely regard this as a sign to pull back.

Stock Market Drops

On September 24, after Microsoft President Steve Balmer said that tech prices were too high, the Dow drops 205.48 points to 10,318.59—the second two-hundred-point-loss in a week. The Nasdaq has the fourth worst trading loss to date.

Edit. At last, one of the major winners in that market is asking for a return to reason.

Big Board Extends Hours

On September 28, it is announced that the New York Stock Exchange be open until 6:35 PM, extending trading by nearly two hours.

Stocks Drop Some More

On October 13, the Dow descends by 231.12 points to 10,417.06. This is a 2.17% loss, the second biggest point drop of the year.

On October 22, Congress Repeals Glass-Steagall

"When he stepped down from his Treasury post this past summer, Rubin left unfinished a legislative effort to re-write the nation's banking laws. Misnamed 'financial modernization' legislation, it was really a deregulatory initiative—reminiscent of the S&L deregulation that led to a corporate crime spree, the collapse of the industry and the subsequent taxpayer bailout of epic proportions.

"The centerpiece of the deregulatory bill, which different fragments of the finance industry have pushed for a decade and a half, is the repeal of the revered Glass-Steagall act, which bars the common ownership of banks on the one hand, and insurance companies and securities firms on the other.

"Although powerful interests have long backed the legislation, it has repeatedly failed to make it through Congress . . . .

. . . .

"Another failure, however, was not acceptable to one company above all—Citigroup. The product of the merger between Citibank and Travelers, Citigroup is operating in apparent violation of the bar on common ownership of banking, and insurance and securities, thanks to a loophole that provides for a two-year transition period.

"Enter Robert Rubin. According to a report in the New York Times, Rubin helped broker the final compromise language on financial deregulation."

Russell Mokhiber and Robert Weisman, November 17, 1999.[153]

Rubin Joins Citigroup

On October 27, Robert Rubin joins the nations's largest financial services company, becoming Chairman of the board's executive committee.

The Base For The Dow Is Altered

On October 27, the Dow Jones Industrials undergo change for the second time in the bubble market. Chevron, Goodyear and Sears and Union Carbide will be out. Microsoft, Intel, SBS, and Home Deport will be brought in.

Critic Explains Rationale Behind Alteration

"Despite the stock market's record runup, most stocks are well off their highs. Wall Street showed how desperate it is to keep the rally going. In an unprecedented move, Dow Jones threw out four stocks from the Dow Industrials Index—and put in several companies not even on the NYSE.

"They did this for one reason. To try to keep the Dow going ever higher—and to hide the fact from the public that the overall market has not kept pace with Internet insanity. As is often the case, Wall Street's desperation will not work. In fact, it will end up backfiring.

Here is what they did. Dow Jones re-jiggered the Dow index. They added what they hope will be the hottest stocks around. At the same time, they threw out stocks that were dragging the index down. This is a huge mistake. The stocks they added already have had their big runup . . . .

"Dow Jones booted out Union Carbide, Goodyear, Sears Roebuck, and Chevron. Taking their place are Intel, Microsoft, Home Depot, and SBC Communication. Talk about a sure-fire indicator of a wipeout. The Dow tried to cook the index. They want it to make bigger, higher moves. But they are trying to do this from the rear-view mirror.

"First, you need to know a key fact about the Dow. To calculate the Dow Jones Industrials average, they use what they call a 'divisor.' The new official divisor is 0.20435952. In other words, Dow Jones divides the prices of each of the Dow stocks by 0.20435952. Then Dow Jones adds the results together, to come up with the Dow index.

Only one problem. When you divide by a fraction, you really are multiplying. For example, with the new divisor a ten-point advance in any one of the 30 Dow stocks gives the Dow a 48.93 advance.

"Obviously, this is absurd. When stock prices are climbing, it multiplies the advances. But it also is a two-edged sword. When stock prices are falling, it makes the drops bigger as well . . . . I like that, because this market is about to collapse. The recent changes in the Dow will increase volatility dramatically. They will make the market come crashing down a lot faster.

"The Dow is doing the exact opposite of what investors

should do. You should buy undervalued stocks and sell overvalued ones."
The Wall Street Underground, Vo. 4, No. 8, December 1999, p. 8.

Government Report Ballyhoos Economy

On October 28, a federal government tally on growth and employer wage costs during the third quarter of 1999 is released. It contends that the economy is growing rapidly without engendering much inflationary pressure.

"'Increases in capacity, along with improvements in productivity performance, have made possible increases in living standards without inappropriate inflationary pressures,' said U.S. Treasury Secretary Larry Summers.

"'This new report shows once again that if we have strong fiscal discipline, strong investment and a strong commitment to education and the new economy, we can get an investment boom and maximize the benefits of the information and technology revolutions now going all over the world,' added President Clinton.

"'There is no question that we've entered a new era,' announces Stuart Hoffman, an economist with PNC Bank. 'The question seems to be how long it will continue, and the jury is still out on that one.'

"'This is a new paradigm,' ventures Joel Kent, an economist with Lehman Brothers. 'The fact that we have higher productivity has allowed the U.S. economy to grow more and grow more rapidly without triggering the usual inflation pressures.'

"'We continue to see very rapid economic growth which has been a problem for the Fed all along,' said Charles Lieberman, chief economist with First Institutional Securities. 'We have not seen a material increase in labor costs and that's what I think is going to be the ultimate problem in the economy somewhere down the road, though clearly it's not imminent.'"[154]

Edit. The publicly expressed reactions of Clinton and Summers are as expected—a loud trumpeting for the new economy. The private sector economists working for these national financial firms exhibit some surprise that the news is that good, but they decide to go along with it. Only Lieberman admits to seeing a problem, but only down the road.

Stocks Rise

On October 29, the Dow soars 227.64 points to 10,622.53. This is because the government reported that GDP grew at 4.8% in the third quarter with few signs of inflation, and the employment cost index increased by .08%. Greenspan, however, grumbles that he needs to see more evidence that the economy is slowing down if he is to keep the Fed from increasing the rates.

Edit. And now for the third time in a row, it happens in late October.

Nasdaq Heads For The Moon

On November 4, the Nasdaq climbs up above the 3,000 level for the 1st time. This takes place mainly on good news from Intel. The Nasdaq has doubled since October of 1998.[155]

German Bank Concerned About Margin

On October 28, Deutsche Bank—Alex Brown's chief economist, Edward Yardeni, suggests that the Fed's 50% margin requirement be raised to 75%. He thinks that this would ascertain how solidly committed investors are to stocks with high price/earnings ratios.[156]

Fed Answers Critics

On November 8, *The Wall Street Journal* carries the Fed's public answer to those who have requested that the Fed raise margin requirements. Fed Vice-Chairman Roger Ferguson announces that "we don't have any intention of raising margin requirements." He explains that "there's a possibility some market participants would read a signal that the Fed is targeting equity markets."

The result is a stampede in which borrowers push margin debt over the $200 billion level for the first time.[157]

ROY A. YOUNG, FEDERAL RESERVE GOVERNOR—MARCH 1928

"I AM NOT PREPARED TO SAY WHETHER BROKERS' LOANS ARE TOO HIGH OR TOO LOW, BUT I AM SURE THEY ARE SAFELY AND CONSERVATIVELY MADE."[158]

Fed Near Goal

On November 17, the Federal Reserve raises the interest rate for the third and last time that year. The goal is to take some of the heat off the stock market, which has obviously blown itself out of proportion—to give it the proverbial soft landing. Very significantly, the Fed also signals that their goal of "markedly diminishing the risk of inflation going forward" is achieved.[159]

Edit. The portrait is that of sound overseeing of the stock market. But isn't there a danger that the market might take the Fed at its word, classify this level as fairly safe, and then use it as a platform for testing higher and more speculative heights? This question might seem a little unfair, since the Fed should give reasons for their actions. But the next ones are not. Why then does the Fed do nothing about margin? Why does Greenspan make speeches encouraging Hi-tech investment?

November Margin Debt

Margin debt is now $206.3 billion. It has increased 13.2% this month, the largest periodic rise since the 1970s.

Euro Declines Against Dollar

On December 3, the euro begins to trade below the dollar. According to *The Wall Street Journal*, "the fall below the parity level reflects concerns that the European economies aren't matching the robust expansion of the U.S."[160]

Margin reaches $228.5 Billion in December[161]

On December 24, *Barron's* editor Alan Abelson muses about Greenspan: "Why he didn't raise margin requirements is beyond me. Just because it hadn't been done since 1974 is hardly a good reason."[162]

Stock Turnover rate Increases

The turnover on the NYSE grows from 42% to 78% between 1982 and 1999. Even more spectacularly, the turnover rate of the Nasdaq increases from 88% in 1990 to 221% in 1999.[163]

Sell Recommendations At Low[164]

Nasdaq Increases 84% over Year[165]

NASDAQ COMPOSITE

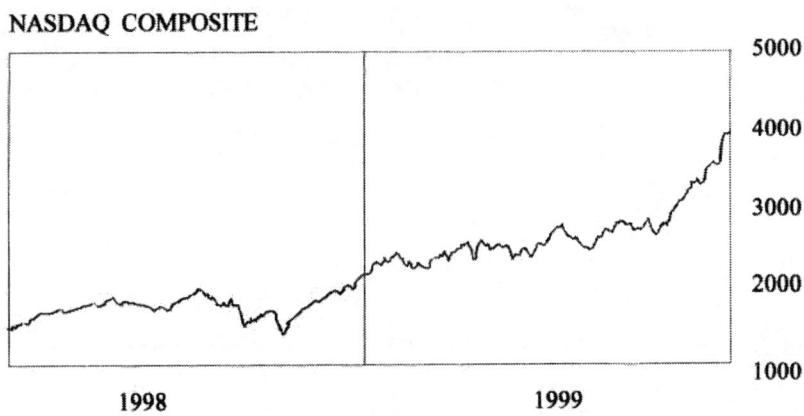

On December 30, the Nasdaq composite breaks the 4,000 barrier, closing up at 4,041.46. The reader should observe how drastically it has grown in the last year, way beyond its trend line. Is it soaring like Icarus?

The Dow increases slightly on the day to 11,484.66, and the S&P 500 adds a few points to become 1,463.46. The Russell 2000 also increases slightly to 497.01.

Gross Federal Debt Increases

During the period, 09/30/1998 to 09/30/1999, the public debt grows by $130 billion, more than it did the previous period. At the end of the new period, it stands at $5,656,270,901,615.43.[166]

CHAPTER X

2000—THE BULL IS LANCED;

THE BUBBLE IS PUNCTURED

Y2K Turns Out To Be A Farce

Editorial: The reader will recall that in his previous State of Union address, the President solemnly promised that he would solve the Y2K problem before the new millennium. Federal, State and Corporate leaders threw between $100 billion and $600 billion at it.[167] Ordinary citizens and small businesses that did not spend a dime on it open their computers that day to discover that there was never anything to worry about. All year the people were told that it would produce havoc in the third world and Russia where old systems were in use. They work just fine. In fact, Fidel Castro laughs that it was all a capitalist plot. Aside from paying people to fix what did not need to fixed, the only thing accomplished by the whole brouhaha is to get people's minds off the bubble advancing against their hopes, making many prisoners of poverty.

Clinton Re-nominates Greenspan

It is the fifth of January. Clinton turns to Greenspan and says, "You know, I have to congratulate you. You've done a great job in a period when there was no rulebook to look to."

"Mr. President,' Greenspan replies, "I couldn't have done it without what you did on deficit reduction. If you had not turned the fiscal situation around, we couldn't have had the kind of monetary policy we've had."

Then Clinton reappoints him. Afterward, the President remarks: "He was also, I think it's worth noting, one of the very first in his profession to recognize the power and the impact of new technologies on the new economy, how they changed all the rules and all the possibilities. In fact, his devotion to new technologies has been so significant, I've been thinking of taking Alan.com public; then, we can pay the debt off even before 2015." Greenspan's willingness to stay in the job should be "a cause of celebration in this country and around the world."

"Mr. President," responds Greenspan, "I first wish to express my deep appreciation to you for the confidence you've shown me over the years . . . . And I must say you have been a good friend to America's central bank. Thank you.'"

Reporter Helen Thomas asks this question of Mr. Greenspan, "Is the market irrational? Do you stick by your previous statements on the stock market?"

"You surely don't want me to answer that," he quips.

"Yes, I do."

"You do?" he asked. "Well, I don't think I will."[168]

Wall Street Journal Comments

"Maybe Alan Greenspan isn't God after all. The Federal Reserve chairman was reappointed yesterday and the financial markets that supposedly think he walks on water promptly staged on their largest selloffs ever . . . .

"Markets closed the millennium at extraordinary heights, of course, and a retreat is in itself no great cause for alarm. In the longer run the Greenspan appointment is reassuring, if only by foreclosing President Clinton from bandying the appointment around as this campaign's Lincoln bedroom. By reappointing Mr. Greenspan six months before his third term expires, Mr. Clinton is wrapping himself and his Vice President in the Greenspan legacy . . . . yesterday Mr. Gore all but nominated Mr. Greenspan for sainthood while endorsing his reappointment, an attempt at virtue by association."

Editorial, *WSJ*, January 6, 2000, P. B1.

Greenspan Pauses To Remark

On January 13, economist Lawrence Parks had this conversation with Greenspan: "I was waiting for him as he alighted the stairs to leave the Hilton's main ballroom. Again, we had some pleasantries . . . . We spoke briefly about the merits of gold-as-money, with which he concurred, and then I asked him why, if he understands what is happening and what the implications are, he doesn't speak out more. His answer had a ring of truth and, also, a tinge of desperation. He said; 'Nobody wants to hear it.' By then, we had reached the elevators on the floor above the main ballroom, and he got in with his wife, Andrea Mitchell, who was most charming."[169]

Examples Of Late Optimism

Thomas Petzinger Jr.—*Wall Street Journal* writer—January 3, 2000.

"The business cycle—a creation of the industrial age—may well become an anachronism. But there were bubbles, panics and crashes long before recessions and recoveries became cyclical. And while the Fed's power over the economy is far less than supposed, its role in sustaining the psychology of our markets has never been greater."[170]

Mark L. Walsh, CEO of Vertical-Net:

"If you knew in 1979 what you know now about the development of cable, wouldn't you have borrowed every dollar you could, mortgaged your house, maxed your credit cards in order to get into cable?"[171]

"The Market Age".

"About 30 years ago, Americans were living in the Age of Aquarius. That's over. The Age of the Market has begun.

"The merger between America Online and Time Warner makes it about as official as these things ever get. The Age of Aquarius was about—well—it's a little difficult to explain if you weren't there. But mainly it was about dropping out, finding yourself, LSD and stuff like that. The age of the Market is about dropping in, vesting stock options, IPOs and stuff like that. We call this progress."

"Until the AOL Time Warner merger, the recent American economy has struck many as a kind of magical mystery tour, the highs mainly deriving from soaring share prices that lifted stock market indices and the value of many individual mutual-fund holdings. The significance of AOL Time Warner is that it brings the market back to earth."

Lead editorial, *WSJ*, January 12, 2000.

Edit. Wow! Levin and Turner and the rest of the Time Warner gang sure are smart to team up with Case's AOl while they still can. Otherwise, the Age of the Market might just pass them by.

Dow Hits All-Time High

On January 17, the Dow Jones Industrial Average reaches a high of 11,722.98

Fed Reaffirms Its Position On Changing Margin Rule Requirements

On January 20, Federal Reserve Governor Laurence Meyer says this before the National Economists Club of Government Economists, meeting, of course in Washington, D.C.: " . . . Margin requirements are simply not an effective ways of dealing with the situation . . . . You can't stop lending for security purchases simply by changing margin requirements."[172]

Senators Question Greenspan

On January 26, during the Senate Banking Committee confirmation hearings, Greenspan is questioned about the recent spikes in margin lending. He answers that "there's no evidence to suggest that changes in margin requirement . . . [have] had any effect on prices."[173]

Prominent Wall Street Economist Disagrees

On January 30, Henry Kaufman replies: "When you raise margin requirements, you express a concern that is telegraphed to the market at large. You express a concern about speculation, the inappropriate use of credit and risks that it may expose the financial regulators."[174]

State Of The Union Speech Proclaims "New Economy"

"We are fortunate to be alive at this moment in history. (Applause.) Never before has our nation enjoyed, at once, so much prosperity and social progress with so little internal crises and so few external threats. Never before have we had such a blessed opportunity—and, therefore, such a profound obligation—to build the more perfect union of our founders' dreams.

"We begin the new century with over 20 million new jobs; the fastest economic growth in more than 30 years; the lowest unemployment rates in 30 years; the lowest poverty rates in 20 years; the lowest African-American and Hispanic unemployment rates on record; the first back-to-back budget surpluses in 42 years. And next month, America will achieve the longest period of economic growth in our entire history. (Applause.)

"We built a new economy."
Bill Clinton, January 27, 2000.

PRESIDENT CALVIN COOLIDGE, FINAL MESSAGE TO
CONGRESS, DECEMBER 4, 1928
"NO CONGRESS OF THE UNITED STATES EVER ASSEMBLED
ON SURVEYING THE STATE OF THE UNION HAS MET WITH A MORE
PLEASING PROSPECT THAN THAT WHICH APPEARS AT THE PRESENT
TIME. IN THE DOMESTIC FIELD THERE IS TRANQUILITY AND
CONTENTMENT, HARMONIOUS RELATIONS BETWEEN MANAGEMENT
AND WAGE EARNER, FREEDOM FROM INDUSTRIAL STRIFE, AND THE
HIGHEST RECORD OF YEARS OF PROSPERITY. IN THE FOREIGN FIELD
THERE IS PEACE, THE GOOD-WILL WHICH COMES FROM MUTUAL
UNDERSTANDING, AND THE KNOWLEDGE THAT THE PROBLEMS
WHICH A SHORT TIME AGO APPEARED SO OMINOUS ARE YIELDING
TO THE TOUCH OF MANIFEST FRIENDSHIP. THE GREAT WEALTH
CREATED BY OUR ENTERPRISE AND INDUSTRY, AND SAVED BY OUR
ECONOMY, HAS HAD THE WIDEST DISTRIBUTION AMONG OUR OWN
PEOPLE, AND HAS GONE OUT IN A STEADY STREAM TO SERVE THE
CHARITY AND THE BUSINESS OF THE WORLD. THE REQUIREMENTS
OF EXISTENCE HAVE PASSED BEYOND THE STANDARD OF NECESSITY
INTO THE REGION OF LUXURY. ENLARGING PRODUCTION IS
CONSUMED BY AN INCREASING DEMAND AT HOME, AND AN
EXPANDING COMMERCE ABROAD. THE COUNTRY CAN REGARD THE
PRESENT WITH SATISFACTION AND ANTICIPATE THE FUTURE WITH
OPTIMISM."175

*Edit. It will be recalled that Mr. Coolidge's successor, Herbert Hoover,
had to deal with the Great Depression.*

Democrat Lauds Alliance With Wall Street

"Given the democratization of money, the Democrats can
be the party of Wall Street *and* Main Street, of the rich *and* the
poor, of Orange County *and* East Los Angeles. To paraphrase
Nixon's embrace of deficit spending, we're all stockholders
now. Democrats who run for any office—president, senator,
governor, representative—can make great use of the

developments of the past decade and run squarely on the Clinton administration's record of managing the markets and improving life for investors.

> "Just as investing personal capital in the markets does, investing political capital in the markets carries equal measures of risk and reward, or upside and downside. In the past decade, Democrats, like the broadening investing public, have reaped far more profits than losses from their ventures. The candidates who understand these slowly emerging truths and make the best use of the leverage they can provide still have the most success in the first election of the new millennium."
> Daniel Gross[176]

NYSE Margin DEBT Reaches Record Levels

At the end of January, the debt is $243.5 billion, or 1.41 percent of market value, the highest ever under current rules.[177]

Edit. This is interesting. By October 1929, brokers' loans through banks and other sources amounted to about $7 billion.[178] Figuring the present dollar is worth about 7.5% of the 1929 dollar,[179] this would be the inflation-corrected equivalent of $93 billion. Of course, the present market is much larger, but still, shouldn't Mr. Greenspan be concerned?

Summers praises New Economy At International Summit

"A few hours before Clinton spoke, Larry Summers, US Secretary of the Treasury, painted a glowing picture of the US economy, prompting grumbling from non-US participants that the 'Americans are descending on Davos to tell the rest of us about the virtues of their 'New Economy.' While not claiming that the US economy, now into its ninth year of expansion, has eliminated the business cycle, Summers drew the portrait of long-term economic expansion, driven by investment, facilitated by budget surpluses, and based on the information revolution. While cautioning against complacency, the Treasury Secretary did not address growing fears about the collapse of the US stock market bubble, simply alluding to the 'resiliency of our financial institutions.'"

Walden Bello, January 30, 2000.[180]

ROBERT P. LAMONT—SECRETARY OF COMMERCE—SEPTEMBER 9, 1929

"NOT ONLY HAS THERE BEEN, SINCE 1921, AN UNUSUALLY PROLONGED PERIOD SUBSTANTIALLY FREE FROM SO-CALLED CRISES, OR UPS AND DOWNS, IN ECONOMIC ACTIVITY REPRESENTING THE SO-CALLED BUSINESS CYCLE, BUT EVEN THOSE VARIATIONS FROM MONTH TO MONTH OF THE YEAR, WHICH ARE THE RESULT OF SEASONAL INFLUENCES AND WHICH WERE FORMERLY CONSIDERED INEVITABLE, HAVE BEEN CUT DOWN IN EXTENT.

"THIS RESULT MUST BE ATTRIBUTED LARGELY TO GREATER FORESIGHT ON THE PART OF BUSINESS MEN PRODUCING AND SELLING COMMODITIES AS WELL AS ON THE PART OF BUYERS OF GOODS."

"WASHINGTON, OCT. 14, [1929]—SECRETARY LAMONT AND OFFICIALS OF THE COMMERCE DEPARTMENT DENIED RUMORS THAT A SEVERE DEPRESSION IN BUSINESS AND INDUSTRIAL ACTIVITY WAS IMPENDING, WHICH HAD BEEN BASED ON A MISTAKEN INTERPRETATION OF A REVIEW OF INDUSTRIAL AND CREDIT CONDITIONS ISSUED EARLIER IN THE DAY BY THE FEDERAL RESERVE BOARD.—NEW YORK TIMES[181]

ANDREW W. MELLON—SECRETARY OF TREASURY—SEPTEMBER, 1928

"THERE IS NO CAUSE FOR WORRY. THE HIGH TIDE OF PROSPERITY WILL CONTINUE."[182]

"Rises in Many Salaries Barely Keep Pace With Inflation:"

"Data Show Wages Have Even Fallen Despite Economic Boom Since 1991" Headline of story by Patrick Barta, *WSJ*, February 1, 2000, p. A2.

SEC Chairman Warns Investors About Margin

On February 12, at Los Angeles, Arthur Levitt says, "Debt in general is an unheralded albatross that will weigh very heavily on investors in the event of a market downturn."[183]

Edit. Here is a warning from Clinton's own Securities Exchange Chairman of the danger of not cutting-back on margin.

One member of the administration could be suggesting that if the unthinkable happens, the blame should be placed elsewhere.

Greenspan Says Market Not Cool Enough

"In his semiannual economic presentation to Congress, Mr. Greenspan drops his opinion—uttered a month ago—that the Fed's attempts to reign in the economy with earlier 'interest rate increases' were 'well advanced.'

"Instead, he said yesterday that investor optimism and a bullish stock market 'to date . . . more than offset' the effects of higher rates and that spending even in sectors of the economy normally considered sensitive to higher rates 'has remained robust.' 'There is,' he said, 'little evidence that the American economy . . . is slowing appreciably.'"

"Greenspan Takes Hard Line on Growth," *Wall Street Journal*, February 18, 2000, p. A2.

Edit. Last year, on November 17, the Fed said its work on tying down the stock market was about complete. Since then the Nasdaq rose 1,500 points and the Dow more than a 1,000. Surely, they must have realized that this expression of satisfaction would only make the speculators feel safe enough to test higher and higher levels. Quite recently, even while the market was peaking, Mr. Greenspan suggested that the whole thing was well under control. Now he talks differently? What gives? He has to know that a falling stock market would hurt Gore's chances for being elected President.

"Venture Capitalists 'R' Us":

"Now, Everyone Is Diving In, Seeing No-Lose Situation" Headline of story by S. Lipin, *W S J*, February 22, 2000, p. C1.

Greenspan Says Margin Debt Does Not affect Stock Prices

On February 23, Greenspan tells Congress during his Humphrey-Hawkins testimony: "Going back to the question of [whether] it were in our interest . . . would not [changing] margins be better? If the evidence indicated that raising margins would affect stock prices, then the answer in that hypothetical question would be yes. But the evidence that we have, going back a long period of time, is that margin requirements per se do not affect stock prices. They do affect borrowing patterns and they affect the prudential safety of brokers and dealers and banks and others. But they don't affect stock prices."[184]

Editorial: Oh Yeah?

Senate Subcommittee Finds An Irregularity

On February 24, the investigative subcommittee of the Senate Governmental Affairs Committee finds in its hearings on day trading that many firms arrange loans between customers and other third parties to evade margin requirements.[185]

Margin Debt $265.2 Billion

By the end of February, margin debt has grown 50 % in six months.

SEC Chief Speaks Out Again On Margin

At a Boston University conference, Arthur Levitt says: "Too often, investors are focusing on the upside—without carefully considering the downside." He adds that many do not realize that brokerages can sell stocks without notifying owners when prices fall.[186]

Edit. Both Greenspan and the Gore are worried about the market. The Gore people want to take it down easily by shaving down a speculative underpinning; Greenspan, as we are seeing, has a different idea. The tension is there, but the public must be kept from sensing it. It is like a couple of opposing swirls in a river; both are going in the same direction, but in the course downward there is some pushing and shoving.

Greenspan Boosts Technology Stocks

"Technological synergies have enlarged the set of productive capital investments, while lofty equity values and declining prices of high-tech equipment have reduced the cost of capital . . . . The fact that the capital-spending boom is still going strong indicates that businesses continue to find a wide array of potential high-rate-of-return, productivity-enhancing investments. And I see nothing to suggest that these opportunities will peter out anytime soon."

"The Revolution in Information Technology," March 6, 2000.[187]

Ed. Here he is at the same Boston University conference at which Arthur Levitt is speaking. What is Greenspan saying? He is telling the most speculative of the small-and middle-sized investors to go ahead; that the opportunities are not petering out. What are those hearing him at the conference in Boston or reading about in the financial press to think? Many of them think that the cautionary words expressed elsewhere do not apply to them—they are on the cutting edge of the future, etc. There may be a correction or two, but the long trend is up.

Nasdaq Above 5,000 For First Time

On March 10, it climbs 149.60 points to reach 5,046.86. This is just two months after having attained the 4,000 level and just four days after Greenspan gave this sort of investment a ringing endorsement.

Excerpt From Diary of Investor David Denby (2000):

"*3/10/00 Henry Blodget Speaks* People are eager to hear what Henry Blodget has to say, but he listens well, too, and over lunch at the Judson Grill, on a very hot day for the market, he leans across the table as I ask a question and stares at me, drawing his mouth down into a small, concentrated circle. Blodget analyzes the value of Internet stocks for Merrill Lynch, and he's good at what he does. His most renowned call came in December, 1998, when Amazon's stock was selling at two hundred and forty dollars a share, and he predicted, in the face of much skepticism, that it would go to four hundred dollars within a year, at which point the stock (adjusting for stock splits) shot to five hundred and fifty within a month . . . .

· · · · · · · · · · · · · · · · · · ·

"'Look,' Blodget says, 'you have to develop calluses. Some of these stocks are going to drop twenty or thirty percent in a day.' For safety, he recommends establishing a core holding of the market leaders—say, a hundred shares of Yahoo or A.O.L.—and buying more shares on the dips, and then selling a comparable number of shares as the price rises.

"I have to ask: 'Do you ever feel like a man riding a stallion to the edge of a cliff?'

'I feel like a man riding a stallion across an endless plain, and someday the horse will begin to slow'"

David Denby, *The New Yorker*, April 24 & May 1, 2000., p. 196.[188]

Edit. Quite a fellow that Blodget. He has made $12 million; and within three years, the stocks he recommended will lose up to $574 billion.[189]

IRVING FISHER—PROMINENT ECONOMIST—OCTOBER 16, 1929

"STOCK PRICES HAVE REACHED WHAT LOOKS LIKE A PERMANENTLY HIGH PLATEAU. I DO NOT FEEL THAT THERE WILL SOON, IF EVER, BE A FIFTY OR SIXTY POINT BREAK BELOW PRESENT LEVELS, SUCH AS MR. BABSON HAS PREDICTED."[190]

Edit. It should be said that Irving Fisher put his money where his mouth was. He lost his fortune in the crash.

The Nasdaq Hits All-Time High

On March 13, 2000 the Nasdaq Reaches 5,048.63.

Greenspan Denies The Fed Is Fighting The Market

"'The Federal Reserve is not jawboning the stock market or targeting stock prices,' Mr. Greenspan said in a letter to Rep. Jim Leach (R., Iowa), chairman of the House Banking Committee. Rather the Federal Reserve is concerned about imbalances between aggregate demand and supply and their implications for inflation and thus sustainability of the expansion.'

. . . .

"Mr. Greenspan also said changes in Fed policy in the short run don't have a 'significant effect' on stock prices. 'Our procedures . . . do tend to smooth short-run fluctuations in short-term rates,' he said. 'However, the risk in investing in equities comes primarily in uncertainty about future earnings and about the longer-term interest rates at which those future earnings should be discounted, and not mainly from the possibility that the short-run cost of financing stock-options could increase,' he said.

"'Consequently, even if our operating procedures were associated with somewhat larger movements in short-term rates, I doubt that investors' perceptions of equity risks would be much affected and thus that equity prices would be significantly influenced,' Mr. Greenspan said."

WSJ, Friday, March 31, 2000, p. A6.

Edit. If that is so, why then does the market so often respond to his statements and actions? He knows that he is the most relied-upon man in the world of money. What about the Plunge Protection Team of which he is a charter member? What of the numerous interventions in the past? The dexterous use of language does not change the underlying reality.

Doesn't Mr. Greenspan realize that there is conflict in what he has been saying? On the one hand, he encourages the ignorant speculator to buy more stocks; on the other, he discourages the experienced trader. Doesn't he see that the two practices must meet in a sharply falling market? The first, because it is brought to a precipitous top; the second, because it promotes selling. This coordination can result in a transfer of wealth from millions of hapless investors to Wall Street insiders and others in the know.

THE LONDON ECONOMIST, MAY 11, 1929

"THE EVENTS OF THE PAST YEAR HAVE SEEN THE BEGINNINGS OF A NEW TECHNIQUE, WHICH, IF MAINTAINED AND DEVELOPED, MAY SUCCEED IN 'RATIONING THE SPECULATOR WITHOUT INJURING THE TRADER.'"[191]

PETER ERICKSON

By End of March, NYSE Margin Reaches $278.5 Billion

April Showers

In this month of stock prices cascading downward, brokers issue more margin calls than ever before. Some don't even bother to notify the borrower and simply liquidate the investment. The Nasdaq is affected most—losing 30% of its value.

On April 6, at the prompting of the SEC, the New York Stock Exchange requests precise information from some big securities firms about margin trading.

On April 14, the Dow and the Nasdaq post record one-day losses; the result is a flood of margin calls, bringing share prices down even further.

On April 17, there is much forced selling, yielding a record-breaking one-month descent. Clients of E*Trade discover that their contracts can be liquidated without advance notification.

On April 18, the Securities Industry Association reports that margin debt was the fastest form of debt in the U.S. in the past years and that twenty percent of the revenues of on-line brokerages came from this source. By the end of the month, margin debt on the NYSE will have dropped $26.8 billion, bringing it to $251.7 billion. Within the following month, it will drop another $11 billion, bringing it to $240.7 billion. A drop of just short of $37.8 billion in 57 days!

In the *ABA Banking Journal* in May, Banc One economist Anthony Chan concludes that "a rise in margin requirement does appear to be followed by a dampening of equity market gains, despite the fact that Greenspan has eloquently stated that such a policy is poised to fail."[192]

Editorial: Greenspan has a point, of course. Taking into account all the exchanges, the amount represented under two percent of the total valuation of the stock market. But that point is rather dull. The amount of margin buying has to affect the prices of the hotter stocks, the kind that make headlines in the financial press and bring in money from those who don't want to be left behind. In this market, it is the purchasers of hi-tech stocks. And they are the first to go over the falls.

Why was this ignored? Alan W. Newman makes a suggestion: "Our take is that Wall Street lobbied frantically to prevent a raise in margin requirements. After all, margin lending is one of Wall Street's most profitable businesses. There was also the perceived 'problem' that a raise in margin requirements would work to the advantage of foreign players who could theoretically borrow on more leveraged terms abroad." [193] *But Mr. Greenspan is supposed to be independent of Wall Street. The Fed has the legal authority to overrule the wishes of the brokerage houses.*

April 2000—Greatest Stock Market Implosion in History Begins

Margin debtors are a small but very important part of those caught up in the trouble. People who own their stocks outright also suffer great loss. The Nasdaq leads the way down the defile. In four days—April 4, 11, 13, and 17—the index loses 1,249.16 points. By the close of the last of these days, it sinks to 3,321.29, losing 35% off the all-time high which it obtained just two months earlier. The Dow Jones Industrial average drops to 10,305.77, almost 11.48% off where it was at the top. To be sure, there will be bear-market rallies, but each one will peak at a lower point, establishing a plateau, from which it will later fall to an even more dismal level. In fact, the Nasdaq will make a comeback on the 19ᵗʰ, recovering 254.41 points. But it will not be able to hold it long. It is not a 'correction'; it is the first pop in the bubble. The New Economy is going to the same way as the "new era" of the 1920s.

In that month, two trillion dollars are wiped out. By end of year, the loss will go much higher.

"The New, Evolving More Savvy American Investor!"

"It started to look like October 1929 all over again in the equities markets this past Tuesday. Stocks were falling like rocks tossed off the empire State building. It really was beginning to look like doomsday! Then, like clockwork, it happened again! Americans began to behave in a psychological manner which until about the 1990's was unknown in the history of man. Suddenly at 1:20 PM, millions of Americans suddenly, spontaneously, collectively and mysteriously understood that stocks were a great bargain precisely when the Dow was down 503.53 and Nasdaq was down 574.57 . . . .

"But now, thanks to the Clinton Administration's excellent management of the economy, and our superiority as Americans, we have evolved to the point where we are able to avoid fear and hence stock market under-valuations. We obviously used that new and great insight . . . at 1:20 PM on April 4th Americans began buying stocks with both hands, confident that once again, they mastered the stock market universe. Once again, those who have sold the idea that 'you can't lose in the long run in stocks' won the argument as did those who are convinced that you should 'always buy on the dips and dives.' Wow! This makes me really proud to be an American because we have the unique and superior ability to understand markets and act rationally. We have managed to eliminate bear markets.

. . . .

"Quietly and perhaps subconsciously, that is what Americans seem to believe. But if you believe the notion about American and Clinton superiority I actually do have a bridge to sell you and it's a great bargain! . . . Any serious student of markets must wonder how it is that Americans have this unique ability to 'catch a falling knife' without getting injured . . . . What some of us have begun to notice is that his unique ability began to take place since 1989 when a former Federal Reserve

Governor Robert Heller spoke about plunging stock markets. He suggested in a speech that year that sharp market declines could and indeed should be avoided by the U. S. Treasury through massive purchases of stocks by the Treasury in the futures markets . . . . In essence, what Mr. Heller was suggesting is that the U.S. Treasury should rig the equities markets because it is for the common good!"

Jay Taylor, Editor of J Taylor's *Gold & Technology Stocks,* April 10, 2000, pp. 1-2.

Edit. April 4 was the first day of the market collapse. Mr. Taylor believes that the Clinton Administration rushed in to place a safety net under investor losses, presumably in order to prevent the market from embarrassing Vice-President Gore, who is running for President. This may well have been the case.

MISS GERTRUDE M. COOGAN—ECONOMIST 1935
"ON OCTOBER 24, 1929, AT 11.00 O'CLOCK SHARP HUNDREDS OF THOUSANDS OF SHARES IN HUNDREDS OF ISSUES WERE OFFERED FOR SALE 'AT THE MARKET.' IT WAS A VERY STRANGE THING THAT COULD HAVE BEEN A MERE ACCIDENT. IT WAS MOST UNUSUAL THAT THOUSANDS OF PEOPLE DECIDED TO SELL AT THE SAME INSTANT. IT WAS ALSO STRANGE THAT THEY ALL DECIDED TO SELL 'AT THE MARKET.' INEXPERIENCED STOCK TRADERS DO NOT PUT IN 'MARKET' ORDER. THAT'S A TRICK KNOWN ONLY TO THE 'WISE BOYS'—THE INTERNATIONALISTS AND THEIR COHORTS . . . ."

Edit. Both Mr. Taylor and Miss Coogan have charged that the stock market was being manipulated on a crucial day—though in opposite directions. Taylor contends that in 2000, the aim of Administration insiders was to bolster up a faltering market, while Coogan had reported that in 1929, the aim of private insiders was to drive it down.

October 1929—1st Great Depression Began

On Thursday, October 24, the bottom fell out of the stock market. Investors lost four billion dollars that day. On Friday, the market rallied; the losses were recovered in part. The headline in the *New York Times* read: "Worst Stock Crash Stemmed By banks; 12,894—Share Day Swamps Market; Leaders confer, Find Conditions Sound." On Black Tuesday, October 29, it was worse. The Headline in the *Times* report on Wednesday, October 30. read: "Stocks Collapse in 16,410,030 share day, But Rally At Close Cheers Brokers; bankers Optimistic, to continue Aid: 240 Issues Lose $15,894,818,894 in Month; Slump in Full Exchange List Vastly Larger."

After that, there was a rally, then a level of resistance would be formed, followed by an even deeper plunge. The losses for the year 1929 would net at about fifteen billion dollars. It would take nearly three years before the market would bottom out.

BENJAMIN M. ANDERSON, JR, CHASE ECONOMIC BULLETIN, NOVEMBER 22, 1929, P. 3.

"WE HAVE FALLEN DOWN A HILL, AND WE FIND OURSELVES BRUISED AND SCRATCHED, AND WITH OUR NERVES UNSTRUNG. BUT NO BONES ARE BROKEN, AND THERE ARE NO INTERNAL INJURIES. WE ARE PERFECTLY ABLE TO GET UP AND WALK. IT IS JUST AS WELL, HOWEVER, THAT WE SHOULDN'T TRY TO RUN VERY FAST IMMEDIATELY. THERE ARE THOSE WHO WOULD LIKE TO HAVE US START RUNNING IMMEDIATELY, BY APPLYING GREAT DOSES OF THE SAME FALSE STIMULANT THAT SET US ON OUR HEADLONG, BREAK-NECK, HEEDLESS RACE WHICH CULMINATED IN THE FALL OVER THE HILL. BUT I THINK THAT MOST OF US WILL AGREE THAT IT IS JUST AS WELL TO QUIET DOWN A BIT, STUDY THE SIGNPOSTS, AND PICK OUT SAFE ROADS TO FOLLOW."

Economist Predicts Great Prosperity Lies Ahead

"Last week's dramatic sell-off in global stock markets is a painful reminder that stocks are risky. But don't be fooled. Historical forces continue to point toward a great Prosperity that could carry the Dow Jones Industrial Average to 35000 by the end of the decade and 100000 by 2020.

. . . .

"To get a sense of the possible, I tracked the progress of the Dow Jones Industrial Average from 1926 through 1999 . . . excluding the 1940s. Over this entire period, the index advanced at an average annual rate of 6.5%. But in the 30 years among those 64 when two or more the three key signposts—taxes, inflation and trade policy—were pointed in a positive direction, the index advanced an average of 11.1% a year. If this rate of growth were to prevail now, the Dow will cross 35000 near the end of the next decade, and reach 100000 around 2020. By then, this latest but far from least correction will be seen for what it is—a minor bump on the road to the great prosperity."

Charles Kadlec, Managing of W.J. & W. Seigman & Co., *WSJ*, April 18, 2000.[194]

IT'LL TAKE MORE THAN THAT TO BLOW HIS HAT OFF
—Hanny in the Philadelphia *Inquirer*.
OCTOBER, 1929.

JOHN D. ROCKEFELLER—OCTOBER 30, 1929

"BELIEVING THAT FUNDAMENTAL CONDITIONS OF THE COUNTRY ARE SOUND AND THAT THERE IS NOTHING IN THE BUSINESS SITUATION TO WARRANT THE DESTRUCTION OF VALUES THAT HAS TAKEN PLACE ON THE EXCHANGES DURING THE PAST WEEK, MY SON AND I HAVE FOR SOME DAYS BEEN PURCHASING SOUND COMMON STOCKS. WE ARE CONTINUING AND WILL CONTINUE OUR PURCHASES IN SUBSTANTIAL AMOUNTS AT LEVELS WHICH WE BELIEVE REPRESENT SOUND INVESTMENT VALUES."

CHARLES M. SCHWAB—CHAIRMAN OF THE BOARD, BETHLEHEM STEEL CORP.—DECEMBER 10, 1929

"NEVER BEFORE HAS AMERICAN BUSINESS BEEN AS FIRMLY ENTRENCHED AS IT IS TODAY. STEEL'S THREE BIGGEST CUSTOMERS, THE AUTOMOBILE, RAILROAD AND BUILDING INDUSTRIES, SEEM TO ME TO JUSTIFY A HEALTHY OUTLOOK. THIS GREAT SPECULATIVE ERA IN WALL STREET, IN WHICH STOCKS HAVE CRASHED, MEANS NOTHING IN THE WELFARE OF BUSINESS. THE SAME FACTORIES HAVE THE SAME WHEELS TURNING. VALUES ARE UNCHANGED. WEALTH IS BEYOND THE QUOTATIONS OF WALL STREET. WEALTH IS FOUNDED IN THE INDUSTRIES OF THE NATION, AND WHILE THEY ARE SOUND, STOCKS MAY GO UP AND STOCKS MAY GO DOWN, BUT THE NATION WILL PROSPER"[195]

Business Week Questions Irrational Exuberance

"Today's talk about irrational exuberance largely misses the point. Sure, many high tech companies will go under, some spectacularly. And it might well be that the Internet does not pay off as big as investors expect, in which case the market will go down. Or the net may far exceed expectations. Either way, the willingness to take risks is what is propelling the U.S. in its longest, expansion in history. And that's no bubble."

"Commentary" by Christopher Farrell, contributing Editor—May 29, 2000.

"Look for companies with the promise of strong future growth"

"But don't fire your broker or cancel that E*Trade account just yet. Although it's likely that 2000 won't end up the most stellar year in the market, some bullish signs will continue to play out during the second part of the year. First, market valuations have improved, especially in growth stocks, with price-earnings rations looking much more favorable. That's because, despite stock prices having come down, corporate profits continue to come in exceedingly strong . . . .

"Technically, the market is on strong footing, with breadth improving dramatically."

Marsha Vickers, "The Right Stocks for a Slowing Economy," *Business Week*, June 26, 2000, p. 209.

Hope Springs Once More For Margin Debtors

In June, it came up $6.5 billion from a May low to $247.2 billion.

Experts Say July Stock Prices Stocks About Right

Abby Joseph Cohen, chief investment strategist at Goldman Sachs Group opines, "Now, we are about where we should be." According to a Wharton School Professor, co-author of 1998 book, *Stocks for The Long Run*, "When the bull market began, I figured that the stock market was at its second-most undervalued point this century, after July 1932, when it was in the depths of the depression. The question now is whether it is overvalued now and if so by how much. My take is that it is pretty fairly valued. My feeling is that long-run investors are going to get about a 5% to 8% return after inflation over a longer-term period."[196]

E,H.H. Simmons—Stock Exchange President—
January 26, 1930.
"The psychological effect of stock market activities
on business is, I think, usually overemphasized . . . . I do not
think that the fall in security prices will itself cause any
great curtailment in consumption, and the trade figures
thus far available seem to bear out this view of the matter."

January 31, 1930—News Dispatch From Washington
"Definite signs that business and industry have turned
the corner from the temporary period of emergency that
followed deflation of the speculative market were seen
today by President Hoover."[197]

Internet Journal Faces Facts

"It may be too late for tough love. By the time the market
closed last Thursday, the Nasdaq composite index had dropped
more than 27 percent from its March 10 peak of 5,050.62. It's
a bear market, the Nasdaq's first decline of more than 20
percent since 1998, and only the ninth since it opened for
trading in 1971.

. . . .

"Indeed, the Nasdaq seems to have lost something far more
valuable than a quarter of its worth. It has lost its seeming
invincibility. That's something it's not likely to recapture
anytime soon."
Anjali, Arora, "Internet Stocks take a Dive," *Industry Standard*,
April 24, 2000.

Not The Pause That Refreshes

"Make no mistake, my friend: This is *not* a 'correction.' This is
not a 'pause that refreshes.' This is not a 'consolidation before

the next leg up.' *This is the start of a series of stock market swings, up and down, that will end in the greatest wipe-out in the history of mankind.* Just over $2 *trillion* of wealth evaporated on Wall Street in the last two weeks—and that's just the start. People who bought into the 'new economy' paradigm are getting killed. This is a crisis that will throw the U.S. economy into its biggest slow-down ever . . . .

"The last time Wall Street suffered a wipe-out like what is happening now, it didn't recover for 12 years—when World War II jump-started the economy and American business started to crawl its way back. But if you had money in the stock market, and left it in the big Dow Jones stocks, you didn't break even (in constant dollar terms, adjusting those dollars for inflation) until 1990. Now, let me ask you a question. How many people do you know who have 40 or 50 years to wait to get back the money they've lost in the stock market?"

The Wall Street Underground, Vol. 4, No. 11, March/April 2000, pp. 1, 5.

Fed Raises Rates

On May 17, the Fed comes out with a half-point increase. Usually, it would proceed in quarter point increments. They warn that there will be more.

Wall Street Journal Changes Bond Measure

"The Journal, for several weeks, has already been including the performance of the 10-year Treasury note in its routine markets coverage and had stopped calling the 30-year bond a 'benchmark.' Starting today, it will replace the 30-year chart with a 10-year chart in the daily Markets Diary . . . ."

WSJ, May 31.[198]

Edit. Time preference is increasing.

Clinton Administration Cooks The Books

"The Fed was in a serious bind. They know they *must* raise rates soon. The Clinton administration has been flat-out cooking the books on key economic reports. For example, according to the latest Producer Price Index (PPI) report released in June, inflation supposedly *fell* 0.8% in April and was just 0.1% in May this year. On June 14, the Clinton Administration released the Consumer Price Index and it showed that prices increased just 0.1% in May. Give me a break! This was despite the *biggest rise in food costs in years* (which the Administration admitted) and *record* high energy prices (which they showed as a DROP). How stupid do they think we are? . . .

Let me tell you how the Clinton administration cooks the books. They showed energy prices *down* 0.05% in May. And they had the gall to claim that liquid petroleum gas dropped 12.1%. They said gasoline prices *dropped!* But you and I both know that gasoline prices have been *climbing* steadily for months. In fact, the Labor Department, in a separate report, said energy prices were *up* 6.5% for the same period. And the Department of Energy, in its report, said that the national average for gasoline is *$1.63 per gallon—the highest price ever.* (In May, the Energy Department predicted top gasoline prices of around $1.40 a gallon. They were wrong, underestimating the present price by about a dollar . . . . Their estimates aren't even keeping up with the price increases. You don't need a government report to tell you there is a *massive* inflation; just hop on over to the local gas station or grocery store.

"When I've confronted Labor Department economists in the past with the evidence that they're cooking the books, they grudgingly admit that the government is lying to the American people. '*Ours orders are to hide inflation as much as we can.*' they say."

The Wall Street Underground, June 2000, Vol. 4, No. 14, p. 2.

Economists Predict Soft Landing

The 55 economists which the *WSJ* rounded up for its semiannual forecasting survey "are confident that the Federal Reserve will engineer a soft landing this year for the U.S. economy, where growth continues to expand, but at a slower, more sustainable pace."[199]

WASHINGTON, JANUARY 13, 1930
"REPORTS TO THE DEPARTMENT OF COMMERCE INDICATE
THAT BUSINESS IS IN A SATISFACTORY CONDITION, SECRETARY [OF
COMMERCE] LAMONT SAID TODAY."[200]

Second Quarter Stock Losses

Second Quarter losses are reported on July 3. The Nasdaq Composite loses 606.72 points; that is down 13.3% to 3,968.11. The Dow Jones Industrials slips 4.3% to 10,447.89.

CRB Futures Price Indices
May 31, 1999 — May 28, 2000
1967 = 100

	May 28	Year Ago	% Change
CRB Futures Index	222.27	186.72	+19.0%
Industrials	208.54	172.70	+20.7%
Grains	173.29	252.55	-31.3%
Livestock & Meats	252.55	219.27	+15.1%
Energy	298.10	169.25	+76.1%
Precious Metals	259.75	227.53	+14.1%

"Prices Skyrocket 19% Over Last year, Energy Up a staggering 76%!"

"The Standard indices of inflation, the Consumer Price Index (CPI) and the Producer Price Index (PPI), are very politicized and easily manipulated by government bureaucrats. No government, no politician, wants to see inflation increase. They want to keep people in the dark as long as possible. But, if you've bought anything recently, from a house to a car to clothing to groceries to gasoline to electricity, you already know that inflation has been climbing significantly. The independent Commodity Research Bureau Index takes key commodity prices in the pipelines as a way of showing real inflation earlier than other indices. The Commodity Research Bureau Index is based on actual prices in the market on a minute by minute, daily basis. And that index has now *soared* to 20 and 30% a year— and in some cases, to record breaking highs!"

The Wall Street Underground, Vol. 5. no. 2, July 2000, p. 4.

Stock Market Drops Again

On Friday, July 31, the Nasdaq composite finishes a week with a 10.5% drop by falling to 3,663. On that day, the Dow went down 74.96 points to 10,511.7.

Republicans Nominate Bush

On August 4, Texas Governor, George Bush, and Richard Cheney, Defense Secretary under Bush Senior, accept nominations as President and Vice-President.

Bill Clinton At Democratic National Convention—2000

"Eight years ago, when our party met in New York, it was a far different time for America. Our economy was in trouble, our society was divided, our fellow citizens were out of work. Interest rates were high. The deficit was $290 billion and rising. After 12 years of Republican rule, the federal debt had quadrupled, imposing a crushing burden on our economy and our children.

. . . .

"First, we proposed a new economic strategy: Get rid of the deficit to reduce interest rates. Invest more in our people. And sell more American products abroad.

"We sent our plan to Congress. It passed by a single vote in both houses. In a deadlocked senate, Al Gore cast the deciding vote . . . .

"The Republicans said they would not be held responsible for the results of our economic policies. I hope the American people will take them at their word.

"Today, we are in the midst of the longest economic expansion in our history. More than 22 million new jobs, the lowest unemployment in 30 years . . . . Today, we have gone from the largest deficits in history—and if we stay on course, we can make America debt-free for the first time since 1835."

. . . .

"Harry Truman's old saying has never been more true: If you want to live like a Republican, you should vote for the Democrats."

August 14, 2000, Los Angeles, California.

Excerpts From Four of Candidate Hoover's 1928 Campaign Speeches

"WHEN WE [THE REPUBLICAN PARTY] ASSUMED DIRECTION
OF THE GOVERNMENT IN 1921 THERE WERE FIVE TO SIX MILLION

UNEMPLOYED MEN UPON OUR STREET. WAGES AND SALARIES WERE
FALLING AND HOURS OF LABOR INCREASING . . . . THE REPUBLICAN
ADMINISTRATION AT ONCE UNDERTOOK TO FIND RELIEF TO THIS
SITUATION. AT ONCE A NATIONWIDE EMPLOYMENT CONFERENCE
WAS CALLED . . . . WITHIN A YEAR WE RESTORED THESE FIVE
MILLION WORKERS TO EMPLOYMENT. BUT WE DID MORE; WE
PRODUCED A FUNDAMENTAL PROGRAM WHICH MADE THIS
RESTORED EMPLOYMENT SECURE ON FOUNDATIONS OF
PROSPERITY; AS A RESULT, WAGES AND STANDARDS OF LIVING
HAVE DURING THE PAST SIX AND A HALF YEARS RISEN TO
STEADILY HIGHER LEVELS.

"THIS RECOVERY AND THIS STABILITY ARE NO ACCIDENT. IT
HAS NOT BEEN ACHIEVED BY LUCK, WERE IT NOT FOR SOUND
GOVERNMENTAL POLICIES AND WISE LEADERSHIP, EMPLOYMENT
CONDITIONS IN AMERICA TODAY WOULD BE SIMILAR TO THOSE
EXISTING IN MANY OTHER PARTS OF THE WORLD."

SEPTEMBER 17, 1928—NEWARK, N.J.

"PROSPERITY IS NO IDLE EXPRESSION. IT IS A JOB FOR EVERY
WORKER; IT IS THE SAFETY AND SAFEGUARD OF EVERY BUSINESS
AND EVERY HOME. A CONTINUATION OF THE POLICIES OF THE
REPUBLICAN PARTY IS FUNDAMENTALLY NECESSARY TO THE FUTURE
ADVANCEMENT OF THIS PROGRESS AND TO THE FURTHER BUILDING
UP OF THIS PROSPERITY."

OCTOBER 22, 1928—MADISON SQUARE GARDEN.

"AS NEVER BEFORE DOES THE KEEPING OF OUR ECONOMIC
MACHINE IN TUNE DEPEND UPON WISE POLICIES IN THE
ADMINISTRATIVE SIDE OF THE GOVERNMENT."

OCTOBER 6, 1928—ELIZABETHTON, TENN.

"THE OUTLOOK OF THE WORLD TODAY IS FOR THE GREATEST
ERA OF COMMERCIAL EXPANSION IN HISTORY. THE REST OF THE
WORLD WILL BECOME BETTER CUSTOMERS."

JULY 27, 1928—SAN FRANCISCO[201]

In September, Administration Intervenes To Support The Euro[202]

Think-Tanker Theorizes About Slump

"Pundits say stocks are weak because of high oil prices, a sliding Euro and concerns about U.S. profits. But there's another more serious worry for investors: the growing possibility that Al Gore will be elected president and bring a Democratic Congress with him . . . ."

"The recent peaks of both the Dow and the Nasdaq occurred around Labor day, when the polls confirmed that Mr. Gore's postconvention surge was no fluke. Mr. Gore's election alone might not trouble the markets. With pressure from a Republican Congress, he could turn out, like Bill Clinton, to be a market guy in a populist masquerade."

James K. Glassman, Resident Fellow At American Enterprise Institute, *WSJ,* September 11, 2000, p. A 6.

Edit. This is a Republican-type intellectual who believes that the near future is bright and the fear of an important Democratic victory is what darkens the horizon.

Harvard Economic Professor Attacks Bush Proposal

"It doesn't make sense to undertake a large tax cut at a time when the economy is at the peak of the business cycle. The result could be inflation and higher interest rates. Certainly we cannot expect to push the growth rate much higher, or unemployment lower, than they are currently. I would save the tax cut for some time in the future when the economy is weak (and after a few more years of surpluses have brought down the outstanding debt).

"One expert's Opinion On Election 2000", Jeffrey Frankel Applauds Al Gore's Economic Plan," Jeffrey Frankel is James

W. Harpel, Professor of Capital Formation and Economic Growth, September 25, 2000.[203] *http://www.ksg.harvard.edu*

Edit. This Democrat-type intellectual thinks the bull is so strong as to render superfluous the injection of a tax cut.

Bear Market Rally

On September 29, the Dow Jones Industrial Average jumps 195.70 points to 10,824,06, a 1.84% increase, and the Nasdaq composite ratchets upwards 122.02 points to 3,778.32, an optimistic 3.34%.

October 4—Fed Stands Pat

October 12—Oil Prices Rise To Post-Gulf War Peak Of $35.14 a Barrel

Stocks Sink

On October 13, the Dow cascades down 379.21 points to 10,034.58, giving up 3.6%—the index's fifth greatest drop to date. The Nasdaq slips to 3,074.68, off 39% from its high. Turmoil in the Middle East is blamed.

Edit. What about the stratospheric stock prices? Couldn't that be why they are fleeing?

Internet Magazine Sees Hope

"'It was once thought that technology was impervious, that there was no cyclicality of it: 'If the economy slows, it doesn't matter,' says Elizabeth Mackay. 'Well, it does matter.'

. . . .

" . . . 'Right now the market is pricing in the worst-case scenario,' says Andrew Barrett, a tech strategist for Salomon

Smith Barney. 'The market needs to sell itself off so it can get back into parity with the fundamentals.'

. . . .

"Barrett and others say that third-quarter numbers, while likely not spectacular, could still stabilize things. 'Earnings are not going to be out of this world, but they will be much better than what the market is pricing in,' says Barrett.

. . . .

"Investors need to be careful, though, to make sure they learn from these harsh lessons. Looking at the pricey and still popular fiber-optics sector, there may be reason to think they haven't. The market has seen a wholesale abandonment of e-commerce and business-to-business stocks—only to find that Net infrastructure stocks, including fiber optics, are the new darlings.

"But while leaders such as Cisco Systems, JDS Uniphase and Juniper Networks are performing well, there are early signs of trouble. Lucent Technologies issued its second earnings warning of the quarter last week, this time citing weakness in sales of fiber-optic products"

Anjali Agora, *The Industry Standard*, October 23, 2000.

" . . . New Economy Leaves Mark On Every Facet Of Campaign 2000 . . ."

"Amid all the shouting and finger-pointing of the campaign that ends today, there has been some consistent background music: the sound of America's New Economy.

. . . .

"Perhaps the most profound effect of the New Economy is

that more and more Americans think they work not for large corporation or organizations, but for themselves. The result: a more independent mind-set that leaves voters less attached to large organizations in general—including organized political parties."

Gerald F. Seib and Bob Davis, *WSJ*, November 7, 2000, p. A1.

Edit. Here we are told by some drummers that this mass New Economy march represents a heightened individuality.

Presidential Race in Doubt

Vice President Gore has won 48.4% of the popular vote, while Governor Bush has only 47.9% of the vote. But because of the nature of the count in the electoral college is somewhat different, the race is to be decided by a recount of the Florida votes.

Edit. Just as Perot (whatever his private intention) was able to deliver the election for Clinton in '92 and help out mightily in '96, so Ralph Nader has turned the tide in 2000. He has received 2.7% of the vote, almost all of which would have gone to Gore. Even if we count Pat Buchanan and the rest and suppose that almost all of their vote would have gone to Bush, together they make up under 1%. The upshot is clear: If Bush should prevail, he can thank Nader for his victory.

Hillary To The Senate

On the bright side for the Democrats: Clinton's wife, Hillary, is elected to the U.S. Senate from New York. An out-of-stater, she followed the precedent that had been begun by Robert Kennedy in 1964, who was elected to the Senate from New York, even though everyone knew he was a resident of another state.

"Feast Will Go On, Say These Economists"

"An array of new forecasts predict a rosy future for the nation's economy, suggesting that recent investor pessimism may be misplaced.

"The stock market has declined much of the year on fears that the economy was slowing too precipitously or that inflationary pressures were building. However, as a blizzard of predictions showed, many economists are confident that a 'soft landing' of slower growth and modest inflation remains within reach.

"Analysts surveyed quarterly by the Federal Reserve Bank of Philadelphia raised their growth forecasts for next year while reducing their inflation predictions.

"The analysts expect the economy to grow at an annual rate of 3.3% next year, far slower than the 5.2% growth predicted for 2000, but a bit higher than the 3.2% growth in 2001 predicted three months ago."

Article by Yochi J. Dreazen, *WSJ*, November 21, 2000, p. A2.

Nasdaq Plummets

On November 29, the Nasdaq Composite falls to 2,734.98, the lowest so far this year. On December 1, it drops to 2,597.93, slumping almost to half of its March record.

"Back To Basics: After Tech Bubble Burst, Value Investing Suddenly Makes Sense Again"

Headline of Article by E.S. Browning and Greg Ip, *WSJ*, November 27, 2000.

Cheney Warns Of Possible Recession

On December 3, Republican Vice-Presidential candidate Dick Cheney says that tax cuts are needed, because "we may well be on the front edge of a recession here."[204]

House Democratic leader Richard Gephardt answers that a tax cut is likely, but will be smaller than one advocated by Bush. "I don't think we are in a recession," he added. "I think things have slowed down a little, and I think they needed to slow down a little."[205]

On "Sixty Minutes," CBS's Scott Pelley said that "some people believe with the markets in the condition they're in, for Dick Cheney to go out and say we're on the front edge of a recession was irresponsible."[206]

Edit. With victory almost certain, it is now possible for the Bush Republicans to talk more candidly to the people about this part of what now faces them.

Nasdaq Rallies

On December 6, reacting to a rumor that Greenspan may consider a decrease, the index flies upward by 274.05 points or 10.48% to a record percentage and point one-day increase. On the 12th, the Nasdaq closes for the first time over 3,000 since November 17.

December 14—Gore Concedes To Bush

Fed Drops Anti-Inflation Stance

On December 20, The Federal Reserve declares that "economic weakness in the future" is a greater problem than that of inflation.

Stocks Ricochet

On December 21, the Nasdaq reacts to bad news on the technology sector by dropping to 2,332.78, a slide of more than seven percent. The Dow falls 2.5%. But, on December 26, the Nasdaq increases to 2,517.02. Analysts, however, stay clear from the comparison with 1929. They instead compare it with the 1970s, pointing out that the Nasdaq's decline from its high of 38.1% simply exceeded the 35.1% drop in that decade.

Edit. The market also crashed in the 70s. But in that decade mainly the well-off and speculators were involved. In the '90s, as in the '20s, by contrast, the general public was also involved. Also, the '90s market was much higher, both in absolute and relative terms, than the one that went down a more than a quarter of a century earlier. The sadder comparison will prove the more accurate.

Investors Losses Estimated At $3 Trillion For The Year[207]

By year's end, the Nasdaq is down 49.3%. The Dow loses 7.3%—down almost 1,000 points from its peak high of 11,722.978 on January 14, 2000. The S&P 500, a broader market average, is down over 12.65% from its record high, closing the year at 1,334.22. The broadest indicator of them all, the Wilshire 5000 Total Market Index, is down 17.45% this year.

Gross Federal Deficit Increases

The public debt for the period 09/30/1999 to 09/30/2000 increases by $18 billion, making it stand at $5,654,178,209,886.86.[208] This is a small increase, only about 14% of the enormity of the previous period. But there is no surplus, let alone a true balanced budget. The debt is still growing. It is, however, as near as this administration comes to honesty on this issue—the very year that the bubble has a great fall. Can the newly elected king's men and the newly elected king's horses put it together again?

CHAPTER XI

2001—IN GREENSPAN THEY STILL TRUST

1st Trading Day Of Year

The Nasdaq falls 7.2% and drops below 2,300 to 2,291.86. The *WSJ* says that reports of tepid manufacturing data and related fears are being blamed.[209]

Edit. Note that The Wall Street Journal does not mention the increasing public awareness of the ridiculously high prices.

Fed Cuts A Rate

On January 4, The Federal Reserve lowers the federal funds target from 6.5% to 6.0% In response, the Dow leaps 299.60 points to 10,945.75. The Nasdaq jumps 14.2% to 2,616.69. This is widely seen as signifying that Greenspan, the one they trust, is worried about a recession.[210]

"Executives Cheer Rate Cut, but Some See Little Immediate Aid To Their Businesses"

Headline, *WSJ*, January 4, 2001, p. A2.

California Utility Defaults

Southern California Edison defaults on $596,000,000 in obligations to bondholders and suppliers. S & P reduces the credit ratings for the parent company, Edison International, to junk.[211]

"Is This Really a Bear Market, or Some Other Kind Of Animal?"

"On one level, it looks as if the bear is upon us. At the Nasdaq Stock Market, where most technology stocks trade, the composite index stands at 48% below its record close . . . on March 10 of last year.

"But what makes this strange is that the general stock market hasn't followed suit, at least yet."

E.S. Browning, *WSJ*, January 16, 2000, p. Cl.

Edit. Wall Street is hoping that it is not like waiting for the second shoe to drop.

On January 22, George W. Bush Takes Oath Of Office

Edit. With the new President, there is definitely a shift from the Wall Street financiers characteristic of his predecessor's administration. The days of Gene Sperling and the "Economic Dream Team" are over. This President campaigned for tax cuts.

Some Large Corporations Cut Jobs In January

AOL Time Warner announces that they will cut 2,000 jobs; Lucent will cut 16,000 jobs after a 28% drop in sales. Daimler-Chrysler will chop off 20% of its work force.[212]

Greenspan, In About-Face, Backs Tax Cuts; Reversal Angers Democrats . . . ."

"Federal Reserve chairman Alan Greenspan, in a striking reversal of a long-held view, said he now sees a place in the federal government's future for significant tax cuts—a pronouncement that gives a big boost to President Bush.

. . . .

"'Have my views changed? Yes, they've changed; they have to change. I see no alternative to that," he explained. 'I still hold the No.1 priority is reducing the debt. The problem is we're going to get that out of the way far sooner than any of us imagined.'"

"Mr Greenspan's testimony before the Senate Budget Committee reflected an extraordinary turnabout . . . .

. . . .

"Mr. Greenspan even sharpened the argument for tax cuts, warning that the surplus projections have grown so enormous that they actually raise economic dangers if they aren't reduced through tax cuts.

"'Large deficits are bad. Large surpluses are bad,' he said.

"Once government pays back as much debt as it can, Mr. Greenspan cautioned, it would have to begin acquiring private assets. Though he didn't says so, that could mean, for example, broad ownership of corporate stocks and bonds. Alternately, a near elimination of debt could lead to a sharp tax or spending boost, perhaps overstimulating the economy. That point, he added, would come before the government had bought back all of its debt outstanding because some debt holders, valuing federal securities' risk free status, wouldn't want to sell."

"Mr. Greenspan has long opposed additional spending because it is politically difficult to stop government programs once they are under way. Yesterday, he said he favored reducing the surplus through tax cuts that started soon but were phased in, to lessen the economic ripples of such huge fiscal transformations. Starting the process 'sooner rather than later likely would help smooth the transition to longer-term fiscal balance,' he said. 'And should current economic weakness spread beyond what now appears likely, having a tax cut in place may, in fact, do noticeable good.'"[213]

Edit. Greenspan knows full well that those surpluses are non-existent. His little speech is baby-talk to fool the Democrats into imagining that his decision to support the new President involves some deep thought. Not so many are fooled. Senator Ernest Hollings,

who had exposed the phony surplus back in 1998, addresses Greenspan:
"You shock me with this statement. You're going to start a stampede
this morning."[214]

Fed Makes Another Cut

On February 1, the Federal Reserve once again reduces interest rates by half a point, thereby lowering the federal-funds rate to 5.5%. So far, this was the most drastic easing since 1982. On this same day, the Treasury announces the discontinuance of the 52-week bill. The Bush Administration scraps the 30-year bond.

"The Fed (Finally) Picks Up The Tempo"

"By knocking down stock prices, the Fed was attempting to level the playing field between new-era and old-era firms. But tight monetary policy is an equal-opportunity destroyer. LTV Steel, Chrysler, General Motors and Sara Lee have been hurt in the same way as Lucent, Motorola and the dot-coms.

· · · · · · · · · · · · · · · · · ·

"The good news is that despite the recognition lag, the economy will come out of this mess in great shape, with the Fed now correcting its mistake and the Bush administration moving rapidly on tax cuts and regulatory rollbacks. The recession should be over by the fourth quarter of this year and the stock market will be back on track for big gains in the years ahead."
Article by economist Brian S. Wesbury, *WSJ*, February 1, 2001, p. A 22.

DR. W. RANDOLF BURGESS—FEDERAL RESERVE BANK OF NEW YORK—JUNE 1930
"THE ECONOMIC MALADJUSTMENT OF THIS PERIOD WILL WITHOUT A DOUBT BE IRONED OUT BEFORE MANY MONTHS HAVE ELAPSED."[215]

Lucent's Accounting Suspect

On February 9, the SEC announces that it has been investigating Lucent's accounting. The investigation focuses on how Lucent booked $679,000,000 in revenue the previous year.

Sad News From Dell

On February 16, Dell warns that earnings will be below expectations and that they will lay some people off.[216]

"Few Economists Are Seeing Recession, Survey Finds"

"Though economists are expecting this year to be the economy's worst since 1991, only a tiny percentage think the economy is in a recession, a new survey has found.

"Just 5% of forecasters surveyed by Blue Chip Economic Indicators think say the U.S. has slipped into a recession.

"Professional forecasters appear to be much more optimistic than the general public."

Greg Ip, *WSJ*, February 12, 2001, p.A2.

JAMES J. DAVIS—SECRETARY OF LABOR—JUNE 30, 1930
"THE WORST IS OVER WITHOUT A DOUBT."[217]

"Greenspan Presents a More Upbeat View"

"He was generally more chipper about the economy than he was in testimony three weeks ago before the Senate Budget Committee. The 'exceptional weakness evident . . . toward the end of last year,' perhaps due to bad weather, 'apparently did not continue in January,' he said. Though consumer confidence has fallen, 'it remains at a level that in the past was consistent with economic growth.'"

Greg Ip, February 14, 2001, p. A2.

ROBERT W. LAMONT—SECRETARY OF COMMERCE—
MARCH 3, 1930
"AS WEATHER CONDITIONS MODERATE, WE ARE LIKELY TO
FIND THE COUNTRY AS A WHOLE ENJOYING ITS WANTED STATE OF
PROSPERITY. BUSINESS WILL BE NORMAL IN TWO MONTHS."[218]

Clinton Speaks Before Corporate Shindig

Oracle Corporation pays Mr. Clinton $100,000 to deliver a
speech on February 21. Among his utterances:"I know there have
been a few dot-coms falling on the NASDAQ for the last several
months, but don't kid yourself, the Internet is still our future."[219]

Nasdaq At Lowest Point In Two Years

On February 22, the Nasdaq Composite tumbles to
2,268.94, the lowest in two years. Fears of more inflation and
troubled corporate earnings was cited as the reason.

President Bush Explains Federal Accounting Standards

At a February 22, press conference: "Let me remind you . . .
that accounting in Washington is a little different than the
way . . . the average person accounts. This is a town where if
you don't increase the budget by an expected number, it's
considered a cut."

" . . . We're going to slow the rate of growth of the budget
down. It should come to no surprise to anybody that my budget
is going to say loud and clear that the rate of growth of the
budget . . . from last year, was excessive. And so we'll be slowing
the rate of growth of the budget down. That, evidently, is a
cut."

Critic Questions These Standards

"What the president described was not a 'cut' but a smaller than anticipated increase in spending. Furthermore, when Mr. Bush presented his Fiscal Year 2002 budget . . . it actually called for a 5.7 percent increase in federal spending—as contrasted with the 3.7 percent increase contained in Bill Clinton's final budget. Were the president, in his role as chief executive officer for the federal government, liable to the same standards being imposed on private CEOs, this single act of fraud would presumably net him a sizable prison term."

William Norman Grigg[220]

Bush Submits Budget of $1.96 Trillion.

This proposed budget is released on March 1. It will be significantly less than what private investors lost in the stock market the previous year.

Stocks Plunge

On March 13, the Nasdaq tumbles 6.3% to 1,923.38; this is its lowest point since December of 1998—just before its tremendous run-up. This puts the Composite Index at 62% below its all-time high. The Dow plunges 4.1% to 10,208.25 and the S&P 500 slips 4.3% to 1,180.16—definitely a bear market.

On the 15th, the Dow drops 317.34 more points, bringing it below 10,000 to 9,973.46, the lowest point so far that year. The Nasdaq continues on its course, dropping to 1,972.09.

By the end of the week, the industrials fall 821.21 points more—7.7%—making it the worst weekly percentage drop in eleven years.[221]

Is Bush Too Negative On Economy?

Leading Democrats are complaining that the President is too critical of the economy: "They're doing it for the short-term political gain of passing a tax cut we can't afford and don't need. They're doing it in a way that I think is very, very harmful to the economy," says Senate Democratic leader Tom Daschle at the Capital Hill news briefing with House Democratic leader Dick Gephardt.

Daschle and Gephardt display a chart which indicates that consumer confidence fell considerably in December after Dick Cheney said, "We may well be on the front edge of a recession here."

Gephardt says, "You see how consistent consumer confidence has been until Dick Cheney started really in December and the President chimed in and everybody began to frankly scare consumers."[222]

WILLIAM RANDOLF HEARST—NOVEMBER 1929

"SOME REASSURING UTTERANCE BY THE PRESIDENT OF THE UNITED STATES . . . WOULD DO MUCH TO RESTORE THE CONFIDENCE OF THE PUBLIC."[223]

TIME Cover Story: "Looking Beyond The Bear"

The cover shows a somewhat ridiculous looking bear. The sub-title is "Yes, it's scary out there, but a recession isn't a sure thing. Here's why." Below is the important part of their argument:

" . . . 'The broad economy's not as bad as the technology economy. More people are starting to wake up to the fact that this is a technology problem,' says Thomas McManus, portfolio strategist at Banc of America Securities in New York City. Consumer sentiment figures released by the University of Michigan Friday suggest that the pessimism may be leveling off. Car and home sales have held up reasonably well, drawing down inventories, a critical issue. Consumers have been refinancing their homes at the fastest clip in several years. Energy prices have stabilized. Despite a rash of announced layoffs, the unemployment rate remains low at 4.2%. And cash is piling up. Mountains of the stuff are accumulating in money funds—a record $2 trillion—presumably waiting to come back into stocks at the first sign of a revival.

"Most important: given time, falling interest rates almost always work, and with inflation low the Fed has room to cut away. Why isn't the stock market responding now? 'In the early innings of a weak economy there's always a battle between lower interest rates and falling corporate profits, and falling corporate profits always win,' says Richard Bernstein, strategist at Merrill Lynch. In that respect, he says, there's nothing unusual about what's happening. Investors are focused on the bad news. Eventually, though, falling rates breathe life into an ailing economy—and into the stock market well in advance.

"Since 1921, in 13 cases in which rates were cut swiftly three times in a row, the Dow has been higher one year after the third cut on 12 occasions. A cut this week would be the third this go-around. The median gain in the 13 cases was 25%, according to Ned Davis Research. The NASDAQ, which came into being in 1971, has never been negative a year after the third consecutive rate cut, and its gains have also been impressive.

"Stats like that give bullish analysts plenty to talk about. 'The economy will be picking up significantly by the fourth quarter,' says Bruce Steinberg, chief economist at Merrill Lynch. 'Corporate earnings should be picking up at the same time, and the stock market, because it looks to the future, is going to be going up well in advance of that. I really think sometime in the spring the market will turn around.'

"As for comparing the U.S. Economy with the

downwardly spiraling Japanese economy, analysts note a host of differences. The main one: The Japan bubble was built on rising real estate values. Banks were heavily exposed through mortgages and commercial-property loans. The U. S. bubble was in a narrow sector of stocks. Some banks are exposed through private equity investments; but for the most part, even if your portfolio tanked, your bank doesn't have much at risk. Healthy banks are vital to the healthy economy.

"Macro issues aside, many stocks now trade at bargain prices. Sell now and you risk selling at the bottom. Ironically, a lot of tech stocks now trade higher relative to this year's earnings than they did before the slide. So they still look expensive. But that's because near term earnings assumptions are falling faster than the stock price. If the earning slump is temporary, as it most likely will be for blue-chip firms like Intel and Microsoft, the near term outlook should be ignored if you are long-term investor. A better metric is the expected five-year growth rate.

"At times like these it can be hard to hang on to your stocks. No one knows if they will go lower before they rebound. But if you sell now for any reason other than to diversify, you probably shouldn't be in stocks in the first place. They work their magic only over long periods of time."

TIME, March 26, 2001, pp. 29, 31.

Edit. The problem, we are told, is impatient investors. What they need to do is wait. Interest rates are going to go down and then the economy will pick up. This, they assert, is not as dangerous as the Japanese bubble, because theirs was based on real estate, while ours was based on stocks.

One marvels at the magazine's continuing optimism, especially in the light of the fact that only one member of the Committee To Save The World remains in Washington, D.C.

"The Old Economy Might Show The New One A Thing Or Two"

"But even against that enormous drop, first-quarter GDP growth still appears to have kept its head above water—if only barely. The point here is that, in the first quarter, Old Economy strength is offsetting much of the New Economy weakness. In the end, consumers will determine which force prevails, and the answer may not be known until well into the summer."

James C. Cooper & Kathleen Madigan, *Business Week*, April 16, 2001, p. 26.

Edit. Wall Street dangles before the investors the idea that the low-tech stuff is O.K., even though the high-tech which was supposed to bring about a new economy didn't pan out.

Fed Cuts Again, But . . .

On March 21, The Fed cuts short-term rates by a half a point to 5%. This is the third rate cut this year. Even so, the Dow drops to its lowest point since March 1999. The Nasdaq is consistent, falling to its lowest point since October 1998.

Bear Market Rally

On April 5, stocks achieve one of their best one-day-gains in years. This follows good earnings reports from Dell and Yahoo, especially the latter. The Dow surges ahead 402.63 points from 9,515.42 to 9,918.05, a 4.2% gain. After the worst quarter hitherto experienced, the Nasdaq is carried upward 146.2 points from 1,638.8 to 1,785.00. This is a far cry from what it was just 12 months earlier, when it stood at 4,446.45, but it is a nifty rise of 8.9%—its third best percentage gain ever. [224]

Wall Street Journal Gets Upbeat

"Analyst's Call on Semiconductor Stock Raises Question: Is It Safe to Buy Tech?"

Susan Pulliam and Dan Goodin, WSJ, April 12, 2001, p. C1.

"Another gain For Tech Stocks raises Hopes Among Investors"
E. S. Browning, WSJ, Thursday, April 12, 2001, p. C1.

"April Rally Sends Investors Looking for a Spring— Earnings May Provide A Sign That Market Is in a Warming Trend"
E. S. Browning, WSJ, April 16, 2001, P. C1.

READY FOR THE NEW YEAR
—Sykes in the New York *Evening Post.*
JANUARY, 1930.

"Investors Stay Cool as Stocks Turn Cold"

" . . . At the market's peak in March 2000, stock-fund managers had just 4% of their portfolios in cash, the lowest level in 28 years.

"Since then, stock-fund managers have sounded the retreat, bolstering their cash holdings by $40 billion, so that they had 5.9% of their portfolios in cash at the end of February. Meanwhile, over the same stretch, investors added $191 billion to their stock-fund holdings, pursuing the sensible strategy of buying more shares as prices tumbled.

If the bear market drags on, that cool-headed buying could turn to frenzied selling. But I suspect the real danger will be when stocks rebound. As investors recoup their losses, they may bail out, rather than risk losing money again.

How much have ordinary investors lost in the market decline? Nobody knows for sure, partly because it's tough to get a handle on investors' holdings of individual stocks. Mr. Markese [president of the American Association of Individual Investors in Chicago] suspects that 'if you looked at individual investors' holdings, they would look more like the broader Wilshire 5000 than a technology-sector fund.'

"We can get a good sense of how investors' stock-fund holdings have fared. According to Chicago researchers Morningstar Inc., U. S. stock funds lost an average 16.9% over the 12 months through March 31, compared with a 24.7% drubbing for the Wilshire 5000 index of most regularly traded U.S. stocks.

"But if you are interested in how badly investors have been hurt, that average decline is misleading, because it gives equal weight to all funds, no matter what their size. Instead, what really counts is how the largest stock funds performed, because that is where many folks have their money invested.

"With that in mind, I asked Morningstar to calculate the return for the 50 largest U. S. stock funds, based on fund assets as of the March 2000 top . . . .

"During the past year, these 50 giant funds, which account for 45.3% of U. S. stock-fund assets, lost an average 27.4%, compared with the Wilshire 5000's 24.7% decline. In other words, fund investors pretty much matched the market before costs, and lost somewhat more once investment costs are figured in.

"'Early last year, money was flowing into tech-heavy growth funds,' notes Russel Kinnel, Morningstar's director for fund analysis. 'But there was already a lot of money allocated to value funds, so investors had pretty well-diversified portfolios.'

"Maybe we shouldn't be surprised that investors have hung tough and that their losses are in line with the market average. The fact is, the image of the tech-crazed, Internet-addicted, IPO flipping, day-trading small investor never quite matched reality.

"Look at the statistics. As of March 31, 2000, margin loans outstanding represented a modest 2.3% of total client assets at Charles Schwab Corp., the big San Francisco discount broker. As of the same date, assets of technology-sector funds accounted for just 4.2% of total stock-fund assets, according to Morningstar.

"What about all those day traders? True, a lot of ordinary investors bought and sold stocks with reckless abandon as the bull market approached it dizzying peak. But very few were trading for a living. Bill Lauderback, a spokesman for the Electronic Traders Association and a vice-president at Momentum Securities in Houston, puts the number of professional day traders at 10,000, unchanged from a year ago.

"'Day trading appeared to be pervasive, from the stories that were written,' Mr. Marese says. 'But, in fact, it was just a small cadre of investors.'"

Jonathan Clements, WSJ. Tuesday, April 17, 2001, p. C1.

JOHN J. DAVIS—SECRETARY OF AGRICULTURE—FEBRUARY 14, 1930
"THE WORST IS OVER WITHOUT A DOUBT, AND IT HAS BEEN A DISCIPLINARY AND IN SOME WAYS A CONSTRUCTIVE EXPERIENCE. PEOPLE HAVE LEARNED ONCE AGAIN THAT ONLY WORK PRODUCES WEALTH."[225]

"Stocks Advance despite Cisco warning"

"'We are starting to maybe view the glass as half-full rather than half-empty,' said Andy Brooks, head of stock trading at Baltimore mutual-fund group T. Rowe Price. 'Especially in Nasdaq-land, I thought it was a particularly strong showing 'considering the down news from Cisco. 'You see that kind of action and you say, maybe we've seen the worst of it.'"

WSJ, April 19, 2001, p. C1.

> Julius H. Barnes, Chairman—National Business Survey Conference—March 16, 1930
> "To the business men of America, the spring of 1930 marks the end of a period of grave concern. They have now weathered the worst of the storm which came in the wake of last autumn's crash on the stock market . . . . American business is steadily coming back to the normal level of prosperity . . . . Article, "Business Turns The Corner."[226]

Edit. Actually, it was just beginning.

The Fed Joins In

On April 19, the Federal Reserve prunes short-term interest rates by a half point. This encourages the market. The Nasdaq leaps by 8.1% to 2,079.44—the first time it attained above 2,000 in almost a month. The Dow grows by 3.9% to 10,615.83.

Edit. Another bear market rally.

"Stock Nightmares? History May Comfort"

" . . . when the bears dwell on the industrials, they neglect to account for dividends . . . .

. . . .

"According to Chicago's Ibbotson Associates, over the 1929-54 stretch, the S&P 500 gained an average of 6.2% a year, once you included dividends.

. . . .

"The bottom line? Over the 1929-54 stretch, a U. S. only stock portfolio might have gained a tad more than 7% a year, while a globally diversified portfolio would likely have returned around 6%. Meanwhile, inflation ran at 1.7% a year, and both bonds and Treasury bills were lackluster performers.

. . . .

"Indeed, if anything, the 1929-54 period provides a ringing endorsement of stock investing. 'Stock returns over that period were quite good, thanks to dividends,' says Jeremy Siegel, a finance professor at the University of Pennsylvania's Wharton School. 'The dividend yield averaged 5% or 6%. That yield was much higher than you could get from other financial assets.'

"By contrast, the 1966-82 stretch was nastier, because of the period's rapid inflation. A U.S.-only stock portfolio might have returned just over 7% a year and a globally diversified fund might have earned 8% annually, while inflation clocked in at 7%.

"In other words, after inflation, stock investors barely treaded water during those grim 16-1/2 years. But they wouldn't have fared any better with bonds or Treasury bills. 'The only assets that did well in that period were land and gold and other real assets,' Prof. Siegel says.

" . . . Both stretches richly rewarded those who had the fortitude to invest regularly in stocks. Suppose that, during both spells, you stashed $100 every month in a portfolio consisting of 75% larger U.S. stocks and 25% smaller companies.

"Ibbotson calculates you would have invested $19,800

during the 1966-82 stretch and amassed $41,944 by the end. But the really impressive result came with the longer 1929-54 period. Over that stretch, you would have socked away $30,300—and had $233,018 by late 1954.

> "Those impressive gains were made possible by the
> market's long plunge, which gave folks the chance to
> buy at bargain-basement prices."
> Jonathon Clements, WSJ, April 24, 2001.

Edit. Every year, the dollar would have been attacked by inflation. Let us take the shorter period. The1982 dollar was worth about a third of its 1966 predecessor. On the average, the $100 invested each month would be worth less than the previous installment. Ibbotson reckons that $100 invested each month from 1966 through 1988 would cost $19,800 and would yield $41,944. Taking inflation into account[227] and proceeding month by month, the 17-year inclusive period would cost in 1966 dollars $38,737.61, a much more modest return— bringing in a profit in the nine-percent range for the whole period, or about a half percent a year in inflation-free dollars. The mistake is not in owning stocks, but in the belief that they take care of themselves. Quite to the contrary: a stock portfolio needs to be weeded like a garden.

Wilshire 5000 Record

The broadest index, comprising five thousand stocks, increased by 8.1% in April, making that the best month, percentage-wise, in almost a decade.

Edit. On May 10, in line with this spate of optimism, there takes place the . . .

Largest U. S. Corporate Bond Sale

WorldCom sells $11.9 billion, the third largest bond sale by any firm in the world to that date.

Edit. The bonds are safer.

"Merrill's Web Fund to Log Off After Brief Life"

"In another cautionary tale for investors who chase the latest hot thing, Merrill Lynch & Co. is pulling the plug on its Internet Strategies Fund.

"Only 13 months after it opened with an avalanche of more than $1 billion in investor money, the mutual fund's directors are asking shareholders to approve a merger into Merrill's Global Technology Fund, which is run by the same manager, Paul Meeks.

"The Internet Strategies Fund was one of Merrill's biggest fund openings ever, but it now has the dubious distinction of having been launched two weeks after what turned out to be the peak in the Nasdaq Composite Index of March of last year. While the planned merger will provide shareholders with a more diversified portfolio within the technology sector, it won't undo the Internet fund's brutal 71% loss from inception until Wednesday evening, a drop that has wiped out more than $700 million in investor capital in the Internet Fund."

Tom Lauricella, *WSJ,* May 4, 2001, p. C1.

May 16: The Fed Cuts Short-Term Rates By ½ Point

"Stocks Surge . . . Industrials Gain 3.15%, Surpass 11,000 Level, As Nasdaq Rises 3.88%"

"The rally followed the curious day-earlier action in which investors had seemed to shrug their shoulders at initial news of the Federal Reserve's fifth interest-rate cut of the year, leaving stocks little changed on a day when the bullish Fed announcement should seemingly have had a bigger effect.

"'One day it doesn't matter, the next day we're off to the races,' noted Bob Bissell, president of Wells Capital Management, Wells Fargo's money-management arm.

. . . .

"'Some of the buying came from previously skeptical professional investors who have been holding money out of the stock market. Some of them appear to have decided, after a night's reflection, to take a part of the money they are holding on the sidelines and put it back into stocks,' said Mr. Bissell.

. . . .

"'The Fed's five interest-rate cuts this year, together with the recent economic numbers, have made many people start to think that 'we have been through the worst' . . . Mr. Bissell said. But like many in his business, he said he remains skeptical that stock-market gains will be more than gradual, and he still expects bonds to do better than stocks."

E.S. Browning, WSJ, Thursday May 17, 2001, p. C1.

ARTHUR BRISBANE—IN HIS SYNDICATED COLUMN, "TODAY"—
JULY 16, 1931
"THIS COUNTRY HASN'T LOST ANYTHING, EXCEPT A FEW BILLION."[228]

Really A Bull Market, They Still Say

"Much has been made of the fact that investors have lost $2.88 trillion since the Nasdaq Composite Index peaked early last year. But a recent study shows just 20 stocks were responsible for more than 76% of those losses. Cisco Systems alone cost investors $333 billion; Intel, $209 billion. Indeed, every one of those 20 stocks are in the technology or telecommunications businesses, according to the study from Bianco Research, LLC in Barrington, Ill.

"By contrast, if tech and the .com stocks were removed from the Standard & Poor's 500, the past few years would have looked like a steady bull market. Without these stocks, the S & P 500 would have actually declined 5.9% last year, instead of the 9.1% decline with them in the index."

Gregory Zuckerman and Peter A. McKay, "Abreast Of The Market," *WSJ*, May 18, 2001, p. C1.

> DR. JULIUS KLEIN—ASSISTANT SECRETARY OF COMMERCE—JANUARY 10, 1930
> "THE STOCK MARKET AFFECTED APPROXIMATELY ONLY 1,000,000 PERSONS, THE SPECULATIVE ELEMENT."[229]

> R. W. WOODRUFF—PRESIDENT, COCA COLA—AUGUST 1930
> "THE GENERAL SLUMP IN BUSINESS, IN MY OPINION, HAS BEEN GREATLY EXAGGERATED."[230]

Now They Tell The Investors, Part I

"TRICKS OF THE TRADE *BIG BATH. HOW IT WORKS* Take large write-off, booking costs now to boost earnings and margins in the future. *DRAWBACK* Unless operations improve, more charges must be taken to maintain earnings. Eventually, investors shun the stock. *WHO'S DONE IT* Cisco, Daimler-Chrysler, Kodak *PLOY* VENDOR FINANCING *HOW IT WORKS* Lends money to financially fragile customers so that they can buy products, pumping sales and profits *DRAWBACKS* Company can be left with bad debts—and falling sales, when it stops lending. *WHO'S DONE IT* Motorola, Lucent, Nortel *PLOY* PENSION GAMBIT *HOW IT WORKS* Decides pension plan is overfunded and cuts company contributions. Hides gain in financial footnotes. *WHO'S DONE IT* IBM, GE *PLOY* BEFORE ITS TIME *HOW IT WORKS* Treats pending sales as if they have already occurred, books sales without subtracting promised rebates. *DRAWBACK* Cuts future sales and earnings, giving appearance of faltering company performance unless operation is repeated. *WHO'S DONE IT* Microstrategy, Informix, Cendant

PLOY BACKDOOR BARGAINS *HOW IT WORKS* Promotes sales by buying a big customer's stock or granting it cheap warrants. *DRAWBACK* investors may be suspicious of stated values; hard to do over again, so future results could falter. *WHO'S DONE IT* Flextronics, Amazon."

David Henry, "The Numbers Game," *Business Week*, May 14, 2001, p. 100.

Now They Tell The Investors, Part II

"That's the hard lesson learned by investors whose portfolios have been hammered 60%, 70% or more in the Nasdaq composite Index Meltdown of the past year . . . .

"Even with recent gains, tech-fund investors are still in the hole and 'it could take years for you to get out,' says Robert Levitt, a financial adviser in Boca Raton, Fla.

The problem is what Vanguard Group Chairman John Brennan calls 'the insidious math' of investing: After a steep loss, it takes a far greater percentage gain to become whole again.

"Take the 70.1% decline suffered by the average tech fund in the almost 13 months between March 10, 2000, and April 4. A 70.1% gain doesn't nearly get the investor back to break-even: indeed, a fund or any other investment down that much has to soar 234%—that is, more than triple—to get back to its initial value.

. . . .

"That means the average tech fund with a 38.5% gain from April 4 through Wednesday, as measured by Lipper Inc., has helped far less than some investors may think. Even after that recent gain, the tech funds are still down an average 59.7% from the March 2000 Nasdaq peak.

" . . . When a fund drops 10%, for instance, to $9,000

from an initial $10,000, it takes an 11.1% advance
to return the stake to its starting size. That's because
investors have less money working for them after
the initial drop."
Article by Karen Damato, *WSJ*, May 18, 2001[231]

Tax-Cut Bill Signed

On June 8, Bush signs a $1.35 trillion tax-cut bill. He
originally sent a $1.6 trillion proposal, but it was reduced due
to Congressional compromise. The Treasury Department will
start mailing rebates in July.
Edit. This will help the wounded upper middle class a tad bit.

Arthur Anderson Fined

On June 20, the SEC fines Arthur Anderson and three
partners because of the way they audited Waste Management.

The Fed Again

On June 28, the Fed cuts interest rates for the sixth time,
this time by just a quarter of a point. The Federal Fund Rate
now stands at 3.5%.

Nasdaq's Good June

The Composite Index finishes the 2nd quarter up 17%, rising
by 1.65% on July 2.

Wall Street Housekeeping

The Nasdaq Stock Market makes its first staff reductions in
fifteen years. The National Association of Security Dealers
proposes that analysts disclose their ownership in any companies
they may cover. Merrill Lynch announces that it will bar its

research analysts from purchasing stocks in companies which
they cover.

Nasdaq Slides, Then Soars

On July 11, the Index loses 3.2%, falling to its lowest level
in three months, to 1,962.79. But, just two days later, it makes
its biggest point increase in nearly three months, surging 5.3%
to 2,075.74. That same day, the Dow delivers its best
performance in almost two months. It increases 2.3% to
10,478.99. This came after news that Microsoft's second quarter
would be slightly better than predicted. [232] Investors are acting
on hope and fear, rather than solid performance.

Good News From Enron

Also, on the 13th, Enron announces that their net climbed
40%. Investors are now being told that strong energy trading
profits offset larger than expected losses at its telecom unit.[233]
Investors like to hear from Enron.

Fed Makes Another Rate Cut

On August 22, the Federal Reserve shaves interest rates by
another quarter point. The reason, the central bank
announces, is because of business weakness and turmoil
overseas.

Critic Charges That Financial News Is Managed

"Look, the guys who bring you the Wall Street news are
Wall Street . . . . Don't you see? A tiny handful of mega-
corporations—Viacom, Sony, Time Warner, Seagram, AT&T/
Liberty Media, Bertelsmann, and GE—control virtually ALL of
the financial news you see. And I mean ALL of it. General
Electric owns CNBC, the financial news network. AOL Time

Warner owns CNN, CNNFN and *Fortune Magazine.* Dow Jones owns both *The Wall Street Journal,* and *Barron's.* "Don't kid yourself. The control is absolute and complete. Even down to individual interviews. Steward Varney use (sic) to anchor CNN's 'Money Line.' That is, he did until he asked some pointed questions about the profit picture at AOL Time Warner, CNN's parent, in an interview with Ted Turner. No more Steward Varney. The anchors at these commercials for Wall Street, disguised as news shows, know the score. You tow the Wall Street line—or else.

"You better believe that this stock market collapse is going to be contested, denied, under-reported and pooh-poohed since the people who are representing themselves as the unbiased media are really Wall Street themselves. It's how they make their money."

The Wall Street Underground, August, September 2001, pp. 4,6.

9/11 And Aftermath

The Fed and other central banks pump more than $80 billion into the financial markets. When the markets open up on the 18th, the Dow plummets 684.81 points, losing 7.13%. The Nasdaq drops 115.83 points, shedding 6.83%. The hardest hit are airline, insurance, and travel stocks.

On the 25th, stocks begin to recover. The Dow closes at 8,603.86, making a partial recovery.

By the end of the week of October 1, stocks are up 7.4%, but the major stock indexes suffer their greatest quarterly loss since 1987.

The Fed chips in by cutting its short-term rate target by half a point.

Market Recovers

Finally, On October 12, the stock market restores the last of the $1.38 trillion lost as a result of 9/11. The Nasdaq climbs 4.6% to 1,701.47, and the S&P 500 rises 1.5% to 1,097.42.

Edit. This market decline was not directly related to the general stock market collapse, which is due to exorbitant prices. The market recovers from 9/11, but will resume its course downward the following year.

"Tough Times: How long?" "How a V-Shaped Rebound Might Materialize"

"AUTOS After several poor quarters, auto makers expect lower interest rates to bring buyers back to the showrooms. COMMERCIAL CONSTRUCTION It's frozen now, but low interest rates and the need for companies to rethink location strategy may push construction next year. CONSUMER SPENDING Although rising joblessness and uncertainty could dampen consumers' exuberance this year, the refinance boom and fiscal stimulus will spark growth by the spring of next year. HOUSING Fed rate cuts mean that getting a mortgage should remain cheap and easy, so housing could get a bounce after consumer confidence returns. TECHNOLOGY Most tech sectors should bottom out by second quarter, 2001—but a strong boom is not anticipated. VENTURE CAPITAL Money should start flowing into new businesses by early next year, but a real revival of VC funding depends on when the stock market starts rising."

Business Week, October 15, 2001, p. 41.

P.E. Crowley—President, New York Central Railroad—June 1930

"PROPHESY IS A VAIN THING AND I HAVE NO WISH TO JOIN THE RANKS OF THE PROPHETS, BUT I CANNOT BELIEVE THAT THIS COUNTRY OF OURS, WITH ITS HUGE CONSUMPTION AND ITS ENORMOUS CAPACITY, CAN LONG REMAIN IN A STATE OF DEPRESSION . . . I BELIEVE . . . THAT WE HAVE TURNED THE CORNER."[234]

Enron Is In Trouble

On October 17, Enron posts a $618 million loss for the third quarter. This is because Enron must take a $1.01 billion charge. There are also questions about irregularities concerning the financial partnerships.

Nasdaq Drops Sharply

On October 18, it has its sharpest drop since the day the market re-opened after 9/11. It falls 4.4% to 1,646.34. The Dow also falls 1.6% to 9,232.97.

More Trouble For Enron

On November 1, Enron discloses that the SEC is investigating their dealings with their partnerships. The S&P drops its ratings on Enron's debt, despite the company having received $1 billion in new credit lines.

Here Comes The Fed

On November 7, the Federal Reserve makes its 10th interest rate cut, lowering the federal-funds rate to 2% from 2.5%. On this news, the Dow leaps 1.5% to 9,591.12 and the Nasdaq jumps 2.31% to 1,835.08.

Enron Implodes

On November 9, Enron discloses to the SEC that it had reduced the net income it had reported as early as 1997 by twenty percent or $586 million. They admit to having used improper accounting procedures.

On November 23, the company is sued by participants in its employee-retirement plan.

Dynegy Considers Buying Enron

"All Eyes On The Enron Prize: If the deal holds, Dynegy will walk away with some juicy assets."

"But the trading profits were obscured in recent weeks by Enron's accounting tricks. The biggest danger for Watson [Dynegy] is that there are other time bombs ticking away. Already, the company has slashed its reported earnings since 1997 by $591 million, or 20% of its total, to account for controversial partnerships involving Enron officials. The Securities & Exchange Commission is still investigating. 'We believe it will take more than just a couple of weeks and a long-term relationship [between Watson and Lay] to do all the necessary due diligence,' says analyst Carol Coalse of Prudential Securities Inc. Dynegy's Bergstrom counters: 'We're pretty certain that most everything of material consideration has been disclosed.' If no? The massive earning boost provides 'a high margin of error,' he says."

Business Week, November 26, 2001, p. 96.

Enron Shrivels

On November 29, its debt is downgraded to junk status. Dynegy, which was on the verge of acquiring Enron, backs out of deal. The value of Enron stock careens 85%.

"Beijing Will Move More Reserves Into Euros"

"SHANGHAI, China—The Country's top foreign-exchange official said China plans to move more of its hard-currency reserves into Europe's common currency, the euro. He also pledged anew to hold the yuan steady following China's entry in the World Trade Organization.

"The comments from Guo Shuqing, head of China's State Administration of Foreign exchange, led to an immediate rally in the euro . . . .

. . . .

"China, bolstered by years of huge trade surpluses and foreign investment, holds the second largest store of foreign reserves in the world after Japan. These funds, valued at $203 billion at the end of October, traditionally have been invested in U.S. dollar-based assets, mostly Treasury bonds."
Article by Karby Leggett, *WSJ*, November 21, 2001, p. A11.
Edit. This move by Red China presages much in America's future. During the time of the Clinton-Greenspan bubble, they supported the dollar against inroads from Europe, all the while making it easy for American companies to transfer their technology into the low-cost Chinese labor market, a market which uses prisoner, i.e., slave, labor.

Mortgage Rates Lowered

Mortgage rates drop on November 11 to their lowest level in at least three decades, the average rate on a 30-year fixed mortgage being 6.45%.
Edit. Hope now springs on the real estate market.

Enron Gets Financing

On December 4, Enron obtains $1.5 billion in new financing from J.P. Morgan and Citibank.

Stocks Soar

Two days later, the Dow goes above 10,000 and the Nasdaq climbs above 2,000 after months of being below these levels. The industrials rise 2.2% to 10,114.29 and the Nasdaq, 4.3% to 2,046.84. This is attributed to good news from Cisco and Oracle.
Edit. Yeah, maybe Enron is a fluke.

Once more, The Fed

On December 12, short term rates are cut for the 11th time that year, to 1.75%. That is the first time they have been below 2% in 40 years.

Gross Federal Debt Rises Again

During the period 09/30/00 to 09/30/01, the public debt rises by $133.3 billion. It stands at $5,807,463,412,200.6.[235] This *increase* is about 7.4 times the increase of the previous fiscal period.

Edit. Since less than three weeks of this period covers the time after 9/11, the vast percentage of the increase concerned other matters. One suspects that a lot of things were deferred last year in order to come in with a low increase.

"Rate Cuts Fail to Stem Market's Slide, Shattering Myth of Fed's Omnipotence"

"Don't fight the Fed. Right?

"That is certainly the oft-cited mantra on Wall Street. It holds that when the Federal Reserve is in a rate-cutting mood, investors should be in a stock-buying mood. The rationale is that lower interest rates help boost the economy and corporate profits, both of which, in turn, helped propel stock prices higher.

"Yet, you would be poorer for having heeded that advice during 2001."

Article by Jeff D. Opdyke, *WSJ*, January 2, 2002.

CHAPTER XII

2002—THE BUBBLE DEMATERIALIZES

Japan Defaults

"In the last days of 2001, Japan announced that it was officially defaulting on its $155 billion in debts.

"Japan's debts are staggering—$7.5 trillion or 2.4 times their GDP, making Japan the most indebted industrial country relative to its size in the world, ever. Of that total, $4.3 trillion is owed by the government, 1.3 times GDP, also the worst in the world. Most dangerous of all; $1.5 trillion of the debts are held by Japan's broken banking system."

Martin Weiss' Safe Money Report, January 2002, p. 1.

Edit. Many Americans still believe in American exceptionalism— that this country is so different that it may blithely ignore historical parallels.

Euro Becomes Fully Operational

On January 2, three hundred million Europeans begin using the new currency. The price of the Euro in terms of dollars is $.8995, and the price of an ounce of gold is $278.20.

Argentina Devalues Peso by 29%

NEW YORK TIMES, PART OF 4-COLUMN HEADLINE—JULY 13, 1931
BERLIN CLOSES BOERSES;
BIG BANK FAILS[236]

"Economic Forecasters Expect Moderate Recovery in 2002"

"The consensus estimate of the 55 economists who participated in The Wall Street Journal's economic-forecasting survey calls for real gross domestic product—the value of the nation's output, adjusted for inflation—to rise at an annual rate of just 0.87% during the first quarter and 2.4% during the second quarter. But the forecasters see the economy picking up momentum during the second half of the year, with growth rising 3.6%.

"The government won't release estimates for growth in the just-ended fourth quarter until later this month, but most economists are expecting a contraction of more than 1%.

. . . .

"In the latest survey, the Wall Street Journal asked the forecasters what caused the current recession. Although 26 of the 55 economists named the sharp reduction in capital spending as the cause of the recession, nearly a dozen economists said the recession was caused by Fed monetary—policy decisions in 2000. Yet when asked to grade the Fed on how it has handled the recession, economists on average gave it a respectable B-plus. Seven economists gave the Fed an A or a B for handling a recession that they believe was mainly caused by Fed policies in the first place. The White House got a B-minus and Congress got a D-plus for their own economic policies.

. . . .

"On average, most economists expect short-term interest rates to rise and long-term interest rates to remain little changed this year. The consensus forecast called for the federal-funds rate to be right around where it is today, at 1.75%. As the economy picks up steam in the second half of the year, economists expect the Fed to gradually increase the federal-funds rate to be between 2.5% and 3%. But with inflation remaining subdued at 2% or less during the years, long-term rates aren't expected to change much. Economists expect yields on 10-year Treasury notes, currently about 5%, to remain at that level by June, then rise slightly to 5.3% by December.

. . . .

" . . . When asked who they thought should succeed Alan Greenspan as Fed Chairman, Robert Rubin . . . received 10 votes, the highest number . . . .

"Economists are modestly bullish on stocks. Of the 55 respondents, 21 said they expected the Dow Jones Industrial Average to end the year between 11000 and 12000; 20 said they expect the Dow to end between 10000 and 11000; seven said they expect the Dow to end between 12000 and 13000. The industrials ended 2001 at 10021.50, down 7% for the year. Nearly half of the economists, 25, said that more than 50% of their personal savings is invested in the stock market, and 19 said they raised the amount invested in the market compared to 2000. Of course, 24 said they lowered the amount they invested in stocks"

Constance Mitchell Ford and Jon E. Hilsenrath, WSJ, pp. A2, A9.

UNLEASHING 'IM

Costello in *Albany News.*

OCTOBER, 1930.

" . . . A Second Dip In The recession? Don't Worry about it: Consumers won't let it happen."

"The Commerce Dept.'s Jan. 30 report on real gross domestic product will most likely show that the U.S. economy contracted at an annual rate in the neighborhood of 1% in the fourth quarter despite a surge in real consumer spending of about 4% . . . . .

"Don't worry. Consumers are not going to lead the U.S. into a double-dip recession or prevent a recovery from taking hold. Certainly, there are risks, but the favorable fundamentals underlying spending argue that households will remain resilient in 2002.

"The double-dip scenario goes like this: After dropping in the final two quarters of 2001, real gross domestic product will manage a gain this quarter, thanks to inventory rebuilding. But further weaknesses in consumer spending will cause the economy to relapse. Consumers will be cowed for several reasons. First, lucrative incentives stole car sales from 2002. Second, labor markets and wage growth will weaken further. Third, two recent props under consumer spending will fall away: mortgage refinancings and cheaper energy. And last, with savings low, consumers will be crushed by their debt loads.

. . . .

"But households are buying more than just cars. Retail sales excluding cars and gasoline rose from October through December . . . . Discounting moved much of the merchandise, but the steady uptrend shows that consumers are willing to shop . . . . December sales of furniture and electronic stores were up nearly 10% from a year ago.

"The second-double dip worry—further deterioration of the job market—is always a risk for consumers. But falling weekly jobless claims strongly suggest that the worst job news is over. The consensus view of economists surveyed by Standard & Poor's MMS is that nonfarm payrolls fell by only 60,000 in January. That would be the fewest layoffs since August.

"True, the increased ability of U.S. companies to generate output from productivity gains suggests that layoffs will continue after the recovery starts. But as Federal Reserve Chairman Alan Greenspan pointed out in a Jan. 11 speech, as productivity strengthens, 'average real incomes could rise, at least partially offsetting losses of purchasing power that stem from diminished levels of employment.' Unemployment is devastating to those directly affected, but better productivity will help to boost real pay for the 94% of the labor force that still has jobs.

. . . .

"To be sure, eroding stock wealth is still taking a toll on consumer spending, and the impact will continue this year. Only about a third of households, however, own stock directly, while more than two-thirds own their homes. Since the first quarter of 2000, the value of corporate stocks and mutual funds directly held by households has declined by $4.8 trillion, based on Fed data on household balance sheets. But at the same time, house values have risen $1.8 trillion, while mortgage debt increased by $700 billion. That gave house owners a $1.1 trillion net gain in the value of most consumer's biggest asset—a nice offset to any stock losses.

"The recent performance of property values is in sharp contrast to the previous recession. During 1990 and 1991, housing net worth fell $200 billion. Homebuilding activity will contribute little to the coming recovery because it didn't fall off during the recession. However, housing's more important contribution may well be its lift to household balance sheets.

. . . .

"Finally, the problem of low household savings is overblown. The Commerce Dept. defines savings as income that is not spent. Except for the boost generated by the tax rebates, the savings rate held at a puny 1% last year, down sharply from about 8% in 1990. But income from realized capital gains, a growing source of cash in the past decade, is not included in that measure. If it were, some economists have estimated the current savings rate is upwards of 8%, down little from about 10% in 1990. That level of savings should provide a healthy cushion for consumers."

James C. Cooper & Kathleen Madigan, *Business Week*, February 4, 2002, p. 23.

ROBERT P. LAMONT—SECRETARY OF COMMERCE—MARCH 3, 1930

"THOSE WHO PREDICT A PROLONGED PERIOD OF DEPRESSION ARE JUST AS FOOLISH AS THOSE WHO PREDICT BUSINESS WILL JUMP MAGICALLY UP TO THE ABNORMAL LEVELS OF EARLY 1929 WITHIN A FEW WEEKS . . . . OUR INFORMATION INDICATES THE PROBABILITY THAT THE DECLINE IN BUSINESS HAS SUBSTANTIALLY IF NOT WHOLLY CEASED."[237]

Another Aspect Of Reality

"Banks received just 55 cents in recoveries from each $1 of defaulted loans last years, far below the historical average of 69 cents and even lower than the 60 cents on the dollar they got back in 2000, according to Moody's Investors Service. The recovery rate hasn't been this bad since 1994, and it is likely to get worse in coming months, hitting a low point by midyear, according to analysts at Moody's.

" . . . However, analysts say the situation is infinitely better than it was a decade ago at the bottom of the last economic cycle, when loan-default recoveries in some months dipped below 60 cents and solvency questions dogged the banking sector.

. . . .

"Still, heightened riskiness in the loan portfolios dates to at least 1997, according to regulators at the Office Of The Comptroller of the Currency in Washington. OCC data from 1997 and 1998 show a sharp rise in leveraged loans, or loans to borrowers whose debt greatly exceed their cash flows, as a percentage of syndicated commercial loans. David Gibbons, deputy comptroller of the currency for credit risk, calls the jumps in 1997 and 1998 a 'radical spike' in leveraged lending, saying it amounts to a 'record easing' in underwriting standards.

" . . . 'Much lending was done in a world of rising leverage where the repayment capacity was not proven,' Mr. Gibbons says. 'And now there is no source of repayment.'

"Mr. Gibbons says the lending to such clients reflected the same optimism that buoyed the stock markets those same years.

. . . .

"Regulators say the now-problematic loans cross a range of the industries, reaching beyond once-hot New Economy sectors like energy trading and telecommunications to Old Economy manufacturing."

Henry Sender, *WSJ*, " . . . Banks Recover Less On Loans," January 4, 2002, p. C1.

"Blue Chips Skid 211.88, Nasdaq Loses all of Year's Gains"

"A drumbeat of bad corporate news sends the Dow Jones Industrial Average to its biggest one-day decline since October, and wipes out all of this years's strong gains for the Nasdaq Composite index."

E.S. Browning, *WSJ*, January 17, 2002, p. C1.

Martin Weiss' Forecasts For 2002

Argentina's default is a sneak preview of debt crises around the globe. America's real budget deficit will be $600 billion; Enron-like time bombs will ravage US companies; Unemployment will soar to 8% and higher; the Dow and the Nasdaq will plummet 50% or more."
Martin Weiss' Safe Money Report, January 2002, p. 1.

"A Market's Woes Give Rise To A New Term For Hitting The Skids"

"When the editors of the Sunday New York Times Book Review needed to find a word to describe a drop in nominations for last year's books, they turned to a new verb. 'This year the process nasdaqed,' the editors wrote in their December story, noting that nominations for the year has tumbled 20%."
Kate Kelly, *WSJ*, January 17, 2002, p. A1.
Edit. What was once was a signatory for progress is now a byword for ruined expectations.

"More Blame Clinton Than Bush For Recession"

"A strong plurality of Americans in a new poll believes that nobody is to blame for the current recession, while among the rest of the respondents, more blame former President Bill Clinton than President Bush for the downturn.

"The poll has a margin of error of 4.9 percent and surveyed 400 registered voters nationwide—a small sample, but enough to show broad trends.

"Only 12 percent blame the terrorist attacks for the downturn, and another 12 percent of respondents blame Mr. Bush. In fact, 17 percent blame his predecessor, Mr. Clinton, for the recession, while 39 percent say nobody is to blame and it is part of a normal economic cycle."

Stephen Dinan, *Washington Times—National Weekly Edition,* Jan. 28,—Feb.3, 2002, p. 8.

Ex-Clinton Advisor Says Democrats Are Sabotaging Economy

"Dick Morris, former adviser to Bill Clinton, has publicly said that the Democrats are working to sabotage economic recovery. In his own words, 'The obvious central political fact of the stimulus package debate now grid-locking Congress is that the Republicans want the recession to end and the Democrats have to pretend to want it to end.' (*The Hill,* 11/ 29/01)."

"Daschle's Lies and His Attempts to Sabotage the U. S. Economy," by Gerald Jackson, *News.Max.com* February 2002, p. 42.

SIMEON D. FESS—CHAIRMAN—REPUBLICAN NATIONAL COMMITTEE—OCTOBER 15, 1930.

"PERSONS HIGH IN REPUBLICAN CIRCLES ARE BEGINNING TO BELIEVE THAT THERE IS SOME CONCERTED EFFORT ON FOOT TO UTILIZE THE STOCK MARKET AS A METHOD OF DISCREDITING THE ADMINISTRATION."[238]

"Enron: Line Between Firm And Accountant Blurred"

Analysts at prestigious outfits like Goldman Sachs, Lehman Brothers, Salomon Smith Barney and UBS Warburg continued to recommend the stock to investors even after Enron's problems became public.

"In the early part of 2000, Jim Chanos, President of Kynikos Associates, an investment firm that sell stocks short made the decision to bet against Enron. To be sure that he was right, he invited 'experts' from the big outfits to come in and tell him wherein his analysis was wrong.

"'It's not that they didn't see what we saw,' Chanos related. 'They either chose to come to the wrong conclusion because it suited them for a variety of other reasons or to put their faith in management.'

"One problem is that the companies being rated pay the agencies doing the rating, such as Finch, Moody's Investor Service, Standard & Poor's. An even bigger problem, according to the analysts, is that these agencies do less than a thorough job of research. For example, it was just two months before Enron officially went bankrupt that the agencies were beginning to threaten it with a low investment grade rating."[239]

Rubin And Enron

"A week ago, it was hard to imagine Treasury Secretary Paul O'Neill looking better than predecessor Robert Rubin, who phoned [the Bush Administration] from his perch at Citigroup, an Enron creditor. Mr. O'Neill boasts that his department refused to rescue the President's buddy and campaign contributor, Enron Chairman Kenneth Lay. Mr. Rubin, often portrayed as the Treasury Secretary we wish we still had, looks like an ordinary banker acting for his company."

"'The America That Says 'No,''' WSJ, Thursday, January 17, 2002, p. A1.

"Citigroup's Enron Sales Draw Suit"

"Citigroup, Inc. lent money to Enron Corp. in October, when the energy company's finances were sliding. At the same time, the Wall Street giant pitched Enron bonds to clients as a solid investment.

"Now, at least one institutional investor who bought the bonds is hopping mad—and has taken the beef to court.

"In a suit filed recently in federal court in New York, Silvercreek Management, Inc., a Toronto investment company that bought Enron bonds in October, accuses Citigroup's

Salomon Smith Barney unit as well as Goldman Sachs Group
Inc. and Bank of America Corp's Banc of America Securities
LLC as promoting securities even when they knew the
company was on the brink of collapse.

"'The brokers were calling our clients telling them that
this was a wonderful opportunity to buy these instruments,'
says Joe Cotchett, a lawyer representing Silvercreek. 'They were
giving our client a sell job.'

"Citigroup, Goldman and Banc of America declined to
comment.

"The suit is one of the first to put the blame for Enron
squarely on Wall Street's role in facilitating Enron's deception.
'Enron's investment bankers sold the securities which propped
up the pyramid,'the suit alleges. 'In the process, these firms
earned $214 million in underwriting fees alone, and more for
lending, derivative trading and merger advice.'

. . . .

"In its suit, Silvercreek says the three financial firms were
pitching Enron securities to Silvercreek as late as October,
including some new bonds that would convert into Enron stock.
The Canadian firm, which invested $175 million in Enron bonds
in October, says it lost $120 million and is seeking compensation
and unspecified damages.

"Sure, Enron had been through a rough patch over the
summer, the Wall Street sales pitch went, according to
Silvercreek's lawyers. But Enron wasn't all that bad off, and
the bonds were selling at a sharp discount. That purported
pitch was mirrored by some of the research reports the
brokerage firms had released during October.

"'We reiterate our Buy rating on Enron,' an Oct. 19
Salomon Smith Barney report on Enron said, 'after untangling
part of a complicated story involving their balance sheet.'

"Enron's story, of course, wasn't nearly so upbeat. Its balance-
sheet high-jinks caused a sudden loss of confidence, bringing

about a liquidity shortage so dire that Enron was forced to draw down an emergency $3 billion credit line on Oct. 25, only a few days after Salomon's report . . . . That move signaled Enron was running short of crucial operating capital.

"Citigroup's lending division knew as well as anybody that Enron was facing trouble, since it had been one of the top banks arranging the credit line. Yet the brokerage companies had Enron securities in their firm's inventory to unload, according to the Silvercreek suit.

"Enron had sold Wall Street firms about $1.9 billion in convertible bonds that firms such as Citigroup were free to sell to investors by June of 2001, the court papers say. But the sales of these securities weren't going so well, Silvercreek alleges.

"So Citigroup's bankers became increasingly aggressive in pushing the Enron bonds on institutional investors. Silvercreek's lawyers say Citigroup sold Silvercreek its last chunk of Enron securites on Oct. 25—the same day that Enron drew down its credit line from Citigroup.

"Executives familiar with Citigroup thinking assert that Silvercreek should have known the risks of investing in Enron as well as any other investor." (*Emphasis omitted*)

Jathon Sapsford, WSJ, February 1, 2002, p. C1, C12.

Edit. Maybe Mr. Rubin won't be nominated to succeed as Fed Chairman, that other member of the Committee to save the World, after all.

"Enron's Rise And Fall Gives Some Scholars A Sense of Deja Vu"

This article is about Samuel L. Insull whose holding company, Middle West Utilities Co., had sunk into bankruptcy in the 1930s amidst allegations of stock fraud and swindle.

"Middle West was made up of a host of interconnected companies with interlocking boards—an arrangement mirrored, in some ways, by the web of off-balance-sheet partnerships that concealed Enron's heavy debt burden. So complicated was Middle West's structure that it took seven years for a team from the newly formed Federal Trade Commission to fully unravel its financial structure.

"Other similarities between Middle West and Enron go straight to the top. Like Kenneth Lay, who resigned last month as Enron's chairman and chief executive, Middle West's Mr. Insull was a big campaign contributor, with powerful friends in Washington. Mr. Insull, for one, 'was careful to regulate the regulator,' Sen. Norris declared in June 1934.

. . . .

"In its era, Middle West's operations were every bit as groundbreaking as Enron's would be with EnronOnline, its Internet-based energy-trading system. Mr. Insull, for example, pioneered the idea that central power plants should operate 24 hours a day to help defray their high fixed costs . . . .

"But, like Enron, Middle West pushed its financial engineering too far. By the early 1930s, it was emblematic of the octopus-like 'power trusts' that were suspected of manipulating the nations's energy markets in unseen ways.

"Middle West withstood the stock-market crash of 1929, and it looked at first like Mr. Insull might emerge relatively unscathed. At one point, he even extended $50 million in credit to the City of Chicago to pay its school teachers and police.

"But Middle West had an Achilles' heel. Its companies had taken on an enormous amount of debt during the go-go years of the 1920s, and the company accelerated its borrowings after the crash. By the middle of 1931, creditors and rivals, including financier J.P. Morgan, were circling. In 1932, Franklin Roosevelt blasted the 'Insull monstrosity' for allegedly inflating the value of its holdings and selling worthless bonds. Middle West and many of its 284 affiliates were placed in receivership.

"Washington quickly got into the act. In rapid order in 1934 and 1935, Congress passed the Securities and Exchange Act and the Federal Power Act. Those laws set out to break up the power trusts and guarantee investors the information they needed to make informed decisions. More than half century later, Enron would figure out ways around part of those same laws."

Rebecca Smith, WSJ, Monday, February 4, 2002, p. C1.

Edit. One difference between Insull and the leaders of Enron is that Middle West was a pioneer in the technical development of the electric utility industry itself while the latter are merely speculators. Furthermore, Insull defeated the criminal charges placed against him, something Enron's executives have yet to do.

"Burst Bubbles Often Expose Cooked Books . . . ."

"The bad news for the stock market doesn't seem to end.

"First there was Enron's collapse, then Kmart's bankruptcy filling, then news from Global Crossing that the Securities and Exchange Commission is investigating its books. Analysts even have raised questions about the accounting at corporate giants Tyco International and Cisco Systems.

"Soon, the optimists say, all these nasty surprises will have to stop, and the budding economic recovery will begin to capture investors' attention.

"They could be right, but don't bet all your retirement money on it.

"History confirms what a lot of stock analysts and investors have been discovering to their chagrin lately-that bubbles and accounting controversies tend to go hand in hand.

"Accounting scandals and bankruptcies, in fact, are one important reason that it can take the stock market years to recover fully from a bubble.

. . . .

"Consider past experience. Corporate bankruptcies and unraveling frauds were among the hallmarks of the 1930s, following the crash of 1929. One accounting trick of that era was to create elaborate webs of holding companies, each helping hide the others' financial weaknesses, all artifices strangely similar to what Enron did with its partnerships . . . .

"'Our view would be that bubbles create greed on the part of investors but they also create greed on the part of management,' says Jeremy Grantham, a co-founder of the Boston money—management firm, Grantham, Mayo, Van Otterloo. That was very much the case in 1929 when holding companies put on leverage and bought other holding companies' stock.

"As the fallout from the 1929 crash spread, former New York Stock exchange President Richard Whitney was sucked in and eventually was arrested and later jailed for fraud.

"A less extensive bubble was inflated in the late 1960s and burst in the early 1970s, when the 'Nifty 50' stocks fell apart. Accounting scandals multiplied again. The Securities and Exchange Commission in 1975 censured Pear, Marwick, Mitchell, one of the largest accounting firms of the day, for failing to perform proper audits of five companies that collapsed soon after getting clean opinions.

"More trouble followed the crash of 1987, although it was shorter-lived than the problems of the '30s or the '70s. The once-hot junk-bond market unraveled, insider-trading scandals proliferated, the savings-and-loan crisis grabbed the front pages and real-estate investments went bust."

E.S. Browning, *WSJ*, February 12, 2002, p. C1.

"As Big Losses Grew, Trader's Solution Backfired'"

"The currency trader blamed for $750 million in losses at the U. S. unit of Allied Irish Banks says he engaged in a series of trades that escalated as he tried to make up for his losses, according to law-enforcement officials involved in the case."

Erik Portagner and Craig Karmin, *WSJ*, February 8, 2002, p. C1.

" . . . A Lehman broker vanishes . . . ."

"Mr. Guttadauria himself suggested that his superiors didn't watch him closely enough. In his letter to the FBI, he said: 'The various firms' greed and lack of attention [to him] on a senior level contributed greatly' to his ability to execute the alleged scam, according to people familiar with the letter. 'I hardly believe that I could have done this without detection for so long.'" [He stole $120 million].

Charles Gasparino & Susanne Craig, *WSJ*, February 8, 2002, p. A5.

Edit. An unusual case of indignation.

" . . . Guttadauria Turns himself In"

Article by Charles Gasprino and Susanne Craig, *WSJ*, February 11, 2002, p. C1.

"Gurus of Growth Stocks Are Stepping Aside . . . ."

"Poor returns since the tech-stock bubble burst in March 2000 have caught up to more than a dozen growth-investing luminaries as mutual-fund managers. Just since the start of the year, three well-known growth-stock-pickers—AIM Weingartern manager Jon Schoolar; Janus Enterprise Fund's Jim Goff; and Charles 'Chip' Morris, manager of T. Rowe Price Science & technology Fund—disclosed they will step away from their portfolios." (**Emphasis** removed.)

Homan W. Jenkins Jr., *WSJ*, February 13, 2002., p. A 21.

"2,467 Listed Companies Suspected of Cooking Books!"

Headline, *Martin Weiss' Safe Money Report*, February 2002, p. 1.

Mutual Fund Holdings In February

"Stock, bond, and money market mutual funds hold $6.97 trillion in assets. In 1980, that figure was $134.8 billion. 52% of U. S. households—an estimated 93.3 million—own the majority of these assets. And 50% of these assets are still in stock funds; the peak level was 59% in December 1999."

"A market that's Clean, Sober, and Disappointing," by E. S. Browning, WSJ, February 19, 2002., p. C1.

Some Investors Are Angry

"A new American social contract arose in the past decade as millions tied their future to the stock market. They exchanged their sweat equity from working 10-and 12-hour days for options, bonuses, and 401(k)s that tracked their own companies' stock and the market in general. It was a high-risk, high-reward deal promoted widely in the era by corporate executives. The idea—a good one—was for the economy to grow more rapidly as rising stock prices generated higher capital investment, greater productivity, more jobs, and bigger incomes.

"The betrayal that class now feels comes not from the two-year bear market that followed the booming '90s nor the bursting of the tech bubble. Until Enron, most people waited patiently for the business cycle to turn up, as it always does. What enraged investors was the revelation that Enron executives and other corporate execs had stacked the deck against them and played by a separate set of rules."

"Editorials: The Wrath Of The Investor Class," *BusinessWeek*, February 25, 2002. p. 150.

Edit. It is simply amazing that these expositors of big business are not using this occasion to blame at least some of it on government dishonesty. Instead, they tell the unhappy investors to hold still and wait until the business cycle turns up again.

Housing Market Up

"Much of the credit for today's buoyant housing market, of course, belongs to Alan Greenspan's interest-rate cuts. Now, with signs that rates may soon start trending higher, a key question is whether housing will falter in the months ahead. Zandi [Mark M Zandi of Economy.com] thinks any weakness will be limited. Morris [Ian Morris of HSBC Securities, Inc.— economist], however, notes that strong price rises could turn into a bubble whose eventual bursting would undermine the recovery. If we're lucky, he says, 'home prices will simply lose some steam as lagging sectors of the economy finally kick in'"

"Home, Sweet Nest Egg: Housing prices offset falling stocks," by Gene Koretz, *Business Week*, February 11, 2002, p. 28.

Edit. Greenspan is now working on the housing market. This requires some watching.

Information Age Said To Speed Up Recovery

"TO SEE HOW rapid responses have changed the way the economy works, you need only look at last year's recession. The quick availability of information on slowing demand caused businesses to cut their inventory levels at an unprecedented rate in 2001. The draw-down in business inventories accounted for all of the contraction in real gross domestic product last year.

"At the same time, officials at the Fed and the White House reacted in record time to supply the economy with stimulus in the form of lower short-term interest rates and tax rebates. St. Louis Fed President William Poole noted in a Feb. 13 speech that the Fed began reacting before the recession began, partly because of anecdotal reports of falling loan demand. He said such reports allow the Fed 'to see what is going on in the economy almost as it is happening.'

"The rate cuts helped to push down mortgage rates, which fueled record home sales last year—a pickup that never occurred in any previous recession. The tax rebates gave consumers the money to keep spending in each quarter of this recession: another unprecedented occurrence. All told, the quicker response times were crucial in making this recession unlike any other in the postwar era.

"That alacrity should likewise make for a unique recovery."

"U.S.: A Slump And A Recovery In Internet Time," by James C. Cooper and Kathleen Madigan, *Business Week*, February 25, 2002, p. 33.

JULIUS H. BARNES, CHAIRMAN OF THE NATIONAL BUSINESS SURVEY CONFERENCE—NOVEMBER 2, 1930

"LAST FALL AMERICA WAS FACED WITH THE DISLOCATION OF ITS GREAT INDUSTRIAL AND FINANCIAL MACHINE. IT SEEMED AS IF THE PANIC SHOCK OF FALLING SECURITY VALUES COULD BE OFFSET BY A BETTER GENERAL KNOWLEDGE OF ACTUAL FACTS AND THEIR DISSEMINATION FROM RESPONSIBLE SOURCES. THAT WAS THE THEORY ON WHICH THE BUSINESS SURVEY CONFERENCE ADJUSTED ITSELF. THE CONFERENCE ASSUMED THAT WE WERE A REASONABLE, EDUCATED PEOPLE; THAT, INFORMED OF ACTUAL FACTS, BUSINESS JUDGMENTS WOULD CONDUCT INDUSTRY INTELLIGENTLY, AND THAT THE ORDERLY EVERY-DAY HABITS OF OUR PEOPLE COULD BE PRESERVED."[240]

Strong Dollar A Problem

"The amazingly strong performance of the U.S. dollar has helped to keep the trade deficit wide. Since the economy began to slow in early 2000, the broad trade-weighted dollar has appreciated 12%, to levels not seen since the superdollar of the mid-1980s . . . . Moreover, since the official start of the recession in March 2001, the greenback has gained nearly 3%, a decidedly atypical recession pattern . . . .

"In the short run, U.S. manufacturers, who now export about 20% of their output, will continue to get hammered by the strong dollar, which makes their goods less competitive in foreign markets. Plus, since the recovery in the rest of the world will lag behind the U. S. upturn, foreign demand will be slow to strengthen."

"There's A Cloud Inside that Silver Lining," *Business Week*, March 11, 2002, p. 23.

Edit. Wow! If the dollar goes down enough, maybe our goods will be cheap enough for us to become another Red China. So far, the Euro has dropped slightly from its January opening and Gold has only increased about $3 per ounce.

"The Calm at the Center Of a Roiling Economy"

"'The Web really was invented. Methods of business really did change. Computers allowed us to do new things,' says Robert Gordon, a Northwestern University economist who spent much of the decade criticizing cheerleaders of the Economy formerly known as new.

"'Consumption really did grow,' he adds. 'Lots of houses were built. Real wages rose at last. The bottom part of the income distribution rate really did decline much further than we had predicted was possible, partly because inflation was so tame.'

"And the pace of productivity growth, which had languished at about 1.4% a year for 20 years, really did quicken. Even after revisions, the government says productivity grew about 2.6% a year between 1995 and 2000.

"The key to the 2000s is determining how much of that productivity spurt was a serendipitous confluence of positive factors—a strong dollar, low energy prices, quiescent health-care inflation, soaring stock prices, the explosion of the Internet—and how much was lasting.

"Productivity pros—including Mr. Gordon, Harvard's Dale Jorgenson and Fed Chairman Alan Greenspan's Daniel Sichel and Stephen Oliner—say the underlying rate of productivity growth now is running at least 2% a year, and maybe higher.

"That's slower than in the late '90s, but still huge. Say productivity grows over this decade 0.6 percentage point faster than it did from 1973 to 1995. By 2010, that would be like getting an extra helping of all the goods and services in the state of Florida.

"First, productivity growth held up during the recession. In most recessions, companies can't cut work forces as fast as they cut production. Output per hour of work fell by about 0.6% on average during post-World war II recessions, UBS Warburg economists calculate. But since the U. S. economy began slowing in 2000, productivity growth has averaged 1.7%. In the fourth quarter, the government estimates, productivity grew at a heartening 3.5% annual rate.

"Airborne, Inc., shows how it is done. The company, parent of Airborne Express, delivered 82,755 packages in the fourth quarter, 2.4% fewer than in the same quarter of 2000. But the company cut its work force even faster. In all, it used 9.3% fewer hours of labor in the recent quarter, partly because of the first layoffs in the company's 55-year history.

"THE RESULT: Airborne shipped 4,218 parcels per employee in the fourth quarter, 7.6% more than it it did a year earlier. Imagine what will happen to productivity when volume picks up "Second, the U.S. economy, though still suffering, is proving so impressively resilient that there's muttering inside the Fed that this downturn doesn't qualify as a recession.

"Mr. Greenspan's hypothesis: Computers did it. 'Alas, the technology has not allowed us to see into the future any more clearly than we could previously,' he said last month. But thanks to information technology, businesses were quicker to realize that sales were faltering and inventories mounting, so they cut inventories much faster than in the past. The result: 'Contractions initially may be steeper, but . . . cyclical episodes'—Greenspan-speak for 'recession'—'should be less severe overall.'

"Third, companies such as Microsoft and Wal-Mart embody some of what went right in the 1990. Microsoft finally made a version of Windows that was more reliable and easier to use. Wal-Mart used information technology to become one of the world's most efficient retailers. They aren't standing still, and neither are their rivals. That bodes well for productivity advances."
David Wessell, WSJ, February 14, 2002, p. A1.

DR. JULIUS KLEIN—ASSISTANT SECRETARY OF COMMERCE—AUGUST 15, 1931
"RADIO WILL PROVE TO BE THE MOST IMPORTANT FACTOR IN BRINGING ABOUT THE RETURN OF NORMAL BUSINESS CONDITIONS AND PROSPERITY TIN THE UNITED STATES."[241]
Edit. Keep those inputs coming in, folks!

"Lessons Of Expansion Are helping Economy Beat Recession, Too"

"The U.S. economy appears to be steaming out of recession, confounding broadbased expectations of a languid recovery and benefitting from a new flexibility woven into its fabric over the last decade.

"The latest upbeat evidence came in two reports Friday: manufacturing surged in February, the first month that sector hasn't shrunk in a year and a half, and household spending rose smartly in January.

. . . .

"The U.S. Economy's ability so far to absorb those traumas and apparently escape with only a mild recession suggest that a fundamental change could be under way. At the heart of the argument is a belief that the economy has become more flexible. Manufacturers are quicker to adjust their inventories and labor force to sales fluctuations. Financial markets are better able to parcel out risk. And policy makers were faster to cut interest rates and taxes in an effort to prevent recession. That could mean that while the business cycle—the wave of alternating booms and busts, that mark of capitalist economies—isn't dead, it has become easier for business executives and economic officials to tame.

"'The recuperative powers of the U.S. economy . . . have been remarkable,' Federal Reserve Chairman Alan Greenspan told Congress last week. He attributed the performance to the economy's 'apparent increased flexibility and resiliency, especially in the financial markets and in companies' access to timelier data such as on sales and inventories."

Greg Ip, WSJ, March 4, 2002, p. A1.

CHARLES M. SCHWAB—OCTOBER 1931
"THE OVERLIQUIDATED PRICES OF MANY SECURITIES ARE A SIGN OF TOO SHORT PERSPECTIVE AND TOO EXCITABLE TEMPERAMENT."[242]

"Productivity Growth Surges Despite Recession"

"Non-farm labor productivity—a measure of output per hour worked—grew by an annualized 5.5% in the final three months of 2001, up from a previous estimate of 3.5%, the department said. For all of 2001, productivity grew by 1.9%, down from 3.3% in 2000 and 2.6% in the late 1990s, but still regarded by economists as an impressive performance in a year marked by a downturn."

Russell Gold, *WSJ*, March 8, 2002.

"Greenspan Brightens Outlook For Economy"

"'The recent evidence increasingly suggests that an economic expansion is already under way,' Mr. Greenspan said in an updated version of this semiannual economic report to Congress.

'We have seen encouraging signs in recent days that underlying trends in final demand are strengthening, although the dimensions of the pickup remain uncertain,' he said."

Article by Jacob Schlesinger and Joseph Rebello, *WSJ*, March 9, 2002.

ROGER BABSON—NOTED STATISTICAL ECONOMIST—MAY 9, 1931

"STATISTICS SHOW CLEARLY THAT BUSINESS REACHED ITS LOW POINT IN DECEMBER OF LAST YEAR. SINCE THEN THERE HAS BEEN A STEADY BUT CONSTANT IMPROVEMENT. EVERYTHING INDICATES FURTHER AND SAYS THAT 1931 SHOULD OFFER THE GREATEST OPPORTUNITIES OF ANY YEAR FOR GENERATIONS."[243]

E.H.H. SIMMONS—STOCK EXCHANGE PRESIDENT—MAY 6, 1931

"PAINFUL THOUGH PANICS AND DEPRESSION MAY BE, THEY ARE REALLY CURATIVE PROCESSES, AND HERALD THE ADVENT OF FIRMER FOUNDATIONS UPON WHICH TO CREATE FUTURE PERIODS OF PROSPERITY. THE RE-ESTABLISHMENT OF EQUILIBRIUM IN THE ECONOMIC WORLD AND THE REPAIR OF DAMAGES WROUGHT BY UNSETTLEMENT ARE BOUND TO TAKE TIME IF THE WORK IS TO BE LASTING."[244]

"How Real was This Recession?"

"With evidence now overwhelming that the recession has ended, some economists argue the decline in output was so mild it didn't qualify as a recession at all. Certainly, the millions of Americans who lost their jobs would beg to differ. But the fact that there is a debate shows how the economy has changed and suggests the meaning of recession may have to as well.

. . . .

" . . . The unemployment rate shot up 1.5 percentage points between March and December. Indeed, it was the plunge in employment that most prompted the nonprofit National Bureau of Economic Research in November to decide that a recession began last March. By that standard, the recession is probably also over. Employment rose in February by 66,000 jobs, the first increase since July, and the unemployment rate dropped for the second straight month, to 5.5% from 5.6%.

"But by the standards of economic output—the volume of goods and services—it is a tougher call. Judging by the latest government figures, this has been the only recession since World War II in which gross domestic product shrank for just one quarter, and it wasn't by much. The reason is productivity . . . . the entire U.S. economy managed to produce more per worker last year. That is rare: productivity almost always declines during recessions.

"This poses a challenge for the NBER, which first began tracking recessions in the 1920s. Its business cycle dating committee, made of six academics, defines a recession as 'a significant decline in activity spread across the economy, lasting more than a few months.' But what is activity? Is it input, such as employment, or is it output—GDP? 'We've never taken a stand on just what this word activity means because we didn't have to,' says committee Chairman Robert Hall, an economist at Stanford University.

. . . .

"True, the productivity growth during this recession may be an anomaly. Committee member Robert Godon of Northwestern University says it may reflect the lagged benefits of steep computer investment in the late 1990s, which is unlikely to be soon repeated. 'You can only invent the web once.' But if strong productivity growth does recur in future downturns, so may divergence between GDP and employment." Article by Greg Ip, *WSJ,* March 11, 2002, p. A1.

JULIAN H. BARNES, CHAIRMAN—NATIONAL BUSINESS SURVEY CONFERENCE—MARCH 30, 1930

"WE REALIZE . . . THAT WE HAVE NOT YET DONE A THOROUGHGOING JOB IN THE ACCUMULATION OF COMPREHENSIVE AND ACCURATE DATA CONCERNING BUSINESS IN GENERAL."[245]

"The Surprise . . . : First-half growth could be three or four times recent expectations"

"The U.S. economy truly has changed. If there is any doubt about that, look at the surprisingly mild 2001 recession—if that's what it really was. Last year's economic reliance defied expectations, even in the wake of the worst [blow] to the U.S. psyche since World War II. Now, a new and more exciting possibility is shaping up: The New Economy forces that helped mitigate the recession may well generate a stronger-than expected recovery.

"Don't expect a reprise of the late-1990s boom. But compared with forecasts of less than 1% growth for the first half that were common as recently as a month ago, economists are increasingly convinced that the US. could turn in a 3%-to-4% growth apart. 'Everything that could be going right for the recovery is going right,' says Ian C. Shepardson of High Frequency Economics."

Business Week, March 18, 2002, p. 12.

COLONEL LEONARD P. AYERS,—VICE PRESIDENT, CLEVELAND TRUST COMPANY—JANUARY 15, 1931

"IT MAY EVEN PROVE THAT THE WORST OF THE DEPRESSION HAS NOT YET BEEN REACHED, BUT, NEVERTHELESS, THE WEIGHT OF PROBABILITY IS DISTINCTLY IN FAVOR OF DURABLE IMPROVEMENT BEGINNING IN 1931"[246]

"Psst, The Recession Is Over"

"It is difficult to say whether the notion of recession continues to be useful in a world where growth is so high and stable that declines in activity are exceedingly unlikely . . . . Given the political importance of the formal declarations, policy debates would be better informed if we collectively agreed to rely upon these new models.

. . . .

"If such a policy were adopted immediately, we would all discover officially that the recession was most likely over earlier this year when we receive the data for first-quarter GDP about a month from now."

Article by Kevin Hasse, Scholar at American Enterprise Institute, *WSJ*, March 28, 2002.

ROY A. YOUNG—FEDERAL RESERVE BANK OF BOSTON—
FEBRUARY 1931
"THE BOTTOM HAS NOW BEEN REACHED." [247]

JULIUS KLEIN—ASSISTANT SECRETARY OF COMMERCE—MARCH
1931
"THE LONG DECLINE HAS AT LAST BEEN HALTED."[248]

"Fannie Mae To Disclose Insider Transactions"

"Fannie Mae, exempt from many securities laws enforced by the Securities and Exchange Commission, will soon begin disclosing information about insider transactions by executives, the chairman of the mortgage-finance company said."

"Fannie Mae will begin posting information about trades by senior managers and certain board members on its web site in April, said Franklin Raines, testifying before the House Financial Services Committee. The House committee is

considering bills to improve oversight of the U. S. accounting industry in the wake of the Enron Corp. collapse."
Article by Patrick Barta, *WSJ*, March 21, 2002.

"The Market Can't Soar Above The Economy Forever"

"The stock market, along with the economy, has rebounded from last year's lows. But by historical standards, it remains seriously overvalued. And there's little reason to believe that profits will grow at a rate that would justify rapidly rising stock values. That suggests the market could remain fairly flat in this decade . . . .

"Despite the bust in tech stocks, price-earnings ratios remain astronomical—about 22 for the standard & Poor's 500-stock index, based on expected earnings, and over 60 based on current earnings. The historic norm is around 14. And in the wake of Enron Corp., it has become clear that corporate earnings have been somewhat overstated, through such gimmicks as failing to count stock options as expenses."
Article by Robert Kuttner, *Business Week*, April 15, 2002, p. 26.
Edit. Sorting it out helps give the right answer.

"Recovery of 2002 May Be Stalling"

"The honeymoon appears to be over.

"After a roaring start in the year, fresh data suggest the U. S. economic recovery is stalling. Sales of existing homes dropped last month from their blistering pace of early 2002, and the government also reported yesterday that upward pressure on wages and benefits was at its lowest point in three years. On Wednesday, a Federal Reserve report showed that while the recovery is geographically broad, it is losing steam."
Article by Russell Gold, *WSJ*, April 22, 2002.

COL. LEONARD P. AYERS—AUGUST 15, 1931

"SUSTAINED IMPROVEMENT IN BUSINESS ACTIVITY IS TO BE
POSTPONED WHILE STILL FURTHER AND MORE EXTENSIVE
READJUSTMENTS ARE BEING EFFECTED BETWEEN WAGES, PRICES,
RENTS, PRODUCTION COSTS, DISTRIBUTION COSTS AND OVERHEAD
CHARGES."[249]

Euro And Gold Prices

On April 22, 2002, the Euro price is $.8896. It has moved
slightly down since the beginning of the year. The gold price
has increased to $303 per ounce. This last is a significant
move—about 9%.

"Bernie Bites the Dust"

"Bernie Ebbers blew it, and under broad pressure has
resigned as CEO of WorldCom. Now there is almost no chance
of saving his baby. With $28 billion in burdensome debt,
WorldCom is wavering on the brink of bankruptcy."
Editorial, *Wall Street Journal,* May 1, 2002.

Blue Chips Rebound

The market was down the morning of May 1st. The Nasdaq
sank so much that some analysts concluded that a bear market
had been reached. Then came the news that auto sales were
greater in April that had been expected. So, the Dow rebounds
230 points to finish at 10,059.63, up 113.41, or 1.14%, over
the previous day. As of now, the blue chips have risen a tiny
amount (0.4%) over the beginning of the year.

The Standard & Poor's 500 gains 0.89%, or 9.54 points, to
finish at 1,086.46. This means that they have lost 5% this year.
The Nasdaq recovers somewhat, but still finishes off 10.70 points
at 1,677.52, a decrease of 14% from the year's start.[250]

On May 8, The Fed Decides
To Leave Interest Rates Alone[251]

Edit. Maybe they are holding back to find out whether or not the market will straighten itself out soon.

Publication Still Sees Bull Market Ahead

"A bull market cannot achieve lift-off until the Fed restores liquidity to the economy. Based on current liquidity, the new bull market liftoff will be impressive and very profitable. Historically, bull markets begin in January, August or October. Better than expected second—quarter corporate profits (to be released in July) could produce an August bull market lift-off.

"The other possibility is an October lift-off that would be produced by faster-than-expected third-quarter economic growth."

"Liquidity Is At Record Levels And Still Rising," *The Wall Street Digest,* July 2002, p. 1.

Edit. That's right, Greenspan. Get back to what you're proficient at—inflating and complaining about the government's deficit!

Major Corporate Mis-statements Besides Enron

Adelphia, a leading cable company admitted that its statements for 1999, 2000, and 2001 were inaccurate. It also admitted not reporting $2.3 billion in loan guarantees it had made on behalf of the family which controls the corporation.

Global Crossing, the telecom company, began exchanging network capacity with Enron, Qwest and other companies in 1999. This was outlined in a 1999 memo by the Arthur Anderson executive whom Global Crossing later hired as its executive vice-president for finance. The scheme allowed the company to overstate its profits by hundreds of millions of dollars by treating these swaps as revenue. At the same time, it recorded capacity which it had "acquired" from others as a capital expenditure. (This also resembles the M1 Sweeps discussed in the Appendix.). Qwest, another Arthur Anderson client which was involved in these swaps, is currently under investigation from the SEC, the FBI, and a U.S. Attorney.

Tyco, another large conglomerate, admitted in February 2001 that it had spent $3.8 billion in 1999 and 2000 on 400 acquisitions which it had not disclosed.

Xerox had to restate $6.4 billion in revenues for the period 1997-2000.[252]

"SEC Forces Executives To Swear By Their Numbers"

"Some of the nation's most powerful CEOs are being forced to sign on the dotted line.

"In a little-noticed move amid the din of corporate-accounting scandals, the Securities and Exchange Commission last week implemented an order that could have major implications—civil penalties or jail time—for errant chief executive officers and chief financial officers at the nation's biggest companies. It also could lead to a spate of financial restatements in the next few weeks as companies scramble to review their recent results.

"The new order requires CEOs and financial chiefs at companies with more than $1.2 billion in revenue last year to swear under oath in writing that the numbers in their companies' recent financial reports are correct. Companies must comply with the order at the time of their next SEC financial filling, which for most companies will be Aug. 14.

"This requirement, which applies to 947 companies, could expose corporate chieftains to civil changes of fraud, or to criminal charges of lying to the government or possibly perjury, if their companies' numbers turn out to be bogus, lawyers say. The SEC can't bring criminal charges itself, but regularly refers cases to the Justice Department for prosecution.

"Meanwhile, the SEC has proposed a rule that would apply to future filings and could require senior executives of all public companies to certify the accuracy of financial results. That proposal will be taken up by the agency after a comment period ends on Aug. 19."

Paul Beckett, *WSJ*, Friday, July 5, 2002., p. A3.

"Qwest faces Criminal Investigation"

Article by Deborah Solomon and Susan Pulliam. *WSJ*, July 5, 2002, p. A1.

"The Twin Deficits Are Back—And As Dangerous As Ever"

"A ballooning federal budget shortfall and a widening trade gap are towering, Godzilla-like, over the nascent recovery. These two deficits, if unchecked, could cause trouble for the financial markets, the U. S. dollar, monetary policy, and U.S. growth."

Article by James C. Cooper & Kathlene Madigan, *Business Week*, July 8, 2002, p. 29.

Edit. How the appraisal of this magazine has changed in a few months!

Business Week asks, "Can Trust Be Rebuilt?"

"Are we fools? Have we jeopardized our futures by buying into Corporate America's idea of a market-driven society only to be deceived by corrupt and unethical behavior on an unimaginable scale?

. . . .

" . . . That trust is now coming undone. It was one thing to see the blowup in dot-coms as an anomaly. Even Enron Corp. could be perceived as a rogue. But the daily drip of scandal is spreading to all parts of the corporate scene. At Tyco International Ltd., there are major accounting problems and its CEO is charged with cheating on sales taxes—even tampering with evidence. There's Merrill Lynch & Co., paying $100 million in fines for misleading investors. People scratch their heads at mainstream companies such as Stanley Works trying to evade taxes by setting up sham headquarters in Bermuda. (Ordinary taxpayers know they must make up the shortfall to pay for homeland defense and education.) They see trust companies such as Merck & Co. booking questionable revenues. Finally there's Martha Stewart, the doyenne of domesticity, tarnished by allegations of insider trading and obstruction of justice, Martha Stewart!

"The latest financial bomb—is WorldCom Inc . . . .

"The danger is that if investors and consumers run, they will take down the economy and the dollar with them. A growing buyers' strike in the stock market, the flight of money into housing, and the rising price of gold all indicate that the early stages of a panic may be building.

"The timing couldn't be worse. The U.S. economy is showing signs of recovery. Momentum is building. Even corporate profits seem to be making a decent comeback. But the cloud over the creditability of all financial numbers is undermining investors' confidence in proclaimed earnings. Are they real or fake? By the fall, the economic upturn could be in full swing. But if the corporate crime wave leads people to pull back from the stock market, the economy could sink into a double-dip recession."

"What worries Americans is that they might find themselves stuck in a long period of stagnation, like the U.S. in the 1970s or Japan in the '90s . . . .

"Perhaps too scared. The U.S. is not Japan. Pessimism is so rife now that people are blinded to how much economic reform is under way. Japan was paralyzed for nearly 10 years, unable to cope with its problems. In America, an enormous cleansing has already started. Boards of directors are firing CEOs left and right. The turnover of chief executives has never been higher. The market is recalibrating, sending capital to companies with transparent, easy-to-understand financial statements while causing the rest to tank. Taking the hint, nearly 1,000 companies have restated their previous earnings, establishing more credible financial base lines. Pushing them along, the Justice Dept. has just given a death sentence to Arthur Anderson . . . .

. . . .

"To most Americans, this goes well beyond being an ethical issue. The high-growth '90s, which generated so many jobs, was based on financial innovation and deregulation. Millions accepted, for the first time in their lives, the conservative argument that they could control their own destinies. and prosper by tying their lives to the markets. They were convinced that they could manage the risk through better information and thus garner more of the profits as well.

"It worked. From 1995 to 2000, a New Economy delivered enormous prosperity to millions of people. Huge productivity gains were made, pushing up real wages and creating opportunities for mobility. Now, people are discovering that, in the bubble years, starting around 1999 or 2000, some CEOs began to fake this information and corrupt the markets. Checks and balances failed, and professional accountants, lawyers, and analysts became greedy. The truth is that markets can work only if information is honest, rules of the games are clear, and people follow them. Realizing that this isn't the case today has left many Americans doubting their own futures and jeopardizing the future of the economy."

Article by Bruce Nussbaum, *Business Week*, July 8, 2002, p. 32-34.

Edit. Why shouldn't they run from people who tell them recovery is around the corner? Underlying all that was a false idea of prosperity, based upon misfortunes abroad and some phony government statistics at home, lifted up by certain genuine technological developments, and set in place by some muttering of low philosophical value about the new millennium. But more about that in the next chapter.

" . . . Return of Big Government?"

"President Bush's tongue-lashing of big business marks a swing of the American political pendulum away from a quarter-century of bipartisan deference to capitalists.

"' We will use the full weight of the law to expose and root out corruption,' Mr. Bush said yesterday to several hundred business leaders at the Regent Wall Street Hotel, once home to the New York Merchants Exchange. 'My administration will do everything in our power to end the days of cooking the books and shading the truth and breaking our laws.'"

Article by J. Cummings, J M. Schlesinger and M. Schroeder, *WSJ*, July 10, 2002, p. A1.

Edit. The "democratization of money" has failed, to be replaced by what—a Republican version of the old Democrat Party paternalism?

Shouldn't Same Standards Be Applied To Government As Business?

"During the late 1990s, when many of the corporate scandals now in the headlines were gestating, Washington, D.C., was awash in talk about the 'budget surplus.' . . .

"But the federal 'budget surplus' was an artifact of accounting fraud: It was created by raiding several so-called 'trust funds' (the largest being Social Security) that were arbitrarily designated 'off-budget.' Between September 1999 and September 2000, a period in which the political class engaged in frenzied discussions of divying up the 'surplus,' the gross federal debt rose by $23 billion. Translated into business terms, this means that the feds falsified corporate profits. On August 1st, agents of the same federal government that perpetuates such fraud arrested Scott Sullivan and David Myers, former financial officers with WorldCom accused of fraud and conspiracy for their role in allegedly hiding $3.8 billion in company expenses."

William Norman Grigg, *The New American*, August 26, 2002[253]

Federal Rules Made Accounting Scandals Possible

" . . . The real Scandal is that SEC rules permit the creative accounting, which enabled the companies to delay public recognition of their failures for several quarters . . . .

. . . .

"Previous reforms aimed at providing investors with more timely information about the profitability and financial condition of public companies. Thus began the focus of quarterly earnings.

"Other reforms tied executive compensation to performance as indicated by the company's stock price. Thus began the use of stock options for executive compensation . . . .

"Two more reforms completed the refocusing of executive attention to short-run performance as measured by share value. These two reforms were put in place in the early 1990s. One capped the amount of executive salary that could be deducted from taxable income at $1 million. Cash compensation larger than $1 million had to be justified by performance or paid out of after-tax profits . . . .

"The other, and final, foundation stone for the current scandals was put in place by the SEC when that agency changed Rule 16b. Previously, executives who exercised their stock options were required to purchase the stock at the option price and hold it for six months before selling. The SEC changed the rule and permitted executives to sell the stock the minute they exercised their options, thus eliminating the executives' exposure to the market.

"These 'reforms' could not have been better designed to produce the current crop of accounting scandals. Reforms tied executives' compensation to short-run stock price, not the health of the company, and SEC rules replaced accounting rules. Misleading accounting is permissible as long as companies and their accountants stay within the SEC rules.

"The old accounting principles were designed to give an accurate picture of financial health. The new rule-based system only requires compliance with rules. As we have again learned, it is possible to comply with the government's rules and still give a misleading picture."

Paul Craig Roberts[254]

Bush Blames Wild Decade

On July 15, President Bush says that the recent contagion is the "hangover we now have as a result of the financial binge" America went through during the 90s. "There was endless profit, there was no tomorrow when it came to stock markets and corporate profits. And now we're suffering a hangover for that binge."

The President says that a 6 percent 1ˢᵗ quarter productivity growth rate is "a pretty good sign that the foundations for growth is there.

"I believe there is a better day right around the corner for all Americans." [255]

FORMER PRESIDENT CALVIN COOLIDGE—JANUARY 20, 1931

"THE COUNTRY IS NOT IN GOOD CONDITION."[256]

NEWS DISPATCH FROM WASHINGTON—JANUARY 21, 1930

"DEFINITE SIGNS THAT BUSINESS AND INDUSTRY HAVE TURNED THE CORNER FROM THE TEMPORARY PERIOD THAT FOLLOWED DEFLATION OF THE SPECULATIVE MARKET WERE SEEN TODAY BY PRESIDENT HOOVER."[257]

Clinton Says Republicans Stopped Reforms

Mr. Clinton blames Republicans for overriding his veto of a 1995 security bill which would have made it more difficult for disappointed stockholders to sue corporations.[258] [See Chapter V].

"The Boom Behind The Bubble"

"The combination of boom followed by bust has left America better off than when it started. That may seem like cold comfort to investors who can't forget the money they've lost in the market over the past couple of years. But the evidence supports the basic premise underlying the New Economy—that investment in information technology, combined with corporate restructuring, can substantially boost productivity and economic performance. Moreover, it suggests that the U.S. economy should be capable of another round of solid growth.

"All this, of course, assumes that the stock market and the economy have bottomed out, which is no sure thing. Another terrorist attack or the discovery of major financial problems at more big companies could send the market into another tailspin. And the economy, while clearly recovering, is vulnerable to a double-dip: Consumer confidence was off 3.5% in June, there's scant evidence yet of a sustained recovery in the labor market, and the dollar is down sharply against the yen and euro.

. . . .

"For now, though, it appears that the U.S. is coming out of its investment boom in far better shape than Japan did. Despite the financial markets' dips and spikes, about half of the stocks in the S&P 500 have produced average annual returns in excess of 10% since the beginning of 1995. Even the tech-heavy Nasdaq turned in an annual return of 8.3% over that stretch.

"Out in the real world, moreover, the economy is doing just fine. Inflation-adjusted wages are up 13% over the past seven years—the best jump in three decades and boon for most Americans. Inflation, outside of food and energy, is only 2.5%, down from 2.9% in 1995. And productivity growth over the past three years is still running at a 3.1% rate—far faster than the 1.5% seen in the first half of the 1990s and the entire 1980s." Michael J:. Mandel, *Business Week*, July 15, 2002, pp. 38-39.

RICHARD WHITNEY—STOCK EXCHANGE PRESIDENT—
SEPTEMBER 10, 1930
"WITH THE EXCEPTION OF THE DIFFICULTIES THAT HAVE ARISEN AS A RESULT OF THE DRASTIC DEFLATION OF COMMODITY PRICES, THE BUSINESS HORIZON IS CLEAR . . . . WE ALL KNOW THAT THE PRESENT PERIOD CANNOT LONG ENDURE."[259]

Greenspan Sees Good Future

On July 16, Greenspan to the Senate: "To sum up, the U.S. economy has confronted very significant challenges over the past year or so. Those problems, however, led to only a relatively brief and mild downturn in economic activity, reflecting the underlying strength and increased resiliency that the economy has achieved in recent years."[260]

Edit. Massive bankruptcies and wholesale unemployment are mild. Check!

"U. S. Is Unlikely to Prop Up Dollar"

"The dollar's slide is raising a question that keeps markets on edge: Will the U. S. enlist Japan and Europe in a joint effort to defend the greenback?

. . . .

"The Bush administration . . . doesn't appear inclined to give it a try. 'The administration believes this is market-determined rate, and intervention is unlikely to have substantial effect,' said Massachusetts Institute of Technology economist Kristin Forbes, a former Bush Treasury official."

Article by Michael M. Phillips, *WSJ,* July 23, 2002, p. A2.

Edit. Just a few months ago, some experts were complaining that the dollar was still too high. Now, the dollar is drifting downward, just like it was in 1995. This time, however, the Government is not likely to use the stock market to prop up the dollar. What will they do?

Euro and Gold Prices

On July 23, 2002, the Euro price moves to $.9818. It is now almost at parity with the dollar, an increase in value against the dollar of about 9% over January. The price of gold has grown to $312.70 per ounce, or 11 %.

Senator Corzine's Firm Named In Stock Scheme

Before May 1999, when he resigned to run for the U. S. Senate from New Jersey, Mr. Corzine was chairman of Goldman & Sachs & Co.; this was also the firm of which Mr. Rubin was co-chairman before he joined the Clinton Administration.

Goldman Sachs is the subject of a class action suit by a former broker who complained to the Securities and Exchange Commission that Goldman Sachs had a scheme to compel unwitting investors to pay unnaturally high prices for certain stocks.

But Nicholas Maier, who was syndicate manager of Cramer & Co. from 1996 to 1998, told SEC investigators that Goldman Sachs had on several occasions forced him to purchase stocks at inflated prices if he wished to buy shares of an IPO (initial public offering).

"Goldman, from what I witnessed, they were the worst perpetrator," said Mr. Maier. "They totally fueled the bubble. And it's specifically that kind of behavior that has caused the market crash. They built these stocks upon an illegal foundation—manipulating up, and ultimately, it really was the small person who ended up buying in."

Senator Corzine has denied knowing anything about it.[261]

RICHARD WHITNEY—N. Y.S.E. PRESIDENT—SEPTEMBER 17, 1931
"THERE HAVE BEEN TOO MANY SUAVE STATEMENTS THAT REASSURE NOBODY, TOO MANY EMPTY PLATITUDES, TOO GREAT A LACK OF FRANKNESS AND REALISM, TOO MUCH OF TRYING TO WHISTLE IN THE GRAVEYARD AT MIDNIGHT"[262] (MR. WHITNEY LATER WENT TO PRISON FOR EMBEZZLEMENT—HE IS REPORTED TO HAVE BEEN A MODEL PRISONER.)[263]

WSJ Calculates Stock Losses Since Market High

According to their study, as of 7/19/02, the Dow has dropped 31.6% from its high on 1/14/00; the Nasdaq, by 73.9%; the S&P 500 by 48.2%.[264]

But of course, there will be another bear market rally and then maybe another or so until it is all over.

WorldCom Files For Bankruptcy

On July 21, WorldCom, the nation's second largest long-distance telephone company with over 20 million customers, filed for Chapter 11. It is the largest bankruptcy to date in American history.[265]

Nasdaq Suffers Biggest Percentage Loss Of Year

On July 23, the Nasdaq lost 4.18% to close at 1,229.05. The next day, *The Wall Street Journal* comments that this is below what it was on December 5, 1996, the day that Greenspan uttered his famous remarks about "irrational exuberance." The Dow also fell, losing 1.06% to close at 7,702.34. Says Andy Brooks, head of trading at Baltimore Mutual Fund, "It is like having a wounded animal in the herd and the others picking on it. They just won't let up."[266]

Another Bear Market Rally

On July 29ᵗʰ, the Dow concludes the most powerful rally since 1933, skyrocketing 447.19 points to 8,711.88. Despite this, it is still down—nearly 26%—from its record high of 11,723 in January 2000. The dollar also gains against the Euro and the Yen.[267]

Edit. Is the plunge protection group still in operation? Space does not permit an investigation of this question.

"Citygroup Deals Helped Enron Disguise Its Debts as Trades"

"Investigators want to determine whether Enron would have been able to defraud investors if not for the willing participation of Wall Street. The documents amount to the most in-depth evidence yet of the extent to which Citigroup, the nation's largest financial institution, helped Enron disguise debt of its balance sheet through some of the complex financial accounting arrangements at the Houston energy company."

Headline story by J. and P.Beckett, *WSJ*, July 22, p. A1.

Democrats Say They Won't Call Rubin

On July 24, Senate Democrats investigating Enron's collapse say they do not intend to question Robert Rubin, the former Clinton secretary of the Treasury. "I don't" is the answer of Senator Joe Lieberman, Chairman of the Governmental Affairs Committee when queried. Senator Carl Levin of Michigan, chairman of the subcommittee investigating Enron's internal practices was asked the same question. He replies that he "probably" would call the chief executive officers of Citigroup and J.P. Morgan, but not Mr. Rubin, because "I'd rather go to the top."

Mr. Rubin is chairman of Citigroup's executive committee. The previous November, he contacted the Bush Administration for support with the credit-rating agencies on behalf of Enron; these agencies were going to downgrade Enron.[268]

" . . . Home-Equity Lending . . . [At] Record Levels . . . ."

"Americans are turning their houses into checkbooks at an unprecedented rate, allowing them to keep spending freely but raising questions about whether they're taking on too much debt.

"The dollar value of home-equity loans and lines of credit is expected to hit a record $1 trillion this year—a 20% increase from last year, according to SMR Research Corp, a market-research firm. An estimated 12 million Americans now have such loans, also a record.

"Lenders have fueled the borrowing binge by making it remarkably easy to get such loans, through speedy approvals and tantalizing teaser rates. They also make it easy to spend the money: While banks have long issued checkbooks tied to their home-equity lines, some are also giving borrowers credit cards."

Ruth Simon, *WSJ*, July 18, 2002, p. D1.

"U.S. assets lose their allure as nervous investors seek security"

"Global capital flows suggest that the U.S. is losing its allure as an investment location but that investors remain reluctant to ditch U.S. assets altogether."

"The fall of the dollar over recent weeks could be interpreted as a sign that capital has been flowing out of U.S. markets. In fact, it is not necessary for investors to sell U.S. assets for the dollar to go down. The ballooning U.S. current account deficit, which is expected to reach Dollars 450 bn this year, means that the US needs to attract a net Dollars 1.7bn every working day just to prevent the dollar from falling.

"Scepticism over U.S. accounting standards and worries over U.S. equity valuations are making this increasingly difficult."

"There is no sign of an exodus from U.S. assets or of panic, but the U.S. has been finding it progressively harder to attract the funds necessary to fund the current account deficit,' said Michael Lewis, senior economist at Deutsche Bank in London. 'The result is that the dollar has had to move lower to attract the necessary overseas investment.'"

Article by Christopher Swann, *Financial Times,* July 18, 2002, p. 20.

Edit. If enough foreign investors desert the Dollar, its value will plummet.

Some Homeowners Have become Renters

"Convinced the housing market is a bubble about to pop, a number of homeowners are deciding to cash out—and stay out, instead of buying new homes, they are renting until prices fall back."

Article, *WSJ,* July 23.[269]

"PRICE-EARNINGS PANDEMONIUM"

"The bear market has brought p-e earnings back to earth. But if companies start expensing options, earnings could drop by roughly 20%, driving p-es back up."

Headline, *Newsweek,* July 29, 2002

Edit. If this were done, the earnings of profit making companies like Microsoft would go down 21%, that of IBM, 16%, Intel, 20%, J.P. Morgan, 36%.

"PROFOUND EFFECT ON ECONOMY SEEN IN A WAR ON IRAQ"

"An American Attack on Iraq could profoundly affect the American economy, because the United States would have to pay most of the cost and bear the brunt of any oil price shock or other market disruptions."

Article by Patrick E. Tyler and Richard W. Stevenson, *New York Times,* July 30, 2002, p. A1

PETER ERICKSON

Commerce Department Admits
Big Errors in 1998 through 2000

According to the report, corporate profits of non-financial firms from current production—profits before tax—had to be revised downwards from the last quarter of 1998 through the third quarter of 2000. This is a significant part of the bubble market which began in January 1996.

These were carefully analyzed by Columnist Robert Novak. He found that the Clinton administration had grossly inflated corporate earnings as reported by the Commerce Department's Bureau of Economic Analysis (BEA) in 1999 and 2000. He also found that they got the direction of corporate earnings wrong. They were in a decline, not an advance. Below is a chart prepared by *Human Events* newspaper, summarizing his findings.[270] They speak for themselves.

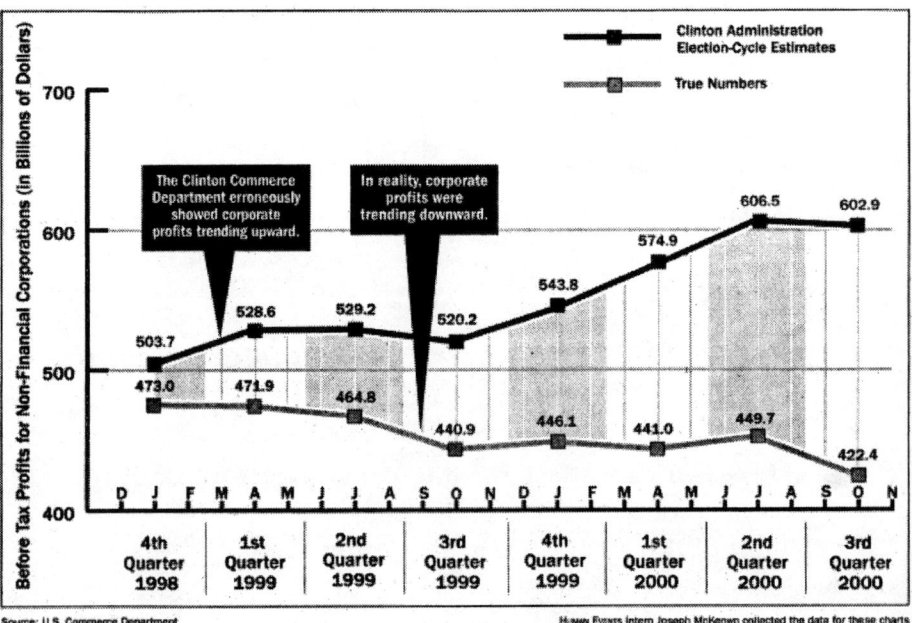

"Saudi moves to shift money out of US raise concerns"

"Moves by Saudi investors to shift tens of billions of dollars out of the US added to market concerns that global fund managers are becoming increasingly disenchanted with the US, analysts said yesterday.

"Most banks, however, emphasized the relatively low level of Saudi holdings of US assets, between Dollars 400 bn and Dollars 600bn according to one estimate, or equivalent to less than 1 percent of total outstanding US assets."

Julie Earle and James Politi, *The London Financial Times*, August 22, 2002, p. 8.

Edit. Whew! They've only started and if they did take it all out, U.S. assets financial assets would still be ninety nine percent intact.

"The Housing Bubble Loses Some Air"

Headline story in *WSJ* article by Motoko Rich, August 1, 2002, p. D1. Subtitle is: "Demand for High-end Homes Drops in Markets that Once Sizzled; a 20-Month Supply in Atlanta."

"Strong July home sales buttress shaky economy"

"Purchases of new homes reach record levels, sparked by low interest rates and a solid appreciation in housing values. Sales of new homes in July climbed to a seasonally adjusted annual rate of 1.02 million, a record monthly sales pace and a 6.7 percent increase from June's level, the Commerce department reported Monday.

"Meanwhile, sales of existing homes—the biggest slice of the housing market—rebounded in July, rising 4.5 percent from the previous month to a rate of 5.33 million units, according to the National Association of Realtors.

"One of the bright spots of the spotty economic recovery has been the housing market, which performed well even during last year's recession, due largely to low mortgage rates."

Article by Jeannine Aversa, "Strong July home Sales buttress shaky economy," *The Associated Press* in *The Oregonian*, August 27, 2002, p. B1.

Edit. The reader may recall that in its March 26, 2001, issue in which it belittled the bear market, Time Magazine said that the U.S. economy will not sink like Japan's, because their bubble was based on real estate. Now, it is hoped that the U.S. market will be held up by home sales. What gives?

"Data Show Growing Trend Toward Permanent Layoffs"

"'These numbers show a relatively high level of job displacement even when the unemployment rate was very low,' said Ryan Helwig, the economist at the Bureau of Labor Statistics who wrote the latest job displacement report. It is based on a survey every two years of 60,000 households."

Article by Louis Uchitell, *NYT*, August 22, 2002, p. 9.

"In Uneasy Times, Consumers Boost a Fragile U.S. Economy"

"If Sept. 11 seemed to signal the American way of life was under attack, American-style spending seemed the proper response: 'The American economy will be open for business,' President Bush assured the nation the evening of Sept. 11. General Motors Corp., kicking off a campaign of no-interest financing on new cars, urged consumers to 'Keep America Rolling.'

"They did—and have continued to do so in the year since.The latest evidence came Friday [Aug. 30], when the Commerce Department reported consumers had increased their spending by 1% in July, the largest advance in nine months . . . .

"The vital question now is whether consumers—whose spending accounts for two-thirds of all U.S. economic activity— will continue shelling out for cars, appliances, furniture and services. As businesses remain reluctant to increase their expenditures, and economic trouble abroad endangers U.S. exports, consumers are more critical than usual to the economy."

"Last fall, consumer purchases saved the U.S. economy from deep recession. The Federal Reserve played a big role by cutting short-term interest rates to a 41-year low. So did the Bush administration and Congress with a tax cut begun last summer with $300 rebate checks and continued with reduced tax withholdings earlier this year. Auto makers and retailers helped with sharp discounts."

Article by Greg Ip and Russell Gold, *W S J*, September 3, 2002, pp. A1-A8.

Edit. And so, the maintenance of the fragile U.S. economy is dependent upon those consumers who did not invest heavily in the stock market. But what about their jobs? Much of that is dependent upon manufacturing, which is now under assault from low-cost foreign competition.

"Imports Hammer Furniture Makers"

"American consumers are buying homes at a record pace this year. However, one industry that historically has benefitted from using home sales—domestic manufacturing—is instead struggling against a wave of imports. Some economists believe the industry's plight partly explains why U.S. manufacturing has faltered even though consumer spending has shown surprising resilience.

. . . .

"According to research by UBS Warburg analyst Margaret Whelan, furniture imports to the U. S. as of the second quarter were 71% higher than they were in 1999. Ms Whelan estimates that furniture imports accounted for more than 40% of the U.S. market. The growth has been especially strong in wood and metal furniture—mainly tables, bedroom furniture, chairs and cabinets. In that sector, imports are up nearly 80% from three years ago, while shipments from domestic manufacturers are down 11%. U.S. makers of upholstered furniture such as sofas, including companies such as La-Z-Boy Inc. of Monroe, Mich., still dominate their market, though imports are rising in that sector, too.

. . . .

"Take Lacquer Craft Manufacturing Co., one of China's biggest furniture exporters. Set up in 1992 in the southern Chinese city of Dongguan by investors from Taiwan, Lacquer Craft describes itself as an 'aircraft carrier for wood furniture.' In other words, it uses China as an export platform to penetrate markets abroad. The company reported $200 million in sales last year—kitchen cabinets, bedroom wardrobes, and other products—most going to the U. S., according to a Lacquer Craft executive.

"With labor costs one-tenth of what they are in Taiwan, Lacquer Craft is expanding aggressively. To add to its manufacturing heft, the company is building a giant new factory, its second in China, outside Shanghai. To bolster U.S. sales, it agreed in June of last year to purchase Universal Furniture Ltd., a retail and distribution unit of furniture maker Lifestyle Furnishing International of High Point, N.C."

Article by Jon E. Hilsenrath and Peter Wonnacott, *WSJ*, September 20, 2002, p. A2.

Edit. The very housing boom on which is to reputed to be holding up prosperity is helping someone knock the legs from under the U. S. furniture-making industry. How can American workers long compete against $100 a month labor housed in dormitories using modern technology?

How Freddie Mac's House Stands"

"But at a time when Fannie Mae is scrambling to recover from a flood of mortgage refinancings, Freddie Mac appears to be doing fine, in part because of its more aggressive use of derivatives and other hedging instruments. Although both companies use such instruments to protect against rare market upheavals—like today's extraordinary low-interest environment—Freddie Mac uses more of them, theoretically giving it more protection."
Article by Patrick Barta, *WSJ*, October 1, 2002, p. C1.

Edit. Derivatives are highly leveraged investments. In the beginning, they were used to insure the other side of large stock, bond, and interest rate positions. Today, they are highly leveraged speculative day-trading instruments, used by the major banks and hedge funds in order to get quick profits.[271] The Long Term Capital Management fiasco discussed earlier in which Greenspan's Fed intervened was a case where one of these operations failed spectacularly. Another one was the collapse of the Barings Bank in England in the late nineties. Enron was also a big derivative player. Many commentators have expressed dismay at the huge amount of derivatives holding up the U. S. financial system. What would happen to the vaunted real estate industry if these derivatives start evaporating?

Here are some of Chairman Greenspan's thoughts on this question:
" . . . the threat of legal damage awards provides dealers with strong incentives to avoid misconduct. A far more powerful incentive, however, is the fear of loss of the dealer's good reputation, without which it cannot compete effectively, regardless of its financial strength or financial engineering capabilities. "[272]

But if enough speculators are willing to take the chance . . . .

"Slowing Activity In Manufacturing Imperils Recovery "

"The manufacturing sector shrank in September for the first time in eight months while car and chain-store sales weakened sharply, suggesting the economic recovery has stalled."

. . . .

"The ultimate path for manufacturing production depends on consumer demand, and those signs aren't good. Total car sales fell to an annual rate of 16.3 million vehicles in September from the 18-million-plus sales rate of the previous two months as dealers sold out of the heavily discounted 2002 models.

"Also in the past few weeks, chain-store sales have fallen sharply, according to several surveys. Sales warnings are troubling because consumer spending has been the economy's bulwark, and discounters such as Target Corp. and Wal-Mark Stores, Inc., both of whom said sales were weaker than expected in September, have been benefitting disproportionately from that. The weakness in chain-stores is especially striking, given how easy it should have been to beat sales of a year ago, which were depressed by the Sept. 11 terrorist attacks.

Article by Greg Ip, *WSJ*, October 2, 2002

"Surge in Exports From China Jolts Global Industry,"

"Today, there are few things in the global marketplace that aren't made in China. Many foreign manufacturers find they must either produce in China or export their purchases from China. The country has become the world's factory floor, with an output so massive and wide—ranging that it exerts deflationary pressure around the globe on everything from textiles to TVs, mobile phones to mushrooms.

"'China's rise as a manufacturing base is going to have the same kind of impact on the world that the industrialization of the U.S. had, perhaps even bigger,' says Any Xie, an economist with Morgan Stanley in Hong Kong."

Article by Karby Leggett, *W S J*," October 10, 2002, p. A1

Edit: Orange China makes 20 % of the refrigerators sold throughout the world, 20% of the washing machines sold throughout the world,

30% of the air conditioners, and 50% of the cameras. They are on the heels of the U. S., Germany, and Japan. (The reason for calling it "Orange China," instead of "Red China" is that one of the men who was recently appointed to the highest level said that China is no longer red, but actually a shade of orange).

U. S. Pension Funds Grossly Underfinanced

"The Pension Benefit Guaranty Corp. (PBGC) revealed in July that U.S. corporate pension plans were underfunded by $111 billion at the end of 2001—a staggering 425% increase from the previous year. To make matters worse, the agency testified to Congress that its own trust fund for bailing out failing pensions has declined 50% in the last 12 months.

"This problem is not in defined contribution plans, such as 401Ks. The problem is in traditional defined benefit plans, in which an employer promises a specific benefit to the employees at retirement. The trouble is that thousands of U.S. businesses don't have enough money set aside to fulfill those obligations. The shortfall, just among 234 companies in the S&P 500, is in excess of $78 billion. At some point in the not-too-distant future, that $78 billion is going to have to come out of earnings— albeit sharply declining earnings.

"With stocks selling at about 34 times earnings, that means market caps for those companies could get hit for 34 times $78 billion or $2.65 trillion (i.e., that's how much could come off those companies' stock market values). Just a few examples illustrate the point: General Motors owes its pension fund $12.7 billion (its stock has crashed over 35% since May); Delta Airlines owes $2.4 billion to its pension fund (its stock has crashed 55% over the past six months); Delphi owes its pension fund $2.4 billion (its stock crashed 43.5% from May to August); Goodyear, Exxon, and other major companies also have severe pension shortfalls." (Emphasis removed).

The McAlvany Intelligence Advisor, November 2002, pp. 6-7.

Edit. Joe and Josephine Six-Pack may have escaped the initial wrath of the bear by staying out of stocks, but they aren't safe, either. The behavior of their supposedly wiser bosses will bring some of them down.

Gross National Debt Boils

During the period 09/30/01 to 09/30/02, the public debt expands by about $421 billion. This is considerably more than the huge increase of about $133 billion in the period 09/30/00 to 09/30/01 over the period preceding it. As of September 30, 2002, it stands at $6,228,235,965,597.16.[273]

"U. S. Carmakers Losing Ground To Imports, Despite Deals"

"The billions of dollars that General Motors, Ford, and Chrysler have spent during the last year on the most generous sales incentives in automotive history have not bought them what they wanted: a bigger share of the market."
Article by Micheline Maynard, *NYT*, October 10, 2002, p. C1.
Edit: The three major U. S. automobile manufacturers have been easing payment terms and even offering cash backs in a frantic effort to keep up sales. Yet, the slide continues. Which brings up the question: how much longer can the American consumer who is drowning in debt continue to take advantage of these special offers?

Home Buyers Becoming Mortgaged To Hilt

"Over the past 10 years, Americans have been refinancing to draw out more and more the equity in their homes—to pay for vacations, boats, second homes, college tuition, etc.
"So now the reality is that millions of American homemakers have less than 10% equity in their homes. So even a small decline in home values could wipe out all their equity . . . .
"A modest $500,000 home falling to $450,000 is not an

extreme drop. It's a very modest 10%. But a modest drop in home prices like that could wipe out all the equity in the homes of millions of Americans.

"And in many cases, Americans have actually taken out loans exceeding the equity in their homes—105%, 110%, even 125% loans. That's mind-blowing. Leverage like this is the clearest sign of a bubble I've ever seen.

"You're going to see a lot more defaults when real estate prices start to tumble. In the 1930s when real estate prices collapsed, the market price of many properties ended up lower than the mortgages . . . .

"Homeowners (and Owners of apartment buildings) often left a note inside their abandoned property for the lien holders: 'Goodbye mortgage company, nice knowing you. Here's the key.'

That's why real estate prices crashed as much as 90% going into 1932 . . . ."

Martin D. Weiss, Ph D., November 20, 2002, *martin_weiss2@weissinc.com*

Edit. But why worry? We have Chairman Greenspan's words on this matter: "While home prices do on occasion decline, large declines are rare; the general experience of homeowners is a modest, but persistent rise in home values that is perceived to be largely permanent. This experience contrasts markedly from volatile and often-ephemeral gains in stock market wealth . . . . Lowering the cost of home ownership is particularly important for increasing homeownership rates among young adults."[274] These were his words in 1999. Isn't he taking the risk of triggering one of those rare large declines by continuing to lower the price of homeownership?

"U. S. Trade Gap Widens"

"A surge in imports showed that domestic spending remained brisk in August despite the sluggish economy, but the trade deficit widened to a record as exports sagged.

"The August trade deficit swelled to $38.46 billion as record amounts of food, clothes and industrial goods poured in.

Analysts attributed some of the surge to a rush by shippers to get goods into the country before the threatened closure of West Coast ports.

"Exports, meantime, fell 1.3% from the July level to $81.86 billion, as economies overseas remained sluggish. August's export slump covered a wide range of products, but vehicles and auto parts led the plunge, falling 4% from July to $6.8 billion."

Headline of article by Neil King Jr. and Greg Ip, WSJ, October 21, 2002, p. A2.

Edit. This is the tell-tale sign of a nation which entered the 20th century as both the largest manufacturing and agricultural nation entering the new one with the planet's biggest trade deficit. Unless something is done to energize its basic industry, it will continue for a while as a wasting battery. And, sometimes after that, a hulk for salvagers to pick at.

"Stagnation in Germany and Japan, unsustainable imbalances in the US . . . will recovery take hold?"

"If the US Current account deficit were to continue at 5 per cent of GDP, net external liabilities would be above 50 percent of GDP in less than five years . . . ."

Article in *Financial Times*, December 18, 2002, p. 11.

Euro And Gold Prices

On December 31, 2002, the Euro price now exceeds the dollar; it stands at $1.05, an increase over its opening January price of about 14%. The gold price is now $347.46, an increase of about 20%.

Home Values And Stock Market Losses

"Home values have not made up for stock market losses. According to the Federal Reserve, home values added $108.8

billion to household wealth in the third quarter. But in the same period, declines in stocks took away $1.811 TRILLION."

Safe Money e-news, December 7, 2002 *edna@weissinc.com>*

Edit. Non-military capital goods orders fell 12.6% in September from the year previous. Consumer borrowing, which has been holding up the economy, is weakening.

"Putting the stock market in perspective"

"Relative to their historic peaks—11,723 for the Dow (January 2000); 1,527 for the S&P 500 (March 2000); and 5,048 for the Nasdaq (March 2000)—by year-end the stock indices had collapsed by 28.8 percent (the Dow), 42.4 percent (S&P 500) and 73.5 percent (Nasdaq). By December 31, the broadest-based stock index, the Wilshire 5000, had dropped 43 percent since its peak. That represents a $7.4 trillion loss of wealth. By way of perspective, that staggering amount is more than twice the size of the national debt held by the public. And it exceeds $25,000 for each man, woman and child in the nation."

Editorial, *The Washington Times—National Weekly Edition,* January 13-19, 2003

But . . .

"As depressing as it is to review the devastation wrought by the three-year-old bear market . . . [since] the greatest bull market began on August 13, 1982 . . . in the wake of a three-year-old bear market, the Dow had increased by nearly 1,000 percent, while both the S&P 500 and the Nasdaq reflected advances of about 7,500 percent. It's all a matter of perspective."

Same editorial as above.

Edit. Which is it, a balanced situation or a legitimate bull market that got replaced by a hissing fraud? For the answer, see the next chapter.

CHAPTER XIII

CONCLUSION

Much has happened since January of 2000 when *The Wall Street Journal* announced that the AOL-Time Warner merger had inaugurated an age which adults were supposed to believe in—"The Age of the Market." To paraphrase a remark made by the royal predecessor of the unfortunate Louis XVI of France, *after that the deluge.*

The common theory of boom and bust is that an excess of credit produces an excess of speculation, which in turn yields a collapse. This accounts for part of what had happened, but not all of it. Most of the money that entered the stock market during the late 90's was not borrowed, but came out of savings. Unquestionably, the expanded credit market did make it possible for that to happen. But possibility is not inevitability. Why did not the people who lost their money sit on their hands and leave it in savings accounts drawing small interest, or at least in less risky adventures?

It is sometimes said that the chief reason for such gambling was the fact that income was too low from savings. This could not have been a major consideration. The safest place to put money for the average person is the three month treasury bill. In 1996, the first year of the bubble, $1,000,000 invested in these T-bills would have earned an income in excess of $50,000—not a fortune to be sure, but an adequate income in those days. Since the official posted urban inflation rate that year was 4.2%, this income would have slightly beaten it. In 1997, the official urban inflation rate was 1.2% and the 3mo.—

T bill would have yielded about the same as the year before. The official inflation rate would have been trounced. In 1998, it would have started getting a little difficult. The year began with T-bills yielding 5.24% and closed with a yield of 4.44%. Surely, they could have gotten $47,500; they would have beat the official inflation rate of 2.3% anyway. Only in 1999, the last full year of the bubble, would it have gotten tight again: They would have earned on their three months T-bills about the same as before and the official inflation rate would have gone to 4%.[275]

But remember that the 3 mo.-T-Bill is what is called a "no-brainer." Every single one of those years, they would have earned more on six-month CDs, which are only slightly more risky. Their income would have been higher than $50,000 every year, sometimes over $60,000.[276] But that too was nearly riskless. Other investments with additional but not great risk would have paid much more. They did not need to have taken to gambling.

Against this, it might be objected that we have shown that the actual inflation would be much higher than the official rate. That is true, but one of the attractions of the stock market during the time of the bubble was the supposedly low inflation. Investors who thought that these rates were false typically did not plunge into stocks. In the 1970s—a time when inflation was widely seen as a major problem—the heavy investment was in precious metals and real estate; the stock market was in the dumps. People who still want to say something good about the bubble market point out that in August 1982, when the market started to run up, the Dow was at 777. They forget that it was much higher in the the late sixties and early seventies, but then fell into disfavor, primarily because of inflation fears.

Why Were So Many Taken In?

In part, it was because they had come to believe that their country had defeated communism, ignoring the fact that it was its inherent inefficiency, rather than the excellence of American leadership, which led to the shucking-aside of that system. An intellectual had written an essay proclaiming that the supposed American triumph was the "end of history." But even if that were the case, it would not of itself suffice for a reason to bid up the stock market way beyond sensible price-earning levels.

Then there was the new technology, the implications of which were hastily imagined by many, but perhaps properly understood by hardly anyone. Yet, even so, this would explain an increase in value in some of the tech stocks, but not the run-up in the common variety—let alone a situation where a stock broker known to this writer could say without fear of much contradiction, that "it is the only game in town."

The truth is that they were led to believe that the stock market was the right place to put their money. It was not primarily the hucksters, speaking of riding the Internet across fields of gold. Such people can be found everywhere at any time, jabbering on just about anything that might have fungible value; and most adults have long since cautioned themselves to take that kind of advice "with a grain of salt." The same can be said for the tub-thumping C.E.O.s. Such are opportunists. And also, the justly criticized relationship between accounting firms and their corporate clients appears to have been legal under the codes then in place.

What brought it together was an alliance between Washington and Wall Street. There was the anomaly of a Democratic President who had seemingly broken with the critical attitude his Party had taken toward the stock market and actually embraced it. This shift fit in with the disarming tactics recommended by Dick Morris of silencing the opposition by seeming to agree with it. During its heyday, a Democrat intellectual would rejoice that "the democratization of money" had been found. But this overblown language by itself would not have been enough for Americans to gamble with three generations of savings. What made that rhetoric seem solid was the deliberately misleading, often false, statistics wrought by persons with few scruples in both the public and the private sector. People thought it should not fail with the Republican Greenspan checking Clinton and the Democrat Clinton balancing Greenspan. And this was not the ultimate motivation, which will be explained at the close of the next section.

Foreigners were also attracted. They knew of the turmoil in Asia and South America; they heard the siren song about the "New Economy;" the media reported to them the supposedly honest government statistics; they thought that they could place their wealth with reasonable assurance of safety. In 2000, the year that the market peaked and began its slide into poverty, they are reported to have invested $175 billion, even in 2001, a year of general decline, they purchased $116 billion. But the purchases during 2002 have been far less.[277]

Today, there is much more desperation of the kind that would lead Americans to gamble their savings than there was in the 1996-2000 period. Because the low inflation myth still has a lot of credibility, interest rates are alarmingly low. As The McAlvany Intelligence Advisor so beautifully puts it: "One million dollars that is invested today in the safest place you and I can find (90 day U.S. treasury Bills) currently earns $7500 annual income (.75%). Therefore our income from a million dollars in T-bills equates to an income of $20.55 a day. Either the million dollars is no good as money, or the current interest rate is phony. This explains why formerly prudent people have been driven to take higher and higher risks in stocks and bonds . . . 'to survive.'"[278]

In 2001, as Alan Greenspan drove down the interest rate, the return on the safest financial instruments got lower and lower, steering people once more toward taking higher and higher risks. Now, rather than then, is the time when gambling is starting to make some sense. Political adventurism might become even more popular.

Why Was It Rigged?

The rigging came from three directions: the Administration, the Federal Reserve, and from the private sector.

The Clinton Administration had shamelessly cooked the books. The C.P.I. was rigged from the start; and when that was not enough, the data was falsified. The same with other economic statistics relating to the nation's economic health. This was especially evident in 1996 when he was up for re-election and 1998 when he was trying to prevent himself from being removed from office.

That this would happen was seen early. James Dale Davidson, a famous investment analyst who had gotten tired of the Republicans and the promises which they so infrequently deliver, voted for Clinton in 1992. At one of the many inauguration balls, he was approached by the freshly sworn-in President. As Mr. Davidson recalled in 1998: "Six years ago when the newly-elected Bill Clinton asked me to prepare a memo for the late Commerce Secretary, Ron Brown, outlining how economic data could be manipulated. I assumed that he intended to correct bogus data. Silly me."[279]

Mr. Clinton was head of state and of government. He was responsible for what was done during his Administration, because he had the power. But responsibility is not the same thing as personal guilt. Could it have been that he did not himself order the dishonest actions done that are recorded on our pages? We know that he was attempted to move his Party in the direction of capitalism—to democratize money. Could it have been that in his rush, he may have hired some people he should not have?

This would not have been the first time in American history that happened. Ulysses S. Grant was a great general. He would not have consciously harmed the country he fought for. But he trusted in the wrong men. He signed the 1873 currency bill. Later on, he said that he "did not know that the Act of

1873 demonetized silver. I was deceived in the matter."[280]
Previously, America was on a bi-metallic standard. The new law
left gold with the double duty of filling in for the work that
silver used to do as a monetary medium. The result was
deflation. This financial crisis lasted almost until the end of
the 19th century.[281] It prepared the way for the inauguration
of the Federal Reserve System.

But Mr. Clinton is no U. S. Grant. The latter was a successful
general, but had to rely on others for complicated financial
advice. Could it have been that Clinton was just innocently
asking Mr. Davidson that question in order to prevent it from
being done in the future? Could it be that he did not order or
know about the actions taken by underlings to foster his re-
election by presenting an illusion of low inflation when it did
not exist? Was there really no collusion between him and
Greenspan that year? Was it all a coincidence? Did he really
not know how false the claims of having balanced budgets and
surpluses were? That he didn't have anything to do with the
machinations involved in protecting him during the
impeachment crisis? That he was ignorant of the fact that the
Commerce Department made it look like corporate profits
were going up the last two years of his administration, when
they were actually going down? That he did none of the
planning in those actions which made a mockery of the so-
called "democratization" of money? That he had no intention
of helping Wall Street insiders transfer to themselves the savings
of three generations of Americans? That all he learned of
importance from the late Carroll Quigley were just a few
Americanisms?

Now, let us turn to the other part of the rigging: the actions
of the Federal Reserve. In his 2002 biography, *Alan Shrugged*,
Jerome Tuccille, the well known libertarian writer, said of
Greenspan that "he will most likely have earned an A" for his
work as Fed Chief.[282] Unless the letter stands for something
like "Amiss," this judgment is wrong.

Last Summer, Mr. Greenspan said that the Fed should not

be blamed for the bubble market. He can certainly show that there were times when he tried to quiet it down; there were other times, however, when he pronounced it stable when it was not.

More recently, Mr. Greenspan said that the jury is still out on how the Fed handled the bubble market. Any jury that is still out on that score is either below highschool age or mentally deficient.

It began, as they say, "innocently enough"—with a dollar crisis. Throughout Clinton's first term of office, the dollar had been in trouble. Interventions had to be made in 1993 and 1994—and again in spring of 1995. One alternative was to jack up the interest rates. This had been done in the 1970s by Greenspan's predecessor, Paul Volcker. At that time, the dollar had sunk so low that investors were fleeing from the currency; the price of gold had increased way beyond ten times its official of price of $35 in less than a decade. To bring the dollar up, Volcker doubled interest rates from the middle of 1980 to the end of 1982, reaching 20% at one point. By doing so, he increased the international value of the dollar 40%.[283] But the cost was high. Every time the prime rate increased, so did the amount of debt borrowers owed to the banks. Simultaneously, the national debt went up in line with the discount rate.[284] As a result, the real estate industry was in a state of depression, and the country as a whole was in a slump.

When the dollar fell again in the early 1990s, the decision was to do something different. Probably, they feared that if they repeated what had been done less than fifteen years earlier, people might get the idea that maybe the gold bugs and those who want the Treasury, not the banks, to create all the new money have something after all—that the modern dollar is inherently unstable.

Greenspan is himself an advocate of the gold standard. It may be that despite his preference for that standard, he sought to do the best he could for the one he had sworn to preserve and protect; that he did not want a crisis; that he preferred a soft landing. His ideal comes out plainly in this confrontation he had with Democrat Senator Paul Sarbanes. It came as a result of Greenspan's testimony that all economic regulations be "sunsetted," i.e., be given an expiration date after which they would cease to exist.

Sarbanes:	"Do you also favor a sunset provision for the authorization of the Federal Reserve?"
Greenspan:	"Yes, I do, Senator."
Sarbanes:	"Do you actually mean that the Fed should cease to function unless affirmatively continued?"
Greenspan:	"That is correct, sir."
Sarbanes:	"All right. The Defense Department?'
Greenspan:	"Yes."
Sarbanes:	"Now my next question is, is it your intention that the report of this hearing should be that Greenspan recommends a return to the gold standard?"
Greenspan:	"I've been recommending that for years. There's nothing new about that. It would probably mean that there is only one vote in the FOMC for that, but it is mine."[285]

This is the kind of a man Greenspan appears to be, one that believes deeply both in total capitalism and a legal transition to it.

That said, let us return to his solution to the dollar crisis of the early '90s.

In 1994 and 1995, the dollar was falling. The first year, he tried a very restrictive policy, repressing economic activity when higher prices had come about. The dollar still fell. So he changed his strategy. He decided to anchor the dollar upon the stock market. To accomplish this, the deficit would need to be reduced. Lowering that would bolster the dollar and maintain the credibility of the whole economy; which would in turn add strength to the currency. On this, he got the cooperation of the President. Though the advertised surplus was non-existent, the annual increase in the deficit was reduced rather significantly during Clinton's second term. This, they did by cutting the military budget as a percentage of GDP in half—from 6 % to 3% [286]—an action which required some assistance from the Republican Congress.

The upshot is that it did not work. Mr. Greenspan seemed to be shocked at the silliness of some investors. He issued more than one warning. Throughout, he retained his conviction about the ultimate soundness of markets. It appears that in the last year or so, he began to pin his hopes on hi-tech.

Then came April 2000. The next year, he abandoned the deficit strategy and accepted the tax cut. The reader may recall the ludicrous justification he gave to the U. S. Senate: that the phantom surpluses, if not trimmed back, might go on to threaten freedom.

There were alternatives available. They could have let the dollar drift. Greenspan may have felt that he had given it an adequate chance in 1994. But the general situation was better then than now. Greenspan's inflationism had only begun. The balance of payments was not as severe then as now. American factories manufactured a greater percentage of their goods in homeland U. S. A. The world had not witnessed the ecstacy and the agony of the bubble market.

Had they done that, Americans would have paid more attention to the trade deficit. Certain practices discussed in the section on the New Economy would have been stopped, or at least greatly retarded. In general, free trade might have been put on hold. And Greenspan is an internationalist and a believer in laissez faire capitalism. He would not have liked that. Furthermore, even if he had been agreeable to it, it would have been against the grain of the entire foreign policy establishment. He couldn't have changed that if he had tried.

Another alternative would have been an international agreement, as some have been advocating all along.[287] Without question, America would have occupied the lion's place at the table. Back then, there was no Euro; the threat from Asia was confined to the Yen. Now, we are the stage where the costs for that fiasco must be borne even by those who had seen through it from the beginning.

But with the capacity for disagreement that exists among the powers, there is no guarantee that such a conference would have produced fruitful results. The Bretton-Woods treaty, the one that lasted for a quarter of a century, was instituted at a time when Europe was prostrate after WWII and only America was strong. The mere fact that America had called such a conference when its currency was under suspicion would have invited trouble. Greenspan did not have the authority to call such a thing, anyway. And if he had, the end result might have been bad for the United States.

In retrospect, it is obvious that his plan did not work. But we know things he did not know then. To use a famous illustration: If Napoleon knew as much about the coming battle of Waterloo as the armchair strategists do now, he would not have lost it.

But there is still the questionable side to it. Greenspan went along with the C. P. I. scam. Indeed, it was he who first said that the published figure needed to be reduced. At a crucial point in Clinton's 1996 reelection campaign, Greenspan and the President's appointees prevented a rate increase, even though the Fed governors wanted one. Years later, in 2002, after Greenspan had issued some words of condemnation for the scandalous C.E.O.s, *The Wall Street Journal,* in a chiding editorial called "Pastor Greenspan," stated: "But one former Fed official we know cites as a crucial mistake an FOMC meeting in September 1996, when the Fed failed to tighten."[288] Several raised objections at that fateful meeting. One of those was Fed Governor Lawrence Lindsay; he said that the markets were held in "gambler's curse."[289] Gertrude Coogan reported a similar situation in 1927, two years before that most famous of crashes.

Even after the 1996 election, Greenspan continued to put

in plugs for the New Economy (although he did not care for that expression).[290] In 1998, he again talked the governors out of a timely rate increase. Although he would occasionally issue warnings against speculation, he refused to do anything about the galloping margin—something that was worrying the World Bank and even important people within the Administration. He trivialized it. The Fed's action in November 1999 helped spur the final tragic three-month run-up in the stock market. Then in March 2000, just before the precipitous fall began, he gave a speech promoting hi-tech—the very thing which would lead the way down. On top of that, throughout the years, he had been "spiking the punch."

The program of the two principals dovetailed. They got along from the start—even though they came from different parties. Bush Senior has said in public that Greenspan's policies led to his electoral defeat. It was Greenspan who proposed to Clinton that he focus on "deficit reduction." Both men favored increased immigration: Clinton, because the majority of the new citizens would probably vote Democratic; Greenspan, because the incoming competition to native-born Americans would keep wage rates down, thereby preventing higher prices, which central bankers like to tag as inflation. Greenspan even went to the extreme of extolling job insecurity as a valuable part in the fight against inflation. Both were big free-traders.

In Greenspan's defense, it could be said that he was not the President; that he had to work with the man whom the people had chosen. Yes, he could have quit. But he may have felt exhilarated by the challenge. Few, if any, had a background, both theoretical and practical, to equal his. He may have had some patriotic feelings as well. *He did try.* Suppose it had worked and the dollar stood high for a many more years? Would the investors have cared? Many of them would have laughed at the purists.

That can be said in his defense. But it is still true that from the standpoint of Christian morality—and even from that of Objectivist ethics, as commonly understood—some of his ways were wrong. Furthermore, from the standpoint of pragmatism, he did not succeed.

And now we have the third direction, sellers who acted badly. That the wild promoter, exemplified so clearly by Enron, should prosper in a situation like that should not be surprising. People wonder about the surprising number of strange characters who have come to the top of huge corporations. A certain kind of person sensed the opportunity. It was made for them. Some individuals in the financial press were less than candid. The stock broker's involvement was more complicated. Many were smart enough to sound convincing, but not cognizant enough to understand why they were turning a blind eye to certain events. One commentator relates an incident when the market was very popular of an individual who told his financial adviser that he wanted to sell his stocks. The advisor's reply: "Don't sell. If everybody sells, the stock market will go down."[291]

From a fourth direction came those who did not do the rigging, but accepted it not simply out of ignorance, but also, in part, out of an affinity with it. These were buyers who not only hoped it would work out, but kept investing, even when they knew it broke with reason. Consider: The most amazing thing about the whole decade is that so many investors bought the yarn about low inflation. Those who had attained adulthood by the 1960s or1970s should have known better.

Many of them rooted for Clinton when he was in trouble; they didn't care whether it was perjury or not. What they wanted to do was keep the thing going. There was also a Greenspan cult, as shown by the dangerous statement, "In Greenspan We Trust."[292] Some thought that the New Economy was producing a New Man, and the anxieties they felt were just part of the inward change.[293] It was not all tra-la-la either. There was at least one murder-suicide. All this helped make the Fed's wager fail so spectacularly.

"The root cause," as Larry Heim put it, "is greed."[294] It was not just the miscalculation, nor the enthusiasm that preceded it. It was the attitude which puts priority on just the *wanting* of more money, more material benefits, more popularity, etc., that provided the original imbalance. Greed misses the mark—

it is a sin. Without that, the doctored statistics, the silly romanticism of the end of the cold war, and the rest could not have done it. The two principals did not create the greed. They were just the men of an evil hour.

And now comes the dénouement. Greed is replaced by fear, and the latter is in danger of hardening into desperation.

What Is The New Economy?

We have all heard about the New Economy promised by President Clinton—how everybody will have more of everything. After President Coolidge made his statement about a "new era" in 1927, there was quite a flap in the press. As Donald Rogers reports in *The Day The Market Crashed*, "There were New Era restaurants, New Era Laundries, New Era duckpin alleys, New Era ice cream parlors, New Era theaters, New Era groceries, New Era poolhalls, and so on, ad nauseam. "[295] But it still crashed.

What did Clinton's "New Economy" mean in reality when we lay aside the Star Trek talk? Millions saw those TV ads put out by Cisco Systems when its Internet stock was the talk of the industry, featuring all those multi-cultural youth asking the audience in an intimidating manner, "Are You Ready?" What really is this new economic era?

During the 1990s, neither the Administration nor the financial press was telling the people what lay behind the alarming trade deficit statistics. The statistics were reported, there were a few sighs, but little analysis was reported by the establishment media. Ross Perot's mention of a "giant sucking sound" was drowned out in the news about lower unemployment, balanced budgets, and the like.

What the trade statistics meant is that ordinary Americans were actually getting poorer, not richer. American know-how was being exported; factories were being built abroad, turning out products designed by Americans in foreign factories. Industrial jobs were being sent overseas, progressively leaving

Americans high and dry with financial and support jobs. To be sure, for a while, Joe and Joan will be receiving fine electronic merchandise at prices below what they would have been had they been made by higher-cost American labor. But this cannot last. The money which they paid for these inexpensive goods goes on, being passed from bank account to bank account and from hand to hand, while the objects which they have purchased wear out and often become obsolete.

And many of them get into debt buying these things. A famous scientist once observed that this interest is not subject to the laws of physics which dictate dissolution for the manufactured objects obtained in trade.[296] The money will continue long after most of that merchandise becomes trash.

Americans were told that they would be manning all the computers; an example of that is Enron, trading electricity instead of producing it. But this strategy won't work for long anyway, even with better people at the helm. Nothing will stop the rulers of those countries from allocating some of their money to build that industry, locally. That is already happening. Indeed, Greenspan offered the argument that immigration would bring to the United States more high-tech people. It is interesting to note that Greenspan's old mentor, Ayn Rand, wrote about America's big businessmen, liberating the people of this land from an approaching serfdom out of motives that were entirely selfish. What we find instead is the self-regarding policy of the contemporary tycoon building factories in the lowest cost suitable labor market they can find abroad. The result is the closure of factories here at home, increasing unemployment, and when things level out, a lower standard of living for most Americans.

According to the free-trade dogmatists, this is all to the good, because they will all balance anyway. It is true that wages will eventually balance out, but with the American sinking to the level of the Coolie, while the wages of the latter will rise somewhat. In the early 90s, the jobs started going to Mexico, but now to Orange China and Indonesia where human life is even cheaper. Readers interested in learning more about this should consult these works: Dr. Ravi Batra's *The Pooring Of America: Competition & The Myth Of Free Trade* and Pat Buchanan's *The Great Betrayal: How American Sovereignty and Social Justice are being Sacrificed to the Gods of the Global Economy.* The first was published in 1993, and the second, in 1998.

Beyond that, one can see that just as the wiping out of much of America's old financial leadership in the early 1930s prepared for FDR's radical departures from American practice, so it might be that as a result of the resent debacle, America will be turned inside out by rulers of foreign countries, working in conjunction with the extremely wealthy people who hold citizenship here. The transfer of trillions of dollars in wealth belonging to American investors can serve as the opening wound in such a tragedy.

While American investors were entranced by the glittering promises of the New Economy, the fruits of America's technologically oriented intelligence were being sucked into Orange China. Among the early casualties were some of the Asian countries whose labor rates were not nearly as low as that of China. *TIME* canonized Greenspan and two members of the Clinton administration, Rubin and Summers, while all they were doing was protecting establishment banks and temporally shoring up the situation over there. Meanwhile, the investors, being told that they were in good hands, went into a state of ecstasy and gambled ever the more.

Would it have mattered if they had succeeded in stabilizing the dollar with respect to the Euro and the Yen? The big corporations would have gotten more money from their out-of country satellites. Foreign capital would have arrived in even greater amounts. The stock market would have behaved like a giant capacitor, sucking in capital all over the world. One is reminded of the phony Shreck generator of Batman II, gulping in electricity. The flacks would have still been out, inviting all to participate in this "human achievement." But what of the average citizen who wasn't part of the glitz, that was not connected with finance, luxury shops, high-class resorts, dude-ranches and the like? Some would fight, shunning the fake non-conformity offered of the urban cowboy. Many more would work on the outskirts, valiantly steadying themselves against the inward pull—hoping to make a stake before their way of life disappeared. Others would quit struggling—not joining their tormentors, but just wait for the compactor.

As it is, unless something is done to reverse the present course, the glorious Republic of Washington and Lincoln is likely to end up another huge hulk, dumped next to post-Soviet Russia.

Comparison With The Bull Market Of The 1920s

Let us compare the present situation with the collapse of the bull market that brought on the great depression of the 1930s. There were some differences. In 1929, the federal government's expenditures represented about 2.6 % of GDP, or about 1/40th of the total. Of late, federal spending was1/4 of the total.[297] This means that Americans were able to keep a greater part of their wealth.

The Americans of 75 years ago had a constitutional government, not merely a labyrinthine network of laws attached to a constitution more honored than observed. One thing they did have in common with the contemporary was the Federal Reserve, which was enacted in law in 1913. And we have no less an authority than Mr. Greenspan himself that it caused the Great Depression. Déjá Vu?

What is a depression? In Chapter I, this was asked, but not defined, only distinguished from a recession. What then is it? I once knew a man slightly who was injured in a traffic accident; he refused a blood transfusion because of fear that the supply was contaminated. Like such a man, the financially stricken can recover, but only with great difficulty. An economic depression is a situation in which the loss of financial capital is so great that the country or region affected by it can regain its former condition, only after great difficulty. This definition is qualitative only; but it will prove to be sufficient for our purposes.

A conservative estimate of the loss in the stock market as of 7/30/02 is $7 trillion dollars. This is the same as the amount of M3 money that was put into the economy from 1946-2000.

This does not mean that the money was extinguished. Most of the money still existed, but in different hands. It is just the loss of realizable value that a losing investor would have had, if they were to have cashed out before the crash had reached current levels.

But that was also the case with the investors of 1929. The question is whether today's losses are great enough to bring about a depression. It is difficult to analyze in terms of mere dollar figures alone. From August 1921 to September 1929, the Dow-Jones Industrial Average rose from 63.9 to 381.17, a rise of 597%.[298] In the 1991—April 2000 period, the Dow increased about 4 times; the Nasdaq, about the same amount as the other index did in 1929.

At its lowest point in 1932, the New York Stock Exchange lost about 82.5% of its value.[299] During the October 1929-32 period, Standard & Poor's 500 Index (without dividends) lost about 72% of its value.[300] Now, let us look at the recent period. As of 7/19/02, the S&P was down 44.5%. On that date, the Nasdaq, which did not exist before 1973, was down 73.9%— very much like those other indices of that by-gone era.[301] The Wilshire 5000 is the most comprehensive index. It was down about 50% from its highs. On this basis, the 7/02 loss was serious, but not as bad as that of the previous era. It should not be overlooked, however, that we do not know what that low point on the present one will be.

The NYSE loss in the 1929-32 period was approximately $74.04 billion. Today, this would be the equivalent of $979.4 billion—which means that the current dollar is worth about 7.55 cents in terms of the 1929 dollar. Using official census data[302] and current dollars, the loss per person in 1929 on the

NYSE was around $8,081; the contemporary NYSE loss as of 6/ 30/02 was approximately $7,513 per person—a difference of under $600.

But the NYSE constitutes a lesser part of the total stock market than it did in 1929. Although there are no figures available of the total market value of all stocks in 1929, an educated guess is $130 billion.[303] Converted into current dollars, this would be about $1.721 trillion. This is not even one third of the $7 trillion which investors have lost during the period 4/00—7/02.

Assuming that the total 1929 stock losses were the same percentage as the NYSE (82.5%), this would be the contemporary dollar equivalent of $1.419 trillion or about $11,707.67 for every man woman and child then living in the United States; contrast with the approximately $24,788 per person lost by the end of July 2002. In comparable terms, the modern loss is over twice as great as the earlier one. Even if it had been a 100% loss, it would have been a loss of about $14,199 per resident, a little more than half as great as the modern figure. By that measure, the modern catastrophe is much greater.

But the distribution is also important. In the 1990s, over half of U. S. families were working or playing the market. The percentage in the '20s was quite a bit less—about 12% of all families. The fact that the stock loss is more widely distributed this time might give some reason for us to hope.

In the 1920s, a greater share of the American economy was owned by families or single proprietorships. That is one reason why tremendous losses by a smaller percentage of the population could bring down the economy. Some might think that with corporate ownership constituting a greater percentage of the private sector, more security now exists; that with the risk more widely spread, the changes of a precipitous collapse are less. But recent figures show that pension fund shortfalls are growing. The Pension Benefit Guaranty Corporation (PBGC) reported in July that by year end 2001, the pension funds of U.S. corporations had been underfunded by one hundred eleven billion dollars ($111,000,000,000). This figure was based on government filings from companies with defined benefit pension funds.

During the recent fiasco, the amount of money which had been invested by foreigners was quite high. Negatively, this was due to the turmoil in Asia and Latin America; positively, it was due to the deceptive aspect of safety presented by the government's statistics. Something similar occurred in the 1920s. Europe had been devastated by WWI; the crowns of Russia, Germany, and Austria had fallen. Bolshevism, which taken over Russia, was hammering at the institution of private property everywhere, but especially in the countries nearby. Germany was prostrate and had to pay enormous reparations; Great Britain was in a depression. France was still solid, but fragile. It did not take any fancy bookkeeping to see that America was safer. Writing twenty years later, Benjamin Anderson, chief economist for the Chase Bank recalled that "the New York stock market had become the central interest, not only for the whole country, but also for the whole world . . . . The tide of investment funds turned definitely from Europe to the United States, whereas in the preceding years it had been from the United States to Europe. Our stock prices were mounting so rapidly that they were an irresistible magnet for a speculatively inclined world. Orders to buy New York stocks came from Asia and Africa."[304] It would be nice to know how close the percentage of foreign investment was then as compared to the very recent past. In that way, a more correct comparison of the losses to America during the two eras could be made. If it was found that the greater percentage was in the 90s, then the loss to Americans would be less and the prospects for a depression would diminish somewhat. Unfortunately, the author has not to date been able to locate them.

But even assuming that the domestic percentage of the recent losses are less in the '90s, it would then follow that America is less worthy of being a world leader than it was a generation or so earlier. A power which induced foreigners to invest and then failed to live up to its promises would be in need of additional grounds to preserve its suzerainty.

Let us ask the question, which period, January 1921 to October 1929 or January 1996 to April 2000 had the more outrageous values? The reader has already seen which one made more sense as a comparison of GNP. A recent study prepared for the Federal Reserve of Bank of Minneapolis argues that stock prices in 1929 were not too high; at their peak, the average stock was trading at 19 times after-tax earnings, much less than what the Stock evaluations were at its recent peak.[305]. In this study, the authors, Ellen McGrattan and Edward Prescott, argue that the culprit was the tremendous money-tightening of the Federal Reserve.[306] A March 1999 "Economic Letter"published by the San Francisco Federal Reserve Bank is in agreement. It points out that at the peak, prices were 30.5 times the dividend yield, just a little above the long-term average. At the peak, stocks were trading at 19 times after tax-earnings [307]

This means that Greenspan was wrong in his famous essay when he claimed that the extension of credit to Britain was an essential precondition for the stock-market crash. The extreme tightening of 1929 was far more important. The situation there was similar to that of 1995 when the market might have held at that level with corrections here and there. The deluge was not inevitable. In 1929, the Rooseveltian era and its troublesome aftermath might never have happened. The much ridiculed economist, Irving Fisher, could have been in the right, when he wrote on October 24, 1929:

"IF IT IS TRUE THAT 15 BILLIONS IN STOCK QUOTATION LOSSES HAVE BEEN SUFFERED IN THE PRESENT BREAK I HAVE NO HESITATION IN SAYING THAT VALUES ARE TOO LOW."[308]

As the reader has probably surmised, this is certainly not the case with the Greenspan-Clinton brouhaha. Stock prices still fell after July 2002—in fact quite a bit. Not until September 30 did the Dow's P/E ratio drop to 19.9 [309]—within the range of 1929 for the broad market. They may still be too high. The modern super-bull was the more bloated. From this point forward, we will instead quote the contemporary representatives in SMALL CAPS.

But that does not prove that there will be a depression akin to it. We have shown that the moderns are deeper in the cold water than those people were. Does it follow that they will also go over the falls? It may be that the U. S. economy is so much richer now that it may survive after common stocks had been reduced an amount greater to that of 1929-32.

After the '29 crash, the Federal Reserve did try to expand the money supply, but to no great avail. The discount rate was cut from 6% to 5% on November 1, 1929, right after the crash. Then it was cut to 4.5% on November 15 and to 4% on January 30, 1930. By the middle of 1931, it had cut the rate to 1.5%. The market responded; there were some five big rallies [310] October 30, 1929 and November 14 of 1929 were among the greatest percentage gainers of record.[311] But none of them held. It was just as it was in 2001: While Greenspan was reducing the interest rate several times; the result was nil. In 2002, the Fed finally cut its interest rate to 1.75%. Same story!

The major difference between the aftermaths is that there have not been any bank failures. During the period October 1929-32, 10,000 banks would fail; this would be 40% of the 1929 total.[312] For some reason, there was a lot of panic, resulting in a strangulation of national financial resources. In 1935, Congress established the Federal Deposit Insurance Corporation, which guaranteed all deposits up to $5,000 per individual account.[313] In terms of contemporary dollars, this would be a guarantee of about $66,225, quite a bit less than today's guarantee of $100,000 per account. But the contemporary protection is in greater jeopardy: With a shrinking dollar; the value of the account balance declines with the unit of account. The fact that the 2002 dollar is only worth about seven and a half cents of the 1929 one speaks poorly for the Fed as the guardian against inflation. FDIC insurance does not guarantee a quick refund.

Stock market failures do not produce deflation; the money that was lost still exists; but it has been transferred to the sellers of the stock and to their suppliers. The bank failures of the early thirties did deflate the money supply, however. It is estimated that the money stock declined by eight billion during the depression.[314] This has not happened, yet. What we have is a greater stock market collapse, but no deflation, yet.

So let us follow the money.

THERE IS A SANTA CLAUS!
—From *Judge*.
DECEMBER 14, 1929.

If Hoover Was Unable To Deliver, Could Greenspan Be Santa?

Whereas the attempts to increase the money supply while Hoover was President were a failure on a net basis, the banking system under Greenspan has increased M3 a lot. In the period of January 2001 through July 2002 inclusive, M3 has increased by $1,107.413 billion.[315] This is a 19-month period. And it is greater than the prior nineteen months of June 1999 through December 2000—that being $935.368 billion—by approximately $172 billion. When one recalls that the entire M3 increase from 1946 to 2000 was $7 trillion, this is indeed a formidable figure. Some people might rush to the conclusion that Greenspan is inflating us out of the crisis.

The average annual M3 monetary expansion of January 1996 through April 2000—the years of the bubble market—was $481.861 billion. On the same basis, the average annual monetary expansion of January 2001 through December 2002 has been $715.813 billion, an annual expansion greater by more than 43%. Yet, Wall Street is complaining that Greenspan is stingy.

Some think that the greatly augmented money supply will be enough to prevent a recurrence of what took place in the thirties of the last century. Are they right? One thing such expansion does is make people more dependent upon the banking system. The extra money goes to those accepted as loan risks by a bank. These would not necessarily be the same people who had lost the most in the stock market. It would go either to the most solvent—either that, or to the person with the best connections. There will be a quiet redistribution of wealth.

But wait! Most of the expansion took place from January 2001 to December 2001: $917.096 billion against $514.529 billion during the period, January 2002 through December 2002[316]—just over 56% of the previous period. But even though Greenspan lowered the prime rate seven times, he was not successful in lifting the stock market—at best only in slowing down its rate of descent. But for how long? The significantly lower expansion this year points to the real possibility that we are indeed at the onset of a deflation, which was why so many banks went under in the early thirties.

M3 figures through December do, however, show that the increase from 1/02 through 7/02 was only 55.6% as great as that from 8/02 through 12/02. So the rate of increase of M3 has itself increased in the last 5 months of the year, but it is still below the comparable five-month period for the previous year. That increase was $371.982 billion against $324.212 billion for the latter period, a rate of increase 13% less. Unless there is quite a bit more inflation in 2003, the prospect for deflation remains.

In our study, we have been using M3. Let us look at M1— the money aggregate in which the actual money creation takes place with a view to determining the course of the money supply. When this is done, we find that most of the latest M1 expansion took place from January 2001 to December 2001.[317] In fact, the figures are more striking than they are with M3. The expansion 1/02-12/02 was only about 43.4% that of 1/01-12/01. The prognosis of possible deflation is confirmed.

There is one more measure of money to be considered: Money Zero Maturity. This measure is purely liquid. It is basically like M3, except it does not contain CDs. MZM is action money. Included in this aggregate are: (1) currency; (2) demand deposits; (3) travelers' checks; (4) savings account balances; (5) MMMF deposits.[318] Excluded are CDs because there the money is tied up for a time.

The average yearly MZM monetary expansion during the bubble market—from January 1996 to December 2000—was $336.67 billion. On the same basis, the average yearly expansion from January 2001 to December 2002 was $746.42 billion. MZM expansion has been much greater during the President Bush II period than it was during the New Economy years. If this were all there was to it, one might think that the prospects of deflation are less.

But wait! The MZM expansion from 1/01 to 12/01 was $1,000.191 billion verses $492.641 billion during the period 1/02 to 12/02, an amount of increase less than 49.25% as great as the year before.[319] This shows a declining rate of increase in MZM. This is what we found to be the case with M3.

The reader should also note that the M3 increase from 1/01 to 12/02—the first two years of the new Bush administration—was $1,431,625 billion, while that from MZM was $1,492,832 billion. This means that the M3 increase has been less than that of MZM, although the former's base is much larger than that of the latter—over $8,500 billion in contradistinction to just over $6,000 billion. How does one explain that the smaller aggregate shows a greater expansion during this larger one?

The answer is that there has been a decline in CDs, that larger deposits have declined during this period. Not as much a percentage is being saved. Americans as a group were spending, rather than saving.

This is consistent with other economic news during this period. Market Vector, a firm which specializes in forecasting long-term economic trends, predicted in July dramatic accelerations in housing starts, beginning in August 2002.[320] Recent reports confirm this: Sales of new homes are at record levels, a 6.7 % increase over June. Sales of existing homes rose 4.5% from the previous month. Experts attribute that to low mortgage rates.

There has also been an acceleration of car sales.[321] This is done through low rates and deep discounts. This is being carried on, primarily, by those who still have jobs and lost little, if any, in the stock market. Although the losses in the stock market exceed $24,000 for every man, woman, and child in the United States, the majority were not investors and were not directly affected by it. Will this be enough to jump start a recovery? *The Wall Street Journal* hopes so.

James Stack of Investech Research is not so hopeful. He recalls an article from the *London Economist* which appeared just 30 months after the Japanese stock market had peaked. In its July 11, 1992 issue there is an article called "How Japan Will Survive its fall. The economic slowdown in Japan should not be confused with a Western-style recession. Which is why Japan will come bouncing back." The article asks and then answers the question: "Is Japan heading into a humdinger of a recession? The answer is no . . . . High employment is helping to support consumer confidence. Much is made of the fact that business investment . . . is falling. But consumer spending, which is almost three times as big, grew by 3.3% in the year to the first quarter . . . The main reason that Japan . . . should be able to dodge a deep recession is that it starts off with the soundest fiscal and monetary policies of any industrial economy. This gives the government more ammunition with which to fend off a recession."[322]

Later on, Japan fell into a deflation, something America's banking system has yet to do.

To rest the future strength of what is today the world's reserve currency upon domestic real estate is a fragile hope. Real estate is tied to a specific parcel of land and/or the improvements upon it. A share of stock is somewhat more universal, especially if the products or services of the firm are purchased around the world. The reader may recall that in its March 26, 2001, article in which it urged its readers to look "beyond the bear," *Time Magazine* said that America would not follow Japan, because prosperity over here is not based upon real estate. As for the automobile, as everyone knows, it is an asset which diminishes as soon as the new owner leaves the sales lot.

Before the year ended, the greater increase of MZM than M3 has been reversed. From August through December, M3 increased by $324.212 billion while MZM grew by only $273.675 billion.[323] In September; the savings rate rose to 4.2% from 3.4% in August.[324]

Greenspan's options are somewhat limited.

During the first quarter of 2003, M1 has returned to the higher levels of increase that prevailed in 2001's first quarter. Those of M3 and MZM have dropped considerably. The M3

increase was less than half of what it was in the last quarter of
2002; during the same period, MZM's increase went down by
two-thirds. The upshot: speculation is out in front. Greenspan
has put bolstering up the dollar and shrinking the deficit on
hold and is now trying to inflate America up and away from
deflation.

Yes, Virginia, There Can Be A Deflation

It is common to say that Orange China is exporting
deflation. This is not incorrect. Deflation is a net *decrease* in the
actual money supply from what it was at an earlier time. They
are not doing this. What they are doing, however, is
impoverishing ordinary Americans. First, jobs are taken away
from many of these people and then the cheaper goods are
sold back to them. This has the temporary effect of enabling
these consumers to pay less, thereby giving them more for their
money. Because prices do not go up as much as they otherwise
would, this in turn disguises dollar inflation. That in turn makes
it easier for the government and Wall Street to continue their
false advertisement of low inflation; which in turn reduces
interest rates, so that a three-month Treasury bill only yields
0.75%, which means that a million dollars only brings $7,500;
which in turn provides an incentive for gambling. All this spells
D-I-S-A-S-T-E-R, but that is not the same thing as deflation,
even if the payoff in both cases is poverty for many, many
Americans.

The possibility of deflation lies not in the accidents of
current history, but in the nature of the banking system itself.

Nearly every bank in existence is a fractional reserve bank.
The Federal Reserve is just an institution, set up under
President Woodrow Wilson in 1913, to control the activities of
this type of bank.

What is the problem with them? It is very simple: They
have the power to create money arbitrarily. There is no secret
in that. It has long been admitted. Marion Eccles, Governor of

the Federal Reserve Board, testified to this effect before the Banking and Currency Committee of the House of Representatives on June 24, 1941.[325]

The fractional reserve bank is best understood by contrast with its logical opposite, the full reserve bank—although the latter may not even exist today apart from memory or imagination. If A were to deposit his money in a full-reserve bank, the bank might lend B the full amount of A's deposits. But while this money were out on loan, A could not make any withdrawals from his account. The date on which the bank's obligations to A fall due must not precede the date on which the bank's corresponding claims on B mature. This is because the same money must be in the same place at the same time. Needless to say, the full-reserve bank would have to pay interest on deposits to entice A. The nearest equivalent to a full reserve bank is a C.D.

A fractional-reserve bank works like this. It may lend part of A's deposit, but while the money is on loan, A may withdraw up to the full amount of his and/or her account. This creates a net increase in the money supply. To obviate conflict, the bank keeps on hand a fraction of its deposits; hence its name. A bank with 20% reserves would be one which could not lend out more than four fifths of its deposits at any given time. This would handle all normal situations and a minor run on the bank as well.[326]

Putting this in concrete terms: if A had deposited $100 in a fractional-reserve bank with a 20% reserve ratio, that would mean that the bank could loan out $80 of this money—all the while A still had the right to withdraw the full amount. If the borrower then took this $80 and redeposited it in the this very bank or another bank with the same reserve requirement, then 80% of the amount deposited, or $64, could be placed on loan. If this too were redeposited, then the bank could loan out 80% of that, or $51.20. What is the maximum possible exposure of a banking system with a twenty percent reserve requirement?[327]

Given a 20% reserve, it is theoretically possible for the banking system to create 4 additional dollars for every dollar deposited in a demand account. Legal reserves today vary 3% to 10%; with a 10% reserve, banks can inflate by a factor of almost 9. Should the bank miscalculate and have withdrawals exceeding reserves, the result would be insolvency. Should the banker be unable to cover through additional sources, there is the potential for a panic.

The deflation of the 1920s resulted from just such a panic.(The question as to whether something spooked them or they fell into it naturally will not be answered here.)

Deflation can happen without a bank panic. It is inherent in the very nature of a fractional reserve bank account. This was well stated many years ago by the Nobel Prize chemist, Frederick J. Soddy:

"This money comes into existence every time the banks 'lend' and disappears again every time the debt is repaid them. So that if industry tries to repay, the money of the nation disappears. This is what makes prosperity so 'dangerous' as it destroys money most when it is most needed and precipitates a slump!

"There is nothing left now for us but to get ever deeper and deeper into debt to the banking system in order to provide the increasing amounts of money the nation requires for its expansion and growth."[328]

This may seem strange. How is it that a payment of a loan would reduce the money supply? Consider: Suppose A borrows $1000 from a fractional reserve bank. He then opens up a deposit account with the same bank. M1 has increased by $1000. This is because the depositors still have the right to the full $1000 that would have been in their accounts if A had never made his loan application. Then, when A pays off the loan, not only is his debt cancelled, but by the very act through which that takes place, so is the new money. Ordinarily, he spends the money he gets from the bank and then obtains the money to buy it back through others. Since the money which he has introduced into the economy outside of the bank is balanced by what he took from it, the net result is zero. But when he turns the money he has gotten from these other people over to the bank, and the institution has received it, the new M1 of $1000 which was created when he took out the loan is extinguished. The bank is back where it was before the loan to him was made. The money supply is now $1000 smaller than it was the day his new account was opened with the proceeds for that loan.

To this it might be answered, "Yes, but now the lending process can start over again with the money A brought into the bank when he repaid the loan!" True, but before there can be any more loans out of the money paid back, M1 must first be reduced by $1000.

To paraphrase the 1960s, what if they offered to make a loan and nobody came? Something approaching this has happened very recently in Japan. The people were unwilling to take out loans even when the interest rate was practically zero. This was because setting up new businesses or expanding old ones was so risky.

Returning now to America: What happens when the consumer has bought up all the new cars he or she needs at the new low financing? What happens when house buyers have bought all that they can afford, when the refinance loans have exhausted their abilities to pay it back? What would happen is that as they went about the sober activity of paying off their loans without taking on any more, the money supply would shrink. Recently (October), a former Federal Reserve governor begged Greenspan in a *WSJ* piece to lower the federal funds rate from 1.75% to 1.25% in order to stave off deflation. Early in 2001, it stood at 6.5%.[329] This could be a grasping after straws.

Since the possibility of a deflation exists, so does a depression—one greater than the one of the thirties. During the stark 1930s, the average returns on stock was—.63%.[330] Yet, in those days, the dollar was much, much sounder; the balance of payments was positive, not greatly negative; American productive resources had not been transplanted overseas, leaving here behind more and more often, financial and service industries. The population was generally more intelligent; for, although the present predicament issued in part from their errors, they would have shunned what this country has been doing since then.

Part Of Problem Lies In Banking System

According to the late economist, Murray Rothbard, who knew Greenspan but did not agree with him on many issues, some of the economic problems which the country is now experiencing are rooted, ultimately, in the fractional reserve system, a disease of which the Federal Reserve is only the biggest tumor.

Rothbard said that the fractional reserve system was fraud.[331] More money claims are issued than the bank can meet. The banker simply hopes that he or she can keep up the front of affluence well enough that not very many will demand their money back. In a commodity money system, it also increases the money supply and is inherently inflationary.

In the 1966 essay which made him famous, Greenspan wrote:

" . . . WHEN THE BUSINESS VENTURES FINANCED BY BANK CREDITS ARE LESS PROFITABLE AND SLOW TO PAY OFF, BANKERS SOON FIND THAT THEIR LOANS OUTSTANDING ARE EXCESSIVE RELATIVE TO THEIR GOLD RESERVES, AND THEY BEGIN TO CURTAIL NEW LENDING, USUALLY BY CHARGING HIGHER INTEREST RATES. THIS TENDS TO RESTRICT THE FINANCING OF NEW VENTURES AND REQUIRES THE EXISTING BORROWERS TO IMPROVE THEIR PROFITABILITY BEFORE THEY CAN OBTAIN CREDIT FOR FURTHER EXPANSION. THUS, UNDER THE GOLD STANDARD, A FREE BANKING SYSTEM STANDS AS THE PROTECTOR OF AN ECONOMY'S STABILITY AND BALANCED GROWTH."[332]

But does the height of the interest rate make the system self-regulating in the way that Greenspan envisioned? "Wild cat" banking was very popular in 19th century America. Strings of banks took whole regions down with them when their inflationary boom was followed by a bust.[333]

Some might answer that such abuses are inevitable for a young nation, struggling to tame the West.

Consider[334], then, these figures from the decade *after* the official closing of the frontier: From 1890-1900, nearly 400 National banks plus 1400 State Banks, private banks, and trust companies were closed out of insolvency.[335] Doubtless the system is self-regulating, but then so is an airplane weathercocked into the ever-tightening turns of a spiral dive.

This scandal, as well as the economic troubles of the first decade of the new century, provided all the excuse that the manipulators needed to hatch their plans for what became the Federal Reserve Act in 1913. The nation entered this new system after first experiencing fractional reserve banking in the raw.

Yet, the result has been even more unstable. As Paul Volcker, Greenspan's predecessor, admitted:

"IT IS A SOBERING FACT THAT THE PROMINENCE OF CENTRAL BANKS IN THIS CENTURY HAS COINCIDED WITH A GENERAL TENDENCY TOWARDS MORE INFLATION, NOT LESS. BY AND LARGE, IF THE OVERRIDING OBJECTIVE IS PRICE STABILITY, WE DID BETTER WITH THE NINETEENTH-CENTURY GOLD STANDARD AND PASSIVE CENTRAL BANKS, WITH CURRENCY BOARDS, OR EVEN WITH 'FREE BANKING.'"[336]

Obviously, the true answer cannot be a return to the free banking which the younger Greenspan had advocated.

But the fractional reserve system itself, flawed as it is, did not out of its own nature create the bubble. I once knew a pilot who flew an airplane with unbalanced wings all the way from Seattle to Fort Worth and landed it safely. A good sailor can cross a sea in a leaky boat. Greenspan might have conducted himself differently and then left office early in 1996 with Clinton appointing someone else in his stead. Most likely, the new appointee would have had more trouble being believed by the investing public. But that person's difficulty getting established would have afforded the public some unintended protection— perhaps enough to prevent the catastrophe we are now experiencing.

Instead, Greenspan stayed on and became an activist— virtually a partner of the President in this endeavor. The end result of their collaboration, in conjunction with the actions of others, was that the savings of upper middle Americans were savaged. A collateral result was that this worthless financial orgy helped conceal the reduction of America's industrial might and the inroads of Orange China.

However bad the monetary system be, it is best that there not be any radical programs. The power might then rest even more than today in the hands of the power-hungry. Better instead that firm laws against chicanery and corruption be instituted, laws which are simple enough that a clever lawyer would have trouble getting a culprit client free, even with a morally weak judge presiding.

Final Words

The upshot is that both post-MacArthur conservatism and post-fifties liberalism are failing. The first thought it could replace patriotism with pure capitalism and create a society open to all peoples; the second believed it could replace it with an open society in which all life styles were allowed to be whatever they can be and in which the traditional Protestant type which founded the country could be safely shunted aside in favor of this diversity. Both rejected the Republic founded by George Washington in which entangling alliances with foreign nations or with international institutions like the United Nations would be eschewed, but in which there were no objections to another nation modeling its own Constitution after the American. During this time, Ronald Reagan's trumpet occasionally called for a return to the old Republic, but his notes were soon overcome by the cacophony that surrounded him.

For the most part, this new conservatism and this new liberalism accepted unlimited immigration, the first to provide cheap labor for business; the second as grist for the mills of the Democratic Party. Both favored free trade, the first on grounds of ideology; the second, because it would work for them.

Both played into the hands of Red—now Orange China. The cooperation between the Clinton Administration and the Federal Reserve not only supported this trend, but added to it.

But for all that, the two political orientations are not compatible. The Fed chief's alliance with Clinton imperiled bourgeois capitalism; without that, it is not likely that the-bull-that-hissed would have been hatched. The great fault of the new conservatism has been that it replaced too much with the type of order which emerges as the market price. In fairness to Ayn Rand and Ludwig von Mises, it must be said that transfoming Marxist miscreants into billionaires is not what they had in mind. Morals matter.

Only days before this line was written, the new administration went to war against Iraq. Some say that victory will be an easy thing. Should that be the case, there may be for a time a revival of the stock market. It should not be forgotten that the wealth lost in the bubble market was not destroyed, but transferred into other hands. In such a case, those who lost big—especially the older people—will not be enjoying this "Prague Spring" very much. Great numbers have already purchased their passport to poverty. Many wait in line. But then there is the rest of the New Economy to take into consideration.

Should there be larger destruction of life and property in the U. S. A., or rocketing oil prices—or difficulties beyond those originally contemplated—the situation will be more desperate for many, many Americans. It should not be forgotten that the Great Depression was followed by American participation in WWII. If this is a repetition, the sequence of events will be compressed, as in an accordion. On the positive side, war spending could prevent deflation; military orders may generate the money creation which would not have come from the civilian economy.

Americans should repair to the ancient signposts of the Republic. One man rule and oligarchies are the common lot among men. The existence of a popular government over a great extent of territory is a rare thing. It requires that ordinary citizen be vigilant. Beyond that it requires a moral outlook on life—and more important than a mere intellectual appreciation or a willingness to criticize others, is a person whose actions are moral. With that, the deceivers can be detected more easily. When that is deficient, the more common types of governmental organization will insinuate themselves. The threat to national existence is too urgent to put on the back burner. It is among those with an informed commitment to America's common good that a realistic hope for the nation's future can be found—if at all.

APPENDIX

Sweeps Adjusted M1

But there is a related problem that should be considered for the sake of accuracy. Let us take the period of the bubble market: January 1996-April 2000: There is a strange fact here. *M1 for the period December 1995 to December 2000 is negative.* December 1995 to December 1996 shows —$47.428 billion; December 1996 to December 1997,—6.943 billion; December 1997 to December 1998, +$24.302 billion; December 1998 to December 1999, +$27.43 billion; and December 1999 to December 2000,—$35.397 billion. Only two of the five years were positive. If this is all there is to it, Greenspan's defenders would be entitled to argue that since M1 was on the average negative during December 1995-December 2000, they were not pumping money into a bubble. If the money creation was negative during that period, how is it possible even to conceive that the period was a classic credit boom, followed by a bust?

What is neglected is that the banks have been using an accounting trick known as a "sweep." In essence, what they do is take bank accounts out of the category of those for which they have to hold back some of the money in reserve—the $10,000 reserve in the example given Chapter III—and switch it into accounts where they do not have to keep reserves. With this trick, they are able to make more loans. The actual way they do this is rather complicated, but that is the essence of the ploy. In moral purpose, it is not too different from the "partnerships" that made Enron notorious.

Professor George Reisman of Pepperdine University explains:

PETER ERICKSON

"Since January 1994, hundreds of banks and other depository financial institutions have initiated sweep programs to avoid statutory reserve requirements on transactions deposits. In a sweep program, a bank's computers analyze customer use of checkable deposits (demand deposits, ATS, NOW, and other checkable deposits) and 'sweep' funds into money market accounts (MMDA). MMDA accounts are personal saving deposits under the Federal Reserve's Regulation D and have a zero statutory reserve requirement ratio."[337]

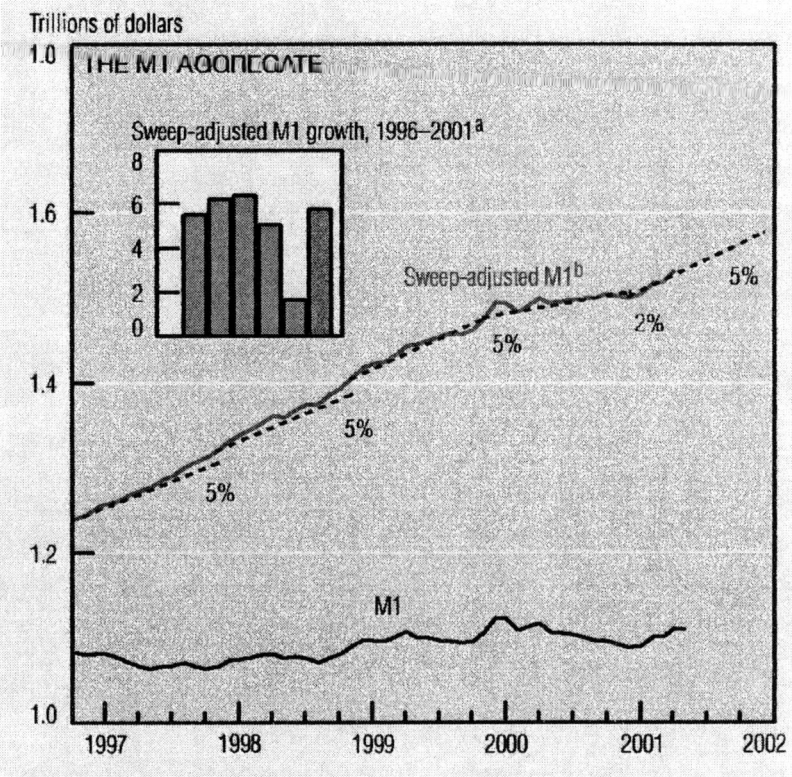

Once the Sweeps are taken into account, the money creation balance turns decidedly in the positive. In recent years, the Federal Reserve has taken notice of this gimmick. Above is a recent chart published by the Federal Reserve Of Cleveland in May 2001[338]:

The footnote(b) in the chart pictured above reads:"The sweep-adjusted base contains an estimate of required reserves saved when balances are shifted from reservable to nonreservable accounts. Sweeps-adjusted M1 contains an estimate of balances temporarily moved from M1 to non-M1 accounts." Note the euphemism, "temporarily," ignoring the fundamental intent to deceive. From the diagram, M1 for 1996 is adjusted upward by about 5.5%; 1997 by 6%; 1998 by around 6.2%; 1999, in the neighborhood of 5%; the year 2000, by approximately 1.5%, and 2001, by something less than 6%. Quite a bundle to sweep under a rug. But these are estimates. At one time, Professor Reisman, like Chairman Greenspan, was a member of Ayn Rand's inner circle. His estimates of the "sweep" are larger than those of the Fed.

In conclusion, Greenspan did preside over the gargantuan monetary growth in the Clinton years. M1, which he has the most direct control over, did expand a lot during those years; this comes out once the Enronical distortions are given reasonable consideration. Greenspan had every reason to understand that it would cause M3 to greatly rise as well.

ENDNOTES

1   Robert J. Shiller, *Irrational Exuberance*, (Princeton, New Jersey: Princeton University Press, 2000), p. xvi.

2   Compiled by Edward Angly, *Oh Yeah?*(New York: The Viking Press, 1931), p. 19.

3   Ellen R. McGrattan and Edward C. Prescott, "The Stock Market Crash of 1929: Irving Fisher Was Right!" Federal Reserve Bank of Minneapolis, Research Department Staff report 294, Revised December 2001, p. 31.

4   Angly, *Op. cit.*, p. 33.

5   The list of sources from whom permission to quote has been granted is available upon request. Send a self-addressed-return-envelope to Economic Depression Consultants, Inc., P.O. Box 8725, Portland, Oregon 97201.

6   "The economy Bush inherited," *The Washington Times; National Weekly Edition*. August 5-11, 2002, p. 36.

7   Carrol Quigley, *Tragedy And Hope—A History Of The World In Our Time*, (New York: The Macmillian Company, 1966), p. 950.

8   Keith Badsher, "A Clinton Aide's farewell to Clients: Keep in Touch," *New York Times* February 5, 1993, p. A1; R. Emmett Tyrrell, Jr., *Boy Clinton: The Political Biography*, (Washington, DC, 1996), p. 140.

9   Ralf Z. Hallow, "GOP challenges Clinton On Oversight," *The Washington Times: National Weekly Edition*, July 29-August 4, 2002, p. 3.

10   *Los Angeles Times*, Washington, April 1, 1994.

11   Ralph West Robey, "The Capreadores In Wall Street," *Atlantic Monthly*, September 1928, p. 396.

12   *Loc. cit.*

13   Bob Woodward, *Maestro: Greenspan's Fed And The American Boom*, (New York: Simon & Schuster, 2000), p.179.

14   Bob Zelnick, *Gore: A Political Life*, (Washington DC: Regnery Publishing Inc., 1999), p. 249.
15   "Dick Morris on Ronald Reagan, George Bush, Hillary and Bill Clinton," *NewsMax.com*, August 18, 2002, p. 30.
16   Jerome Tuccille, *Alan Shrugged: Alan Greenspan, The World's Most Powerful Banker*, (Hoboken, NJ: John Wiley & Sons, 2002), pp. 207-208.
17   Bob Woodward, *Op, cit.*, p. 108.
18   *Ibid.*, p. 110.
19   Nathaniel Branden, *Judgment Day: My Years With Ayn Rand*, (Boston: Houghton Mifflin Company, 1989), pp. 131, 133.
20   Alan Greenspan, "Gold And Economic Freedom", in *Capitalism: The Unknown Ideal*, by Ayn Rand and Others, (New York: Signet Books, 1967), pp. 99-100.
21   Tuccille, *Op. cit.*, pp. 140-143.
22   John Cassidy, "The Fountainhead: Alan Greenspan faces the biggest challenge of his career," The New Yorker, May 1, 2000, p. 168.
23   Tuccille, *Op. cit.*, pp. 138-39, 149-51.
24   Lawrence Parks, *What Does Mr. Greenspan Really Think?* pp. 7-10.
25   It is common to state stock exchange numbers without the comma, but in order to make the figures stand out better, they are inserted.
26   Woodward, *Op. cit.*, p. 196.
27   Lawrence Parks, *Op. cit.*, p. 27.
28   "M1", M2", "M3", *investorwords.com www.investorwords.com/cgi-bin/getword*
29   A "repo" is a contract in which a seller of securities agrees to repurchase them at a specified time and price, also called a "repurchase agreement".
30   NOW (Negotiable Order of Withdrawal)—an interest-bearing checking account at a bank or savings and loan.
31   Marion Eccles, in testimony before the Banking and Currency committee of the House of Representatives, June 24, 1941, quoted in *Citadels Of Chaos* by Cornelius Carl Veith (Boston: Meador Publishing Company, 1949), p. 31.
32   There is a small complication here. A large shift toward savings can mean that more money creation has been taking place than

the annual increase in M1 may lead one to suppose. Suppose the increase in M1 that year were X dollars. Suppose further that some of the checking account in existence at the end of the previous fiscal year had been moved into saving accounts. As a result of this subtraction and removal into savings, the base from which the M1 increase is calculated is smaller than it would have been, had this change not taken place. Therefore, since the actual base from which the X dollars increase is smaller, the actual increase is greater than X. When a checking account (M1) is cancelled and the proceeds are placed into a savings account or a CD (M2 & M3), the actual increase in money creation will be greater from the end of one period to the end of the next one than it would have been if M1 had increased the same amount, though without any switch into a savings account.

33   "ALAN GREENSPAN: IS HE A DEMOCRAT OR A REPUBLICAN?" *The Wall Street Digest*, September 2002, p. 6.

34   "M3 Money Stock Seasonally Adjusted," *St. Louis Federal Reserve*, p. 7 *http://research.stlouis.org/fred/data/monetary/m3sl*

35   Parks, *Op. cit.*, p. 94.

36   Tuccille, *Op. cit.*, p. 210.

37   Loc. cit.

38   *Ibid.*, p. 211.

39   Justin Martin, Greenspan: The Man behind Money, (Cambridge, MA: Perseus Publishing, 2000), p. 202.

40   H.F. Langenberg, C.F.A., *Notes: 1994 . . . 1995. . . . 1996?* (St. Louis, MO: Smith Moore & Co., 1995), pp. 29-30.

41   *Ibid.*, p. 30.

42   *Ibid.*, p. 52.

43   "In a study made by the stock market over a period of years, i.e., 1872-1979, the author, Steven C. Lenthold, divided up the 108 years into six different periods, namely extraordinary inflation, relatively high inflation, moderate inflation, stability, moderate deflation, relatively high inflation, moderate inflation, stability, moderate deflation, and extraordinary deflation. According to these criteria, common stocks did poorly in periods of extraordinary inflation, relatively high inflation, and extraordinary

deflation, but did well in periods of moderate inflation, stability, and moderate deflation." H.F. Langenberg, *Fall Notes 1991—46th Year*, (St. Louis, Mo: Smith Moore & Col, 1992), p. 81.

44   All news citations in this work presented, without being end-noted or otherwise identified, are from "Year-End Review of WHAT WAS NEWS" from the appropriate year. This feature regularly appear in the first January issue of the following year in *The Wall Street Journal.*

45   "What was News" *Wall Street Journal,* January 2, 1996, p. R3.

46   L. Patterson, "NPT Interview," *C.R.*, March 1995, pp. 10-11.

47   Ambrose Evans-Pritchard, *The Secret Life Of Bill Clinton: The Unreported Stories.* (Washington, D.C., Regnery Publishing, Inc.), 19970, p. 3.

48   Michael M. Phillips, "U.S. Is Unlikely to Prop Up Dollar," The Wall Street Journal, July 23, 2002, p. C1.

49   Paul Blustein, Japan disputes meaning of trade pact," *The Washington Post,* June 29, 1995

50   Robert D. Hershey Jr., "Payrolls Swelled By 215,000 In June: Jobless Rate Fell," *NYT,* July 8, 1995, p. 1

51   "Transportation Average," *WSJ,* July 17, 1995, p. C3.

52   L.Patterson, *C.R.* July 31, 1995, p. 24.

53   Ralf Z. Hallow, "GOP challenges Clinton On Oversight," *The Washington Times: National Weekly Edition,* July 29-August 4, 2002, p. 3.

54   Woodward, *Op. cit.*, p.153.

55   H. F. Langenburg, *Notes: 1994 . . . 1995 . . . . 1996?* (St. Louis, MO: Smith, Moore& co., 1995), p. 91.

56   Federal Reserve Bank of Chicago, "Conference on Asset Price Bubbles, 22-24 April, 2002, p. 3.

57   Jonathon Chait, "Clinton: What went Right," *The New Republic ON-Line, 1/11/01 www.thenewrepublic.com/012201/jud012201.html*

58   Steven Pearlstein, *Washington Post,* January 5, 1996. *www.poop.org/natldebt/default/rubin.htm*

59   Bob Woodward, *Op. cit.*, p.165.

60   Calvin Coolidge, quoted in *The Day The Market Crashed* by Donald I. Rogers (New Rochelle, New York: Arlington House, 1971), p. 207.

61   Gertrude M. Coogan, *Money Creators Who Creates Money? Who should*

Create It? (Hawthorne, CA: Omni Publications, 1998 reprint of 1935 original), p. 69.

62   *The Underground Wall Street,* March 1996, pp. 12-13. *Http:// www.wallstreetunderground.com/NewsLetter/Filles/0396.asp*

63   Virginia Deane Abernathy, "Chronicles Intelligence Assessment: Immigration Misinformation," *Chronicles: A Magazine of American Culture,* August 2000, p. 22.

64   *Loc. cit.*

65   Daniel Gross, *Bull Run: Wall Street, The Democrats, and the New Politics of Personal Finance,* (New York Public Affairs, 2000) p. 100-101.

66   Woodward, *Op. cit.* p.178.

67   *Loc. cit.,* p. 178.

68   Gertrude M. Coogan, *Op. cit.,* pp. 67-68.

69   Gross, O*p. cit.,* p. 101.

70   "Analysis: Would U.S. Make decision based on Investments" by David E. Sanger http:equity.stern.nyu.edu/~nroubini/NYT/ SS3NYT.HTM

71   Angly, *Op.* cit., pp. 6-7.

72   Daniel Gross, *Ibid,*

73   Deloitte & Touche December 8, 1996 *www.dtonline.com/tnv/1996/ December/tnv1209.htm*

74   Or did she?

75   *Www.thenewamerican.com/tna/1997/vol1/vol13no11_charade.htm*

76   Robert J. Shiller *Op. cit.,* p. 113.

77   Bob Woodward, *Op. cit.,* p. 188.

78   Eliott Platt, Quoted in Larry Kahaner's *The Quotations Of Chairman Greenspan* (Holbrook, MA: Adams Media, Corporation, 2000), p. 224.

79   Gross, *Op. cit.,* pp. 102-103.

80   Robert J. Shiller, *Op. cit.,* p. 245.

81   Gross, *Op. cit.,* p. 103.

82   Jonathan Peterson and Robert A. Rosenblatt, "In Wake of Wall St. Decline, Rubin Reassures Investors," *Los Angeles Times,* October 28, 1997, p. 2.

83   *Loc, cit.*

84   Suzanne McGee, "Stocks Burst back by 337.17 Points On record Volume as bonds Drop," *WSJ,* October 29, 1997, p. C1.

85   All Politics—CNN TIME. Tuesday, October 28, 1997 *http:// images.cnn.com/ALLPOLITICS/1997/10/28stock.market/*

86   Bill King, Quoted in "the rig is in" by James Dale Davidson, *Strategic Investment,* November 18, 1998, p. 1.

87   Alan Greenspan, "Before the Task Force on Social Security of the committee on the Budget, U.S. Senate," *www.federalreserve.gov/ boarddocs/testimony/1997/19971120.htm*

88   *London Financial Times,* October 20, 1997. Cf., C.R., October 31. 1997, p. 27

89   Shiller, *Op. cit.,* p. 490.

90   "The Right Answers," *The New American,* August 3, 1998, p. 9.

91   "Historical Debt Outstanding—Annual 1950 - 2000, *Bureau of the Public Debt on line, www.publicdebt.treas.gov/opd/opdhisto4.htm*

92   Suzanne McGee, "Bonds Fall As Investors Take Profits—Steep Stock Losses Curbed late in Day," *The Wall Street Journal,* January 8, 1998, p. C1.

93   Bill King, quoted in James Dale Davidson, *op. cit.,* p. 7.

94   Christopher Ruddy and Bryan Troup, "Economist: Inflation Rate Is Double Official Number", *Blanchard,* March 14, 2000, pp. 4-6 *www.blanchardonline.com/beru/bul;letin29.html*

95   Senator Ernest Hollings, "What Surplus?" *The Washington Post,* February 5, 1998, p. 1 http://infoweb.newsbank.com/iw-search/ we/InfoWeb?p_action=print&p-docid=0EB2CEA39

96   *Http://www.poop.org/www/ctzcrank/2000/hollings.html*

97   Senator Ernest Hollings, *Op. cit.,* p. 2.

98   Alan Greenspan, quoted in Tuccille, *Op. cit.,* p. 151.

99   Cf., "New Stock Exchange Preparing for Serious trouble," *C. P.,* February 7, 1998, p. 28.

100   Cf., L. Patterson, "Devaluation In Asia Raises Possibility Of Worldwide Depression," *C. P.,* November 30, 1997, p. 22.

101   "The Right Answers," *The New American,* January 18, 1999, p. 27; citing December 14, 1998, article in *Forbes.*

102   Quoted in Lawrence M. Parks, *op. cit.,* p. 8. Cf., C.R., November 30, 1997, p. 23.

[103]   Bill King, quoted in James Dale Davidson, *Op. cit.*, p. 7.

[104]   *Ibid.*, p. 8.

[105]   Jerome Tuccille, *Op. cit.*, pp. 236-237

[106]   Michael M. Phillips, *Op. cit.*, p. C1

[107]   J. Orlin Grabbe, "And Now, the Financial Apocalypse," *www.orlingrabb.com/Apocalp.htm*

[108]   Angly, *Op. cit.*, p. 12

[109]   Alan Greenspan, quoted in Kahaner, *Op. cit.*, p. 46.

[110]   Bob Woodward, *Op cit.*, p. 208.

[111]   *Ibid.*, pp.198- 202.

[112]   *Ibid.*, p. 47.

[113]   Ambrose Evans-Pritchard, *London Telegraph*, September 2, 1998, quoted in Davidson, *op. cit.*, p. 9.

[114]   "Margin Timeline," FMC Publications, p. 7. *www.fmcenter.org/fmc_superpage.asp?ID=376*

[115]   David Smith, "All good things do come to an end," July /August 2000 *www.economicsuk.com/articles/proinv/ju00.html*

[116]   "What was News," WSJ, January 4, 1999, p. R. 16.

[117]   Bill King, quoted in James Dale Davidson, *Op. cit.*, p. 8. A comma was removed from the sentence which begins: "Massaging the deflator, and savings rate. . . ."

[118]   "What's News," *The Wall Street Journal*, November 4, 1998, p. A1.

[119]   Everett Caril Ladd, quoted in James Dale Davidson, *Op. cit.*, p. 10.

[120]   Bob Woodward, *Op. cit.* 212.

[121]   James Dale Davidson, *Op. cit.*, p. 11.

[122]   "Clinton favors using stock market to pump up social security," CNN.com, December 9, 1998, *http://www.cnn.com/US/9812/09/social*Http://www.cnn.com/US/9812/09/social.security/

[123]   Laurin R. Rubin, "Liftoff Ahead," *Barron's*, January 10, 1999, p. 17. Drawing by Stuart Goldenberg.

[124]   *Loc. cit.*

[125]   Robert J. Shiller, *Op. cit.*, p. 23.

[126]   "Historical Debt Outstanding—Annual 1950-2000," *Op. cit.*, p. 1

[127]   Gross, *Op. cit.*, pp. 81-83.

[128]   "State of Shame," *The Wall Street Journal*, Thursday, January 21, 1999, p. A 18.

129 Lester Thurow, "Clinton Snookers Republicans at Their Own Economical Game, *USA TODAY,* February 1, 1999.
130 Tuccille, *Op. cit.,* p. 245.
131 Christopher Ruddy, "1990s: The Socialist Decade", NewMax.*com Vortex,* November 1999, in *Bitter Legacy NewsMax.com Reveals The Untold Story Of The Clinton-Gore Years,* ed. by Christopher Ruddy and Carl Limbacher Jr., (West Palm Beach, FL: NewMax.com Inc., January 2001), p. 272-273.
132 "Year-End Review of WHAT WAS NEWS, *The Wall Street Journal,* January 3, 2000, p, R12.
133 Russel Mohiber and Robert Weissman, An Excerpt from Corporate Predators (Common Courage Press, 1999). http://www.thirdworldtraveler.com/Book_Excerpts/DailoutBanks_CP.html
134 William F. Jasper, "Feeding the Red Dragon," *The New American,* February 15, 1999, p. 26
135 "Margin Timeline: January 1999-July 2000," Financial markets Center, p.1. *http://www.fmcenter.org/fme_superpage.asp?ID=376*
136 *Ibid.,* p. 2.
137 Shiller,*Ibid.,* p. xv.
138 "Margin Timeline," *Op. cit.,* p. 1
139 "End Of The Millennium," *Wall Street Journal,* January 3, 2000, p. R4.
140 "Clinton" ' I do believe in the New Economy,' *BusinessWeek on line,* (July 12, 1999), p. 1.
141 Angly, *Op. cit.,* p. 55.
142 Gross, *Op. cit.,* p. 185.
143 Mark Weisbrot, "No Change at Treasury, But Sure is Needed," *Knight-Ridder/Tribune Media Services (May 13, 1999) www.cepr.net/treasurychange.htm*
144 Federal Reserve Chairman Alan Greenspan's semi-annual economic report to Congress before the House Banking Committee, (July 22, 1999), Question and Answer period.
145 Abernathy, *Op. cit.,* p. 21.
146 *Loc. cit.*
147 Dwight R. Lee and Richard B. MacKenzie, 'How to (Really) Get

Rich in America," USA *Weekend,* August 13-15, 1999, p. 6, quoted in Shiller, *Op. cit.,* p. 50.

148 Samuel Crowther, "Everybody Ought to be Rich: An Interview With John J. Raskob, *Ladies Home Journal,* August 1929, pp. 9, 36.

149 Gross, *Op. cit.,* p. 67.

150 "Margin Timeline," *Op. cit.,* pp. 2-3.

151 *Ibid.,* p. 2

152 John Kenneth Galbraith, Money: *Whence It came, Where It Went,* (Boston: Houghton Mifflin Company), 177-179.

153 Russell Mokhiber and Robert Weisman, "Teflon Bob And Banking Deregulation," *Focus On The Corporation,* November 17, 1999. *www.eatthestate.org/04-05/FocusOncorporation.htm*

154 M. Corey Goldman, "Is it really a new era?," October 28, 1999, *http://money.com/1999/1028/news*

155 "Year-End Review of WHAT WAS NEWS," *The Wall Street Journal,* January 3, 2000, p. B16.

156 "Margin Timeline," *Op. cit.,* p. 2.

157 *Ibid.,* p. 2.

158 Roy A. Young, quoted In Eustace Mullins' *The Secrets Of The Federal Reserve,* (Staunton, VA: Bankers Research Iinstitute, 1983), p.142.

159 "Year-End Review of WHAT WAS NEWS, January 3, 2000, p. B. 12.

160 'Year End Review Of What was News', January 3, 2000, p. R. 14.

161 *Loc. cit.*

162 *Ibid.,* p. 3.

163 Shiller, *Op. cit.,* p. 39.

164 "According to data from Zacks Investment Research about analysts' recommendations on some 6,000 companies, only 1.0% of recommendations were 'sells' in late 1999 (while 69.3% were 'buys' and 29.9% were 'holds'). This statement stands in striking contrast to that indicated by previous data. Ten years earlier, the fraction of sells, at 9.1%, was nine times higher." Robert J. Shiller, *Op. cit.,* p. 30.

165 Michael Santoli, "The Morning After—What a swell Nasdaq party that was—and what a necessary hangover," *Barron's,* January 10, 2000, p. 17. Chart by Stuart Goldenberg for *Barron's.*

166 "Historical Debt Outstanding—Annual 1950- 2000", *Op. cit.,* p. 1

167   "What's New—Business and Finance," *WSJ,* January 3, 2000, p. A1.

168   Bob Woodward, *Ibid.,* p. 224.

169   Lawrence Parks, *Ibid.,* p. 84.

170   Thomas Petzinger, Jr., "SO LONG, SUPPLY AND DEMAND," *Wall Street Journal,* January 3, 2002,.

171   David Denby, "The Quarter of Living Dangerously," *The New Yorker,* April 24 & May 1, 2000, p.195.

172   "Margin Timeline," *Op. cit.,* p. 3.

173   *Loc. cit.*

174   *Loc. cit.*

175   Angly, *Op. cit.,* pp. 5-6.

176   Daniel Gross, *Op. cit.,* pp. 24-25.

177   "Margin Timeline", *Op. cit.,* p. 3.

178   Galbraith, *Op, cit.,* p. 177.

179   For the justification of this, see Chapter XIII.

180   Walden Bello, "Davos 2000: An All-American Show?" January 30, 2000. www.focusweb.org/public . . ./ Davos%202000-%20An%20All-American%20Show.ht

181   Angly, *Op. cit.,* p. 24.

182   *Ibid.,* p. 22.

183   "Margin Timeline," *Op. cit.,* p. 3.

184   Loc. cit.

185   *Ibid.,* p. 4.

186   *Loc. cit.*

187   Alan Greenspan, The Revolution in Information Technology," March 6, 2000, quoted in James Grant's "Blame Greenspan," *Forbes Magazine,* September 9, 2003, *http://www/internetional.se/ Grant1992.htm*

188   David Denby, *Op. cit.,* p. 196.

189   Martin Weiss, *Safe Money Report,* quoted in *The McAlvany Intelligence Advisor,* January 2002, p. 22,

190   Angly, *Op. cit.,* p. 38.

191   *The London Economist,* quoted in Mullins, *Op. cit.,* p. 147.

192   Ibid., pp. 5-6.

193   Alan M. Newman, "The One Way Fed," *http://www.flash.net/~rhmjr/ c0410.html*

194   Charles Kadlec, "Market Mayhem: Don't Worry, the Great Prosperity Is Still Coming," *The Wall Street Journal*, April 18, 2000.

195   Angly, *Op. cit.*, p. 28.

196   E.S. Browning, "Stocks face hurdles in bid to Match Years Past," *Wall Street Journal*, July 11, 2000., p, C1

197   Angly, *Op. cit.*, p. 17.

198   Gregory Zuckerman, "Ring in a new bond Bellwether: 10-Year," WSJ, May 31, 2000, p. C1.

199   Constance Mitchell Ford, "Economists Split on Fed's Strategy to Curb Inflation," *Wall Street Journal*, July 2, 2000, p. A2.

200   Angly, *Op. cit.*, p. 24.

201   Angly, *Op. cit.*, pp. 9-10.

202   Michael M. Phillips, *Op. cit.*, p. C1

203   Jeffrey Frankel, September 25, 2000. *www.ksg.harvard.edu/news/ experts/frankel_economy_qa.htm*

204   "Election 2000", 12/03/00. *Www.suatoday.com/news/vote2000/ pres186.htm*

205   *Loc. cit.*

206   "Cyberaltert," December 6, 2000 *www.mediaresearch.org/cyberalerts/ 2000/cyb2001206.asp*

207   E. S. Browning, "Is This Really A Bear Market or Some Other Animal?" *Wall Street Journal*, January 16, 2001, p. C1; "Business & Finance," *Wall Street Journal*, November 29, 2000, p. A1.

208   "Historical Debt Outstanding—Annual 1950-2000," *Op. cit.* p. 1.

209   *Year-End Review* of WHAT WAS NEWS," *The Wall Street Journal*, January 2, 2002, p. R 12.

210   *Loc. cit.*

211   *Loc. cit.*

212   *Loc. cit.*

213   Alan Greenspan, quoted by John McKinnon and Greg Up, "Greenspan, In About-face Backs A Tax Cuts," *WSJ*, January 26, 2001, p. A1.

214   *Loc. cit.*

215   Angly, *Op. cit.*, p. 41.

216   *Loc. cit.*

217   *Ibid.*, p. 57.

218 Angly, *Op. cit.*, p. 25.

219 f2) network, February 21, 2001, p. 1. *www.smh.com.au/news/0102/ 21/pageone/pageone13.html*

220 www.thenewamerican.com/tna/2002/08-262002/ vol8no17_mishandling_print.htm

221 *Loc. cit.*

222 http://www.cbsnews.com/stories/2001/03/15/politics/ printable279141.shtml

223 Angly, *Op. cit.*, p. 15.

224 Gregory Zuckerman, "Whiff of Good News, *WSJ*, April 6, 2001, p. A1.

225 Angly, *Op. cit.*, p. 22.

226 *Ibid.*, p. 47.

227 H.F. Langenberg, *Op. cit*, p. 84.

228 Angly, *Op. cit.*, p. 35.

229 *Ibid.*, p. 52.

230 *Ibid.*, p. 42.

231 Karen Damato, "Doing the Math: Tech Investors' Road to Recovery Is Long," *WSJ*, May 18, 2001, p. C1.

232 *Loc. cit.*

233 *Loc. cit.*

234 *Ibid.*, p. 41.

235 "National Debt," http://www.poop.org/Natl-Debt/nd-main.html

i Angly, Op. cit., p. 45.

ii *Ibid.*, p. 25.

iii *Ibid.*, p. 27.

iv *The Oregonian*, Sunday, January 20, 2001. "Enron: Line between firm and accountant blurred," p. 1.

v Angly, Op. cit., p. 8.

vi *Ibid.*, p. 53.

vii *Ibid.*, p. 59.

viii *Ibid.*, p. 36.

ix *Ibid.*, p. 30.

x *Ibid.*, p. 47.

xi *Ibid.*, p. 54.

xii *Ibid.*, p. 59.

xiii   *Loc. cit.*

xiv   *Ibid.*, p. 54.

xv   E. S. Browning, "Blue Chips Surge Past 10000 Level," *Wall Street Journal,* May 2, 2002, p. C2.

xvi   Greg Ip, "Fed Keeps Interest rates Unchanged," *The Wall Street Journal,* May 8, 2002, p. A2.

xvii   Editorial, *The Washington Times: National Weekly Edition,* July 29-August 4, 2002, p. 36.

xviii William Norman Grigg, "Mishandling 'The People's Money,'" *The New American,* August 26, 2002. www.thenewamerican.com/tna/2002/08-26-2002/vol8no17_mihandling_print.htm

xix   Paul Craig Roberts, "How Federal Accounting Rules Created Corporation Scandals," *Human Events,* July 29, 2002, p. 9.

xx   "'Economic binge' during the '90s led to crisis, Bush says:, *The Washington Times: National Weekly Edition,* July 22-28, pp. 1, 22.

xxi   Angly, *Op. cit.,* p. 61.

xxii   *Ibid.,* p. 17.

xxiii Ralf Z. Hallow, "GOP challenges Clinton On Oversight," *The Washington Times: National Weekly Edition,* July 29-August 4, 2002, p. 3.

xxiv   *Ibid.,* p. 30.

xxv   "Democrats Talk Economy Down" by Terence P. Jeffrey, *Human Events,* August 5, 2002, p. 8.

xxvi   "Democrat's firm named in scheme to inflate stock prices," by Dave Boyer, *The Washington Times: National Weekly Edition,* July 22-228, 2002, pp. 1, 22.

xxvii Angly, *Op. cit.,* p. 30.

xxviii Donald I. Rogers, *The Day The Market Crashed* (New York: Arlington House, 1971), pp. 306-307.

xxix   "Stock Slide: Tallying the Pain," *Wall Street Journal,* July 22, 2002, p. C1.

xxx   "WorldCom Files For Bankruptcy," *Wall Street Journal,* July 22,2002, p. A3.

xxxi   E.S. Browning, "Nasdaq Stocks Sustain Biggest Loss of year," *The Wall Street Journal,* July 24, 2002, p. C1.

xxxii "What's News," *The Wall Street Journal,* July 30, 2002, p. A1.

xxxiii David Boyer, "Democrats Won't Question Rubin," *The Washington Times: National Weekly edition,* July 29- August 4, 2002, p. 1.

xxxiv Ray A. Smith, "Fearing a bubble, Homeowners Cash Out; A Return to Renting," *Wall Street Journal,* July 23, 2002, p. D1.

xxxv "D id Clinton (or Liberal bureaucrats) Cook Books?" *Human Events,* August 19, 2002, p. 3.

xxxvi *The McAlvany Intelligence Advisor,* January 2003, p. 23.

xxxvii Alan Greenspan, "The Regulation of OTC Derivatives," Before the Committee On Banking And Financial Services, U.S. House Of Representatives, July 24, 1998, quoted in Larry Kahaner's *The Quotations of Chairman Greenspan: Word from the Man Who Can Shake the World,* (Holbrook, MA; Adams Media Corporation, 2000), p. 43.

xxxviii "National Debt," *Op. cit.,* pp. 1,3.

xxxix Alan Greenspan, At a Mortgage Conference Sponsored by American's Community Bankers, Washington D.C., November 2, 1999, quoted in Kahaner, *Op. cit.,* p. 119.

275 "3 month Treasury bill rate—Secondary Market Average of Business Days, Discount Basis *http://researchstlouisfed.org*

276 Cf., "6-month CD Rate. Average of Business Days," *http://researchstlouisfed.org*

277 Gregory Zuckerman and Craig Karmin, "Foreigners' Ardor for U.S. Stocks Is Waning," *The Wall Street Journal,* May 20, 2002, p. C1.

278 *The McAlvany Intelligence Advisor,* January 2003, p. 24.

279 Davidson, *Op. cit.,* p. 8.

280 President U.S. Grant, quoted in Carl Veitch's *Citadels Of Chaos* (Boston: Forum Publishing Co., early 1950s), p. 133.

281 M. W. Walbert, *The Coming Battle: A Complete History of the National Banking Money Power In the United States* (Chicago: W.B. Conkey Company, 1999); Reprinted by Walter Publishing & Research (Merlin, OR, 1998), pp. 62-148.

282 Tuccille, *Op. cit.,* p. 266.

283 F.W. Maisel, *The Great American Ripoff: An Indictment of the Federal Reserve Board,* San Diego, CA: Condido Press, 1983), p. 35.

284 *Ibid.,* p. 79.

285 Tuccille, *Op. cit.,* p. 242-243.

286   Christopher Ruddy, *Bitter Legacy: NewsMax.com Reveals The Untold Story Of The Clinton-Gore Years*, edited by Christopher Ruddy and Carl Limbacher, Jr. (West Palm Beach, FL: NewsMax.com Inc., 2001), p. 271.

287   Principally Lyndon LaRouche.

288   Editorial, "Parson Greenspan," *The Wall Street Journal,* July 18, 2002, p. A 12.

289   Alan M. Newman, "The One way Fed", *http://www/flash.net/~rhmjr/ c0410.html*

290   Kahaner, *Op. cit.*, p. 151.

291   Lawrence H. Heim, "Crash (How to survive And become Wealthy In The New Depression)" March 2001, p. 9.

292   F. Kreigle, "In Greenspan We Trust," January 23, 1998. web.mit.edu/fik/Public/essays/greenspan.html

293   David Denby, *Op. cit.*, p. 190.

294   Heim, *Op. cit.*, p. 8

295   Rogers, *Op. cit.*, p. 207.

296   "Debts are subject to the laws of mathematics rather than physics. Unlike wealth, which is subject to the laws of thermodynamics, debts do not rot with old age and are not consumed in the process of living." Frederick Soddy, Wealth, Virtual Wealth And Debt, (London: George Allen & Unwin Ltd., 1926), p. 70.

297   William P. Hoar, *The New American*, May 13, 1996

298   G. Edward Griffin, *The Creature from Jekyll Island: a Second Look at the Federal Reserve*, (Westlake Village, CA: American Media, 1998), p. 493.

299   "Stock Slide: tallying the Pain," *WSJ,* July 22, 2002, p. C1

300   Walter F. Lineberger, III, CLU, ChFC, *The Stock Market Since 1928: History and Analysis,* (Internet: Personalized Brokerage Service, Inc., 1997) Pl 4.

301   "Stock Slide: Tallying the Pain," *Op. cit.*, p. C1.

302   U.S. Census Bureau. Estimate for April 21, 2002,was 282,421,906. The official figure for 1930 is 121,202,604.

303   Ellen R. McGrattan and Edward C. Prescott, *Op. cit.*, p. 6. This is an estimate of the value of all U.S. corporations.

304   Benjamin Anderson, *Economics And The Public Welfare*, p. 198.

305 Ellen McGratten and Edward Prescott, *Op. cit.*, p. 1.

306 Sam Vaknin, "Why is the Stock Market falling: Is this the Crash of 1929?" *The Idler: A Web Periodical, p. 5. www.the-ideler.com/IDLER-02/ 8-1.html*

307 Vaknin, *Op. cit.*, pp. 5-6.

308 Angly, *Op. cit.*, p. 39.

309 *The Wall Street Digest,* November 2002, p. 3.

310 Edward Thomas Trading Company, "An Admonition From History," p. 3. *www.edwardthomas.com/alert1.htm*

311 "Dow Jones: Daily Gains and Losses," *www.globalfindata.com/articles/ bestusa.htm*

312 "Timelines Of The Great Depression," *www.hyperhistory.com*

313 Veitch, *Op. cit.* p. 171.

314 Congressman Wright Patman, "A Primer On Money" in Eustace Mullins, *The Secrets Of The Federal Reserve,* (Staunton, VA: Bankers Research Institute, 1983), p. 145.

315 Federal Reserve, *http://research.stlouis.org/fred/data/monetary/m3sl*

316 Federal Reserve Of St. Louis, M3 08/27/2002 *http:// research.stlouisfed.org/fred/data/monetary/m1sl*

317 Cf., Federal Reserve of St. Louis, 08/27/02 *http:// research.stlouisfed.org/data/monetary/m1sl*

318 Frank Sostak, "The Mystery Of The Money Supply Definition," *The Quarterly Journal Of Austrian Economics Vol. 3, No 4* (Winter 2000), p. 72.

319 Cf., Federal Reserve of St. Louis, *http://research.stlouisfed.org/data/ monetary/m1sl*

320 U.S. Housing Starts Outlook—September 2001- January 2003, *Market Vector, www.marketvector.com/leading-indicator/housing-starts.htm*

321 Gregory L. White and Karen Lundergaard, "U.S. Auto sales Accelerated 13%, Driven by Deals,' The Wall Street Journal, September 5, 2002, p. A1.

322 "Maximum Greenspan," *The Daily Reckoning,* September 4, 2002, p. 3 "The Daily *Reckoning"<Pop-Ups@agoramail.net>*

323 Series Title M3 Money Stock: Billions of dollars; SA. Series Title MZM Money stock; Billions of Dollars:SA. *www.Economagic.com*

324 Daily Reckoning 11/04/02 *http://www,agora-inc.com*

325 Cornelius Carl Veith, *Op. cit.*, p. 31.

326   Murray N. Rothbard, *What Has Government Done to Our Money?*
       (Auburn, Alabama: Praxeology Press, 1990, orig. 1963), pp. 47-52.
327   *Ibid.*, pp. 47-52.
328   Frederick J. Soddy, quoted in Veitch, *Op. cit.*, p. 158.
329   Wayne Angell, "Greenspan's Deflation," *The Wall Street Journal*,
       October 29, 2002, pl A22.
330   "Info-Stock Market History," Stock Picks System, p. 1
       www.stockpickssytem.com/stock_market_history.htm
331   Rothbard, *Op. cit.*, pp. 47-52.
332   Alan Greenspan, "Gold and Economic Freedom," *Op. cit.*, p. 98.
333   Charles Holt Carroll, *Organization of Debt Into Currency and Other
       papers*, ed. by Edward C. Simmons, (Princeton, NJ: D. Van Nostrand
       Company, Inc., 1964), pp. 74-94; 136-175; 349-358.
334   Peter Erickson, *The Stance Of Atlas: An Examination Of The Philosophy
       of Ayn Rand*, (Portland, OR: Herakles Press, Inc. 1997), p.305; Peter
       Erickson, *Introduction To the Tripartite System: A Monetary Program for
       Americans*,(Privately Printed, 1975).
335   Thomas McClary, "Banking and Currency Reform. Its Necessity. Its
       Possibility." 62nd Congress, 2nd Session, *Document No. 295*.
336   Paul Volcker, quoted in Robert Pringle and Marjorie Deane, *The
       Central Banks* (New York: Viking, 1994), p. vii, in Parks, *Op. cit.*, p.
       56.
337   George Reisman, "Adjusted Money Supply Data," *Reisman, BSM
       477, Spring 2001*, p. 5.
338   "Money and Commercial Markets," *Federal Reserve Of Cleveland*, May
       2001, p. 5.